Mometrix
TEST PREPARATION

# TExES

## History 7-12 (233) Secrets Study Guide

# DEAR FUTURE EXAM SUCCESS STORY

First of all, **THANK YOU** for purchasing Mometrix study materials!

Second, congratulations! You are one of the few determined test-takers who are committed to doing whatever it takes to excel on your exam. **You have come to the right place.** We developed these study materials with one goal in mind: to deliver you the information you need in a format that's concise and easy to use.

In addition to optimizing your guide for the content of the test, we've outlined our recommended steps for breaking down the preparation process into small, attainable goals so you can make sure you stay on track.

We've also analyzed the entire test-taking process, identifying the most common pitfalls and showing how you can overcome them and be ready for any curveball the test throws you.

Standardized testing is one of the biggest obstacles on your road to success, which only increases the importance of doing well in the high-pressure, high-stakes environment of test day. Your results on this test could have a significant impact on your future, and this guide provides the information and practical advice to help you achieve your full potential on test day.

**Your success is our success**

**We would love to hear from you!** If you would like to share the story of your exam success or if you have any questions or comments in regard to our products, please contact us at **800-673-8175** or **support@mometrix.com**.

Thanks again for your business and we wish you continued success!

Sincerely,
The Mometrix Test Preparation Team

# TABLE OF CONTENTS

# Introduction

**Thank you for purchasing this resource**! You have made the choice to prepare yourself for a test that could have a huge impact on your future, and this guide is designed to help you be fully ready for test day. Obviously, it's important to have a solid understanding of the test material, but you also need to be prepared for the unique environment and stressors of the test, so that you can perform to the best of your abilities.

For this purpose, the first section that appears in this guide is the **Secret Keys**. We've devoted countless hours to meticulously researching what works and what doesn't, and we've boiled down our findings to the five most impactful steps you can take to improve your performance on the test. We start at the beginning with study planning and move through the preparation process, all the way to the testing strategies that will help you get the most out of what you know when you're finally sitting in front of the test.

We recommend that you start preparing for your test as far in advance as possible. However, if you've bought this guide as a last-minute study resource and only have a few days before your test, we recommend that you skip over the first two Secret Keys since they address a long-term study plan.

If you struggle with **test anxiety**, we strongly encourage you to check out our recommendations for how you can overcome it. Test anxiety is a formidable foe, but it can be beaten, and we want to make sure you have the tools you need to defeat it.

# Secret Key #1 – Plan Big, Study Small

There's a lot riding on your performance. If you want to ace this test, you're going to need to keep your skills sharp and the material fresh in your mind. You need a plan that lets you review everything you need to know while still fitting in your schedule. We'll break this strategy down into three categories.

## Information Organization

Start with the information you already have: the official test outline. From this, you can make a complete list of all the concepts you need to cover before the test. Organize these concepts into groups that can be studied together, and create a list of any related vocabulary you need to learn so you can brush up on any difficult terms. You'll want to keep this vocabulary list handy once you actually start studying since you may need to add to it along the way.

## Time Management

Once you have your set of study concepts, decide how to spread them out over the time you have left before the test. Break your study plan into small, clear goals so you have a manageable task for each day and know exactly what you're doing. Then just focus on one small step at a time. When you manage your time this way, you don't need to spend hours at a time studying. Studying a small block of content for a short period each day helps you retain information better and avoid stressing over how much you have left to do. You can relax knowing that you have a plan to cover everything in time. In order for this strategy to be effective though, you have to start studying early and stick to your schedule. Avoid the exhaustion and futility that comes from last-minute cramming!

## Study Environment

The environment you study in has a big impact on your learning. Studying in a coffee shop, while probably more enjoyable, is not likely to be as fruitful as studying in a quiet room. It's important to keep distractions to a minimum. You're only planning to study for a short block of time, so make the most of it. Don't pause to check your phone or get up to find a snack. It's also important to **avoid multitasking**. Research has consistently shown that multitasking will make your studying dramatically less effective. Your study area should also be comfortable and well-lit so you don't have the distraction of straining your eyes or sitting on an uncomfortable chair.

The time of day you study is also important. You want to be rested and alert. Don't wait until just before bedtime. Study when you'll be most likely to comprehend and remember. Even better, if you know what time of day your test will be, set that time aside for study. That way your brain will be used to working on that subject at that specific time and you'll have a better chance of recalling information.

Finally, it can be helpful to team up with others who are studying for the same test. Your actual studying should be done in as isolated an environment as possible, but the work of organizing the information and setting up the study plan can be divided up. In between study sessions, you can discuss with your teammates the concepts that you're all studying and quiz each other on the details. Just be sure that your teammates are as serious about the test as you are. If you find that your study time is being replaced with social time, you might need to find a new team.

# Secret Key #2 – Make Your Studying Count

You're devoting a lot of time and effort to preparing for this test, so you want to be absolutely certain it will pay off. This means doing more than just reading the content and hoping you can remember it on test day. It's important to make every minute of study count. There are two main areas you can focus on to make your studying count.

## Retention

It doesn't matter how much time you study if you can't remember the material. You need to make sure you are retaining the concepts. To check your retention of the information you're learning, try recalling it at later times with minimal prompting. Try carrying around flashcards and glance at one or two from time to time or ask a friend who's also studying for the test to quiz you.

To enhance your retention, look for ways to put the information into practice so that you can apply it rather than simply recalling it. If you're using the information in practical ways, it will be much easier to remember. Similarly, it helps to solidify a concept in your mind if you're not only reading it to yourself but also explaining it to someone else. Ask a friend to let you teach them about a concept you're a little shaky on (or speak aloud to an imaginary audience if necessary). As you try to summarize, define, give examples, and answer your friend's questions, you'll understand the concepts better and they will stay with you longer. Finally, step back for a big picture view and ask yourself how each piece of information fits with the whole subject. When you link the different concepts together and see them working together as a whole, it's easier to remember the individual components.

Finally, practice showing your work on any multi-step problems, even if you're just studying. Writing out each step you take to solve a problem will help solidify the process in your mind, and you'll be more likely to remember it during the test.

## Modality

*Modality* simply refers to the means or method by which you study. Choosing a study modality that fits your own individual learning style is crucial. No two people learn best in exactly the same way, so it's important to know your strengths and use them to your advantage.

For example, if you learn best by visualization, focus on visualizing a concept in your mind and draw an image or a diagram. Try color-coding your notes, illustrating them, or creating symbols that will trigger your mind to recall a learned concept. If you learn best by hearing or discussing information, find a study partner who learns the same way or read aloud to yourself. Think about how to put the information in your own words. Imagine that you are giving a lecture on the topic and record yourself so you can listen to it later.

For any learning style, flashcards can be helpful. Organize the information so you can take advantage of spare moments to review. Underline key words or phrases. Use different colors for different categories. Mnemonic devices (such as creating a short list in which every item starts with the same letter) can also help with retention. Find what works best for you and use it to store the information in your mind most effectively and easily.

# Secret Key #3 – Practice the Right Way

Your success on test day depends not only on how many hours you put into preparing, but also on whether you prepared the right way. It's good to check along the way to see if your studying is paying off. One of the most effective ways to do this is by taking practice tests to evaluate your progress. Practice tests are useful because they show exactly where you need to improve. Every time you take a practice test, pay special attention to these three groups of questions:

- The questions you got wrong
- The questions you had to guess on, even if you guessed right
- The questions you found difficult or slow to work through

This will show you exactly what your weak areas are, and where you need to devote more study time. Ask yourself why each of these questions gave you trouble. Was it because you didn't understand the material? Was it because you didn't remember the vocabulary? Do you need more repetitions on this type of question to build speed and confidence? Dig into those questions and figure out how you can strengthen your weak areas as you go back to review the material.

Additionally, many practice tests have a section explaining the answer choices. It can be tempting to read the explanation and think that you now have a good understanding of the concept. However, an explanation likely only covers part of the question's broader context. Even if the explanation makes perfect sense, **go back and investigate** every concept related to the question until you're positive you have a thorough understanding.

As you go along, keep in mind that the practice test is just that: practice. Memorizing these questions and answers will not be very helpful on the actual test because it is unlikely to have any of the same exact questions. If you only know the right answers to the sample questions, you won't be prepared for the real thing. **Study the concepts** until you understand them fully, and then you'll be able to answer any question that shows up on the test.

It's important to wait on the practice tests until you're ready. If you take a test on your first day of study, you may be overwhelmed by the amount of material covered and how much you need to learn. Work up to it gradually.

On test day, you'll need to be prepared for answering questions, managing your time, and using the test-taking strategies you've learned. It's a lot to balance, like a mental marathon that will have a big impact on your future. Like training for a marathon, you'll need to start slowly and work your way up. When test day arrives, you'll be ready.

Start with the strategies you've read in the first two Secret Keys—plan your course and study in the way that works best for you. If you have time, consider using multiple study resources to get different approaches to the same concepts. It can be helpful to see difficult concepts from more than one angle. Then find a good source for practice tests. Many times, the test website will suggest potential study resources or provide sample tests.

# Practice Test Strategy

If you're able to find at least three practice tests, we recommend this strategy:

## Untimed and Open-Book Practice

Take the first test with no time constraints and with your notes and study guide handy. Take your time and focus on applying the strategies you've learned.

## Timed and Open-Book Practice

Take the second practice test open-book as well, but set a timer and practice pacing yourself to finish in time.

## Timed and Closed-Book Practice

Take any other practice tests as if it were test day. Set a timer and put away your study materials. Sit at a table or desk in a quiet room, imagine yourself at the testing center, and answer questions as quickly and accurately as possible.

Keep repeating timed and closed-book tests on a regular basis until you run out of practice tests or it's time for the actual test. Your mind will be ready for the schedule and stress of test day, and you'll be able to focus on recalling the material you've learned.

# Secret Key #4 – Pace Yourself

Once you're fully prepared for the material on the test, your biggest challenge on test day will be managing your time. Just knowing that the clock is ticking can make you panic even if you have plenty of time left. Work on pacing yourself so you can build confidence against the time constraints of the exam. Pacing is a difficult skill to master, especially in a high-pressure environment, so **practice is vital**.

Set time expectations for your pace based on how much time is available. For example, if a section has 60 questions and the time limit is 30 minutes, you know you have to average 30 seconds or less per question in order to answer them all. Although 30 seconds is the hard limit, set 25 seconds per question as your goal, so you reserve extra time to spend on harder questions. When you budget extra time for the harder questions, you no longer have any reason to stress when those questions take longer to answer.

Don't let this time expectation distract you from working through the test at a calm, steady pace, but keep it in mind so you don't spend too much time on any one question. Recognize that taking extra time on one question you don't understand may keep you from answering two that you do understand later in the test. If your time limit for a question is up and you're still not sure of the answer, mark it and move on, and come back to it later if the time and the test format allow. If the testing format doesn't allow you to return to earlier questions, just make an educated guess; then put it out of your mind and move on.

On the easier questions, be careful not to rush. It may seem wise to hurry through them so you have more time for the challenging ones, but it's not worth missing one if you know the concept and just didn't take the time to read the question fully. Work efficiently but make sure you understand the question and have looked at all of the answer choices, since more than one may seem right at first.

Even if you're paying attention to the time, you may find yourself a little behind at some point. You should speed up to get back on track, but do so wisely. Don't panic; just take a few seconds less on each question until you're caught up. Don't guess without thinking, but do look through the answer choices and eliminate any you know are wrong. If you can get down to two choices, it is often worthwhile to guess from those. Once you've chosen an answer, move on and don't dwell on any that you skipped or had to hurry through. If a question was taking too long, chances are it was one of the harder ones, so you weren't as likely to get it right anyway.

On the other hand, if you find yourself getting ahead of schedule, it may be beneficial to slow down a little. The more quickly you work, the more likely you are to make a careless mistake that will affect your score. You've budgeted time for each question, so don't be afraid to spend that time. Practice an efficient but careful pace to get the most out of the time you have.

# Secret Key #5 – Have a Plan for Guessing

When you're taking the test, you may find yourself stuck on a question. Some of the answer choices seem better than others, but you don't see the one answer choice that is obviously correct. What do you do?

The scenario described above is very common, yet most test takers have not effectively prepared for it. Developing and practicing a plan for guessing may be one of the single most effective uses of your time as you get ready for the exam.

In developing your plan for guessing, there are three questions to address:

- When should you start the guessing process?
- How should you narrow down the choices?
- Which answer should you choose?

## When to Start the Guessing Process

Unless your plan for guessing is to select C every time (which, despite its merits, is not what we recommend), you need to leave yourself enough time to apply your answer elimination strategies. Since you have a limited amount of time for each question, that means that if you're going to give yourself the best shot at guessing correctly, you have to decide quickly whether or not you will guess.

Of course, the best-case scenario is that you don't have to guess at all, so first, see if you can answer the question based on your knowledge of the subject and basic reasoning skills. Focus on the key words in the question and try to jog your memory of related topics. Give yourself a chance to bring the knowledge to mind, but once you realize that you don't have (or you can't access) the knowledge you need to answer the question, it's time to start the guessing process.

It's almost always better to start the guessing process too early than too late. It only takes a few seconds to remember something and answer the question from knowledge. Carefully eliminating wrong answer choices takes longer. Plus, going through the process of eliminating answer choices can actually help jog your memory.

**Summary**: Start the guessing process as soon as you decide that you can't answer the question based on your knowledge.

## How to Narrow Down the Choices

The next chapter in this book (**Test-Taking Strategies**) includes a wide range of strategies for how to approach questions and how to look for answer choices to eliminate. You will definitely want to read those carefully, practice them, and figure out which ones work best for you. Here though, we're going to address a mindset rather than a particular strategy.

Your odds of guessing an answer correctly depend on how many options you are choosing from.

| **Number of options left** | 5 | 4 | 3 | 2 | 1 |
|---|---|---|---|---|---|
| **Odds of guessing correctly** | 20% | 25% | 33% | 50% | 100% |

You can see from this chart just how valuable it is to be able to eliminate incorrect answers and make an educated guess, but there are two things that many test takers do that cause them to miss out on the benefits of guessing:

- Accidentally eliminating the correct answer
- Selecting an answer based on an impression

We'll look at the first one here, and the second one in the next section.

To avoid accidentally eliminating the correct answer, we recommend a thought exercise called **the $5 challenge**. In this challenge, you only eliminate an answer choice from contention if you are willing to bet $5 on it being wrong. Why $5? Five dollars is a small but not insignificant amount of money. It's an amount you could afford to lose but wouldn't want to throw away. And while losing $5 once might not hurt too much, doing it twenty times will set you back $100. In the same way, each small decision you make—eliminating a choice here, guessing on a question there—won't by itself impact your score very much, but when you put them all together, they can make a big difference. By holding each answer choice elimination decision to a higher standard, you can reduce the risk of accidentally eliminating the correct answer.

The $5 challenge can also be applied in a positive sense: If you are willing to bet $5 that an answer choice *is* correct, go ahead and mark it as correct.

**Summary**: Only eliminate an answer choice if you are willing to bet $5 that it is wrong.

## Which Answer to Choose

You're taking the test. You've run into a hard question and decided you'll have to guess. You've eliminated all the answer choices you're willing to bet $5 on. Now you have to pick an answer. Why do we even need to talk about this? Why can't you just pick whichever one you feel like when the time comes?

The answer to these questions is that if you don't come into the test with a plan, you'll rely on your impression to select an answer choice, and if you do that, you risk falling into a trap. The test writers know that everyone who takes their test will be guessing on some of the questions, so they intentionally write wrong answer choices to seem plausible. You still have to pick an answer though, and if the wrong answer choices are designed to look right, how can you ever be sure that you're not falling for their trap? The best solution we've found to this dilemma is to take the decision out of your hands entirely. Here is the process we recommend:

**Once you've eliminated any choices that you are confident (willing to bet $5) are wrong, select the first remaining choice as your answer.**

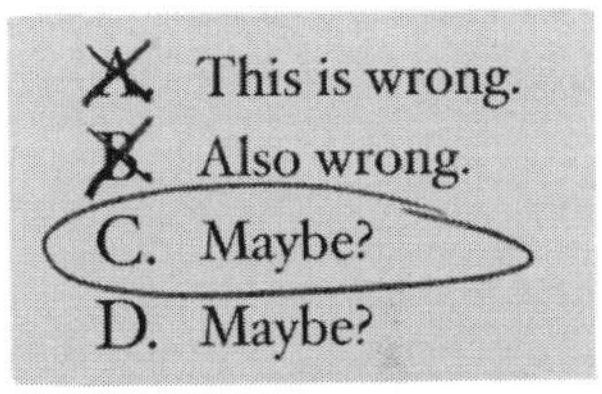


Whether you choose to select the first remaining choice, the second, or the last, the important thing is that you use some preselected standard. Using this approach guarantees that you will not be enticed into selecting an answer choice that looks right, because you are not basing your decision on how the answer choices look.

This is not meant to make you question your knowledge. Instead, it is to help you recognize the difference between your knowledge and your impressions. There's a huge difference between thinking an answer is right because of what you know, and thinking an answer is right because it looks or sounds like it should be right.

**Summary**: To ensure that your selection is appropriately random, make a predetermined selection from among all answer choices you have not eliminated.

# Test-Taking Strategies

This section contains a list of test-taking strategies that you may find helpful as you work through the test. By taking what you know and applying logical thought, you can maximize your chances of answering any question correctly!

It is very important to realize that every question is different and every person is different: no single strategy will work on every question, and no single strategy will work for every person. That's why we've included all of them here, so you can try them out and determine which ones work best for different types of questions and which ones work best for you.

## Question Strategies

### ✓ Read Carefully

Read the question and the answer choices carefully. Don't miss the question because you misread the terms. You have plenty of time to read each question thoroughly and make sure you understand what is being asked. Yet a happy medium must be attained, so don't waste too much time. You must read carefully and efficiently.

### ✓ Contextual Clues

Look for contextual clues. If the question includes a word you are not familiar with, look at the immediate context for some indication of what the word might mean. Contextual clues can often give you all the information you need to decipher the meaning of an unfamiliar word. Even if you can't determine the meaning, you may be able to narrow down the possibilities enough to make a solid guess at the answer to the question.

### ✓ Prefixes

If you're having trouble with a word in the question or answer choices, try dissecting it. Take advantage of every clue that the word might include. Prefixes can be a huge help. Usually, they allow you to determine a basic meaning. *Pre-* means before, *post-* means after, *pro-* is positive, *de-* is negative. From prefixes, you can get an idea of the general meaning of the word and try to put it into context.

### ✓ Hedge Words

Watch out for critical hedge words, such as *likely, may, can, often, almost, mostly, usually, generally, rarely,* and *sometimes.* Question writers insert these hedge phrases to cover every possibility. Often an answer choice will be wrong simply because it leaves no room for exception. Be on guard for answer choices that have definitive words such as *exactly* and *always.*

### ✓ Switchback Words

Stay alert for *switchbacks.* These are the words and phrases frequently used to alert you to shifts in thought. The most common switchback words are *but, although,* and *however.* Others include *nevertheless, on the other hand, even though, while, in spite of, despite,* and *regardless of.* Switchback words are important to catch because they can change the direction of the question or an answer choice.

### ⊘ Face Value

When in doubt, use common sense. Accept the situation in the problem at face value. Don't read too much into it. These problems will not require you to make wild assumptions. If you have to go beyond creativity and warp time or space in order to have an answer choice fit the question, then you should move on and consider the other answer choices. These are normal problems rooted in reality. The applicable relationship or explanation may not be readily apparent, but it is there for you to figure out. Use your common sense to interpret anything that isn't clear.

## Answer Choice Strategies

### ⊘ Answer Selection

The most thorough way to pick an answer choice is to identify and eliminate wrong answers until only one is left, then confirm it is the correct answer. Sometimes an answer choice may immediately seem right, but be careful. The test writers will usually put more than one reasonable answer choice on each question, so take a second to read all of them and make sure that the other choices are not equally obvious. As long as you have time left, it is better to read every answer choice than to pick the first one that looks right without checking the others.

### ⊘ Answer Choice Families

An answer choice family consists of two (in rare cases, three) answer choices that are very similar in construction and cannot all be true at the same time. If you see two answer choices that are direct opposites or parallels, one of them is usually the correct answer. For instance, if one answer choice says that quantity *x* increases and another either says that quantity *x* decreases (opposite) or says that quantity *y* increases (parallel), then those answer choices would fall into the same family. An answer choice that doesn't match the construction of the answer choice family is more likely to be incorrect. Most questions will not have answer choice families, but when they do appear, you should be prepared to recognize them.

### ⊘ Eliminate Answers

Eliminate answer choices as soon as you realize they are wrong, but make sure you consider all possibilities. If you are eliminating answer choices and realize that the last one you are left with is also wrong, don't panic. Start over and consider each choice again. There may be something you missed the first time that you will realize on the second pass.

### ⊘ Avoid Fact Traps

Don't be distracted by an answer choice that is factually true but doesn't answer the question. You are looking for the choice that answers the question. Stay focused on what the question is asking for so you don't accidentally pick an answer that is true but incorrect. Always go back to the question and make sure the answer choice you've selected actually answers the question and is not merely a true statement.

### ⊘ Extreme Statements

In general, you should avoid answers that put forth extreme actions as standard practice or proclaim controversial ideas as established fact. An answer choice that states the "process should be used in certain situations, if..." is much more likely to be correct than one that states the "process should be discontinued completely." The first is a calm rational statement and doesn't even make a definitive, uncompromising stance, using a hedge word *if* to provide wiggle room, whereas the second choice is far more extreme.

### ⊘ Benchmark

As you read through the answer choices and you come across one that seems to answer the question well, mentally select that answer choice. This is not your final answer, but it's the one that will help you evaluate the other answer choices. The one that you selected is your benchmark or standard for judging each of the other answer choices. Every other answer choice must be compared to your benchmark. That choice is correct until proven otherwise by another answer choice beating it. If you find a better answer, then that one becomes your new benchmark. Once you've decided that no other choice answers the question as well as your benchmark, you have your final answer.

### ⊘ Predict the Answer

Before you even start looking at the answer choices, it is often best to try to predict the answer. When you come up with the answer on your own, it is easier to avoid distractions and traps because you will know exactly what to look for. The right answer choice is unlikely to be word-for-word what you came up with, but it should be a close match. Even if you are confident that you have the right answer, you should still take the time to read each option before moving on.

## General Strategies

### ⊘ Tough Questions

If you are stumped on a problem or it appears too hard or too difficult, don't waste time. Move on! Remember though, if you can quickly check for obviously incorrect answer choices, your chances of guessing correctly are greatly improved. Before you completely give up, at least try to knock out a couple of possible answers. Eliminate what you can and then guess at the remaining answer choices before moving on.

### ⊘ Check Your Work

Since you will probably not know every term listed and the answer to every question, it is important that you get credit for the ones that you do know. Don't miss any questions through careless mistakes. If at all possible, try to take a second to look back over your answer selection and make sure you've selected the correct answer choice and haven't made a costly careless mistake (such as marking an answer choice that you didn't mean to mark). This quick double check should more than pay for itself in caught mistakes for the time it costs.

### ⊘ Pace Yourself

It's easy to be overwhelmed when you're looking at a page full of questions; your mind is confused and full of random thoughts, and the clock is ticking down faster than you would like. Calm down and maintain the pace that you have set for yourself. Especially as you get down to the last few minutes of the test, don't let the small numbers on the clock make you panic. As long as you are on track by monitoring your pace, you are guaranteed to have time for each question.

### ⊘ Don't Rush

It is very easy to make errors when you are in a hurry. Maintaining a fast pace in answering questions is pointless if it makes you miss questions that you would have gotten right otherwise. Test writers like to include distracting information and wrong answers that seem right. Taking a little extra time to avoid careless mistakes can make all the difference in your test score. Find a pace that allows you to be confident in the answers that you select.

### ✓ KEEP MOVING

Panicking will not help you pass the test, so do your best to stay calm and keep moving. Taking deep breaths and going through the answer elimination steps you practiced can help to break through a stress barrier and keep your pace.

## Final Notes

The combination of a solid foundation of content knowledge and the confidence that comes from practicing your plan for applying that knowledge is the key to maximizing your performance on test day. As your foundation of content knowledge is built up and strengthened, you'll find that the strategies included in this chapter become more and more effective in helping you quickly sift through the distractions and traps of the test to isolate the correct answer.

Now that you're preparing to move forward into the test content chapters of this book, be sure to keep your goal in mind. As you read, think about how you will be able to apply this information on the test. If you've already seen sample questions for the test and you have an idea of the question format and style, try to come up with questions of your own that you can answer based on what you're reading. This will give you valuable practice applying your knowledge in the same ways you can expect to on test day.

**Good luck and good studying!**

# World History

## World History Pre-1400

### Lower Paleolithic Period

The **Paleolithic period** is the earliest period of human development, as well as the longest. It is also commonly referred to as the **Old Stone Age**. It lasted from about 2.5 million years ago until about 300,000 years ago. Development during this period was excruciatingly slow. The Paleolithic period is usually divided into three sections: the Lower, Middle, and Upper. The **Lower Paleolithic period** is characterized by the appearance of stone tools; the chopping tools found at the Olduvai Gorge in Tanzania are from this period and date back over a million years. They were probably made by **Australopithecus**, an ancestor of modern humans. Anthropologists have also found stone tools believed to have been made by Homo erectus between 100,000 and 500,000 years ago.

### Middle and Upper Paleolithic Periods

The Middle Paleolithic period occurred about 300,000 years ago until about 40,000 years ago. During this time, the Mousterian culture of Neanderthal men was active in Europe, North Africa, Palestine, and Siberia. These ancestors of modern man lived in caves and had the use of fire. They hunted prehistoric mammals and had slightly more sophisticated tools than their forebears, including crude needles for sewing furs together. These people may have practiced some sort of religion. In the **Upper Paleolithic** period, about 40,000 years ago until about 10,000 years ago, Neanderthals were replaced by varieties of Homo sapiens, including Cro-Magnon man and Grimaldi man. A number of diverse cultures flourished during this period, and the first manmade shelters arose. This was also the period in which people first crafted jewelry and illustrated drawings on the walls of caves.

#### *Solutrean and Magdalenian Phase of the Paleolithic Period*

During the **Upper Paleolithic period**, hunters entered Europe from the east and conquered the more primitive cultures living there. These victorious hunters were known as the **Solutreans**. These people are noted for their fine spearheads, which they used to hunt wild horses. The Solutreans were, in turn, replaced by the **Magdalenians**, the most advanced phase of the Paleolithic period. The Magdalenians subsisted mainly through fishing and reindeer hunting. They developed extremely precise tools and sophisticated weapons, such as the atlatl, a device that made it possible to throw a spear over a great distance. Most of all, though, the Magdalenians are known for their cave paintings in modern-day France.

### Mesolithic Period

The Mesolithic period, otherwise known as the **Middle Stone Age**, began roughly 10,000 years ago and ended with the introduction of farming (dates vary by culture). In some areas, the use of farming was already beginning at the end of the Paleolithic era, and therefore there may not be a true **Mesolithic period**. The most extensive examples of this kind of culture are found in Northern Europe, where the end of the **Ice Age** created much greater changes in the ability to live off of the land. The remains of the Mesolithic period are mainly just middens (rubbish heaps), as well as some deforestation. The people of the Mesolithic period made small tools out of flint; fishing tackle, canoes, and bows have been found at some sites.

## Neolithic Period

The Neolithic period, also known as the **New Stone Age**, refers to that stage of human cultural evolution in which man developed stone tools, settled in villages, and began making crafts. In order to begin living in towns, man had to learn how to domesticate animals and sustain agriculture; formerly, in the Paleolithic and Mesolithic periods, man had subsisted through hunting, fishing, and gathering. The **Neolithic period** is said to have ended when urban civilizations began, or when metal tools or writing began. Because the designation of Neolithic depends on these factors, anthropologists date its occurrence differently for different regions and populations. At present, anthropologists believe that the earliest Neolithic culture was in southwest Asia between 8000 and 6000 BC.

### *Spread of Neolithic Culture*

Most anthropologists date the beginning of **Neolithic culture** at somewhere between 8000 and 6000 BC. It began with the domestication of plants (wheat, barley, and millet) and animals (cattle, sheep, and goats). The Neolithic culture in the valley between the Tigris and Euphrates Rivers gradually evolved into a more urban civilization by 3500 BC. Meanwhile, Neolithic cultural advances spread through Europe, the Nile Valley, the Indus Valley, and the Huang He Valley. In these regions, the innovations of the Neolithic period were intermixed with the particulars of the region; in the Huang He region, for instance, rice cultivation was a product of advances in agriculture. By 1500 BC, Neolithic culture had spread to Mexico and South America. In these areas, corn, beans, and squash were the major crops.

## Sumerians of Mesopotamia

Mesopotamia, the region between the Tigris and Euphrates Rivers in what is now considered the Middle East, contained several different early civilizations of which the **Sumerians** were one of the more prominent. They developed the system of writing known as **cuneiform**, by which they elaborated their theories on mathematics and astronomy. The Sumerians also had a detailed system of **laws** and traded widely with other groups throughout the region. They even traded with civilizations as far away as Egypt and India. There was no coin or currency system at this time, thus trade was conducted on the barter system, in which goods are exchanged for one another, directly.

## Babylonian Civilization of Mesopotamia

After the Sumerian civilization declined, the next dominant civilization was **Babylon**. The Babylonians conquered the Sumerians and established a city on the Euphrates River in approximately 1,750 B.C. One of the most famous Babylonian rulers was **Hammurabi**, who established the famous **Code of Hammurabi**, an extremely detailed set of laws. This marked the first time that a set of rules governing every aspect of social life was applied to an entire people. The Babylonians are also known for their construction of **ziggurats**, long pyramid-like structures that were used as religious temples. Over time, the Babylonians acquired a reputation as a sensuous and hedonistic people, and the name Babylon has come to stand for any debauched civilization.

**Review Video: Early Mesopotamia: The Babylonians**
Visit mometrix.com/academy and enter code: 340325

**Review Video: Early Mesopotamia: The Sumerians**
Visit mometrix.com/academy and enter code: 939880

## Pyramids of Egypt

The incredible engineering skills of the Egyptians are most famously displayed in the **pyramids** clustered along the Nile River. These were built roughly between 2700 and 2500 BC. The largest of the structures, the **Khufu pyramid** at Giza, is estimated to have taken 20 years and 100,000 laborers to construct. Today, it stands at 450 feet; some of its height has been lost to erosion. These pyramids were built as burial sites for the pharaohs, who were believed to continue their rule in the afterlife. Peasants worked on the pyramids in exchange for food and shelter. The shape of the pyramids was meant to symbolize the slanting rays of the sun, with sloping sides meant to help the ka (soul) of the pharaoh climb to the sky and join the gods.

**Review Video: Ancient Egypt**
Visit mometrix.com/academy and enter code: 398041

### Religion in Africa

**Sub-Saharan Africa** was composed of disparate tribes. Most of Africa practiced **animistic religion**, in which it is believed that deities are embodied in the animals that people depend upon for food and service. Ritual and participatory worship were important; common activities included drumming, dancing, divination, and sacrifices. These religions typically had well-developed concepts of good and evil; they believed that some evil, disasters, and illnesses were produced by witchcraft, and that specialists (known as diviners) were required to combat the power of these malevolent beings. Many African peoples shared an underlying belief in a **creator deity**, whose power was expressed through the **ancestors** who founded the tribe. These deceased ancestors were a link between the living and the deities. African tribal religions showed a remarkable resilience when they began to come into contact with monotheistic religions.

### Indus Valley Civilizations

The **Indus River Valley** is an area bordered by the Himalayan Mountains in what is now Pakistan. The people of this region developed a system of writing, as well as systems of weight and measurement which were useful in trade. They exchanged goods with the people of Mesopotamia in the west, as well as with the people of Tibet in the east. The Aryans invaded this region and brought with them iron technology and the Sanskrit language. The introduction of iron tools made it possible to cultivate the forests of the **Ganges River Valley** in what is now India.

### Early Cities of Mohenjo-Daro and Harappa in the Indus Valley

Both the Indus Valley and Egyptian civilizations featured extremely well-planned **cities**. In the Indus Valley, the cities of **Mohenjo-Daro** and **Harappa** were located along the Indus River, in what is now Pakistan. Each of these cities was built around 2500 BC and housed approximately 30,000 citizens. They were each designed in a grid-like pattern, with streets running east-west and north-south. Both Mohenjo-Daro and Harrapa had bathhouses, sewer systems, and organized garbage collection. The structures in these cities were built with oven-fired bricks, which made them durable. Unlike in Egypt, where technological advances were used to enhance religious practice, the people of the Indus Valley used their technology to improve sanitation.

### Earliest Civilization in What Would Become China

The earliest civilizations in what would become China flourished along the banks of the **Huang He (Yellow) River** before the year 2000 BC. The first Chinese dynasty was the **Xia** (Hsia), succeeded by the **Shang** dynasty. In this period, the rulers established an intricate system of government and a comprehensive judiciary. The basic components of this system would be preserved in Chinese civilization for centuries. The distinctive Chinese style of writing also developed during this period. Like Egyptian hieroglyphs, the Chinese pictographs were meant to resemble their definition. Over time, though, the Chinese characters have come to resemble their definitions less and less.

## Zhou Dynasty

The Zhou dynasty, which ran from roughly 1030 to 221 BC, is generally considered to be the third Chinese dynasty, after the Shang. The **Zhou** were brought into power by the commander **Wu**, who declared that the decadent Shang monarchs had forfeited the mandate of heaven (in other words, God's approval of their reign). The Zhou dynasty is generally divided into two parts: The **Western Zhou** ran a feudal-type state in the central plain and the area around the Yellow River. The later **Eastern Zhou** had a more difficult time maintaining control of rival states within its control. The Zhou dynasty was the period in which Chinese civilization spread to most parts of Asia. Both **Confucius** and **Lao Tzu** were active during this period. China became the preeminent state during this period.

## Han Dynasty

The Han dynasty ran from approximately 206 BC to AD 220. It began when a peasant, **Liu Pang**, led a successful insurrection against the Qin dynasty leaders. The **Han** shifted the capital of China to Changan (Xian). This was the period in which **Confucianism** became the dominant political and social ideology in China. The Han developed a code of laws and a form of government based upon the proper Confucian relations between king and subject, husband and wife, and father and son. The Han dynasty saw China accrue fantastic wealth and become one of the most sophisticated and resplendent countries the world has seen. Eventually, though, peasant revolts weakened the Han and made them susceptible to overthrow.

## Daoism

Next to Confucianism, **Daoism** (also Taoism) is the most important philosophy to have emerged out of China. **Taoist thought** is based on the 6th century-BC writings of **Lao Tzu**, specifically on the Tao Te Ching. Lao Tzu was a student of Confucius and taught that individuals should discover the essential nature of things and of themselves and should not seek to challenge the natural harmony of life. A proper Taoist should be patient and austere. Unlike Confucianism, Daoism contains an element of mysticism and so may be called a religion. Taoism introduced the concept of the **yin and yang**, the contrasting male and female elements that make up everything in existence and which must be harmonized in order to achieve self-realization.

## Early Civilizations of Mesoamerica and South America

Mesoamerica, which is now known as Central and South America, were both host to developed civilizations 3,000 years before the arrival of Columbus. These civilizations were largely dependent upon water-supported agriculture. The most important crop in the region was **maize**. The first dominant group in this region, the **Olmecs**, was based in what is now the gulf coast of eastern Mexico. The Olmecs were known for making large and elaborate stone carvings. There were also major civilizations at this time in what is now Peru. In the Andes Mountains of that region, the **Chavin** culture developed intricate stone temples and pyramids. These sites have been explored carefully by archaeologists.

## Hinduism

Hinduism is the traditional religion of India. It is expressed in an individual's philosophy and behavior, rather than in the performance of any specific rituals. **Hinduism** does not claim a founder but has evolved slowly over thousands of years; the first Hindu writings date back to the third millennium BC. There are a few concepts that are common to all permutations of Hinduism, such as the **Vedas**, which are considered to be the sacred texts of the religion. The chief aim in life for a Hindu is to be liberated from the cycle of suffering and rebirth. Hindus believe in **reincarnation** and that a person's conduct in this life will affect his or her position in the next (**karma**). Although Hinduism is frequently associated with the caste system, the two are actually unrelated.

## Hindu Caste System

The Hindu caste system is a means of organizing society. It divides the populace into four groups, each associated with a part of the body of the Hindu god Purusha. The highest class is the **Brahmins**, associated with the mouth of the god. In the original system, the brahmin class was made up of priests. The second caste is the **Kshatriyas**, made up of rulers and soldiers; this caste is associated with the arms of Purusha. Next are the **Vaishyas**, associated with the legs of the god. This caste was composed of landowners, merchants, and artisans. The last group is the **Shudras**, associated with the feet of the god. This caste was composed of servants and slaves. Women do not have a place in the traditional Hindu caste system.

## Judaism

Judaism was founded by **Abraham** in the 20th century BC. Abraham was called out from among the Chaldeans to enter into a covenant with God, whereby he and his descendants would receive special treatment and an inheritance of land. Abraham then moved to Canaan (near present-day Israel). Later, his descendants would move to Egypt and be enslaved. They were eventually liberated from slavery in Egypt by God through Moses, and they conquered the land of Canaan under the leadership of Joshua. Moses received from God a set of strict laws, the **Ten Commandments**; all of this is described in the **Torah**, the essential Jewish Scripture. There are also several other important books, including the Talmud, and many important commentaries by learned Jewish theologians.

## Creation of Ancient Israel

Around the year 1020 BC, **Saul** became the first king of the Jewish nation, known as **Israel**. Saul's successor **David** conquered the city of Jerusalem and united all of the tribes of Israel, making Jerusalem their capital. In the 10th century BC, David's son **Solomon** built the first Jewish Temple in Jerusalem; this building was used to house the **Ark of the Covenant**, which housed the original Torah. Israel would be taken over by the **Assyrians** in the 8th century BC, and later by the **Babylonians**. Finally, in 538 BC, the Persian King Cyrus allowed the Jews to return to Jerusalem and rebuild the Temple. Israel would subsequently be taken over by the **Greeks** under Alexander, and later by the **Romans** under Pompey.

## Vedic Age

The Vedic Age is the period recounted in the Indian Vedas, the earliest known records of Indian history. The dates of the **Vedic age** are considered by most to be between 2000 and 1000 BC. The oldest Vedic text is the **Rig-Veda**, which bears many Indo-Iranian elements. It is a collection of religious hymns and stories and describes a nomadic people who were ruled by a king who depended on their consent. His main duty was to protect the people. Religion in this period primarily consisted of chanting and the performing of sacrifices. During this period, elaborate rules concerning marriage were created, and the rigid social stratification that would become known as the **caste system** evolved.

## Buddhism

Buddhism was created by **Gautama Siddhartha** (otherwise known as Buddha) in about 528 B.C. It was in part a response to Hinduism, which Buddha felt had become bloated with worldliness and politics. Traditional Buddhism is based upon the **Four Noble Truths**: existence is suffering, suffering is caused by desire, an end of suffering will come with Nirvana, and Nirvana will come with the practice of the **Eightfold Path**. The steps of the Eightfold Path are as follows: right views, right resolve, right speech, right action, right livelihood, right effort, right mindfulness, and right concentration. Buddhism has no deities. Buddhism did not receive any official sanction for a long time but did eventually spread and take hold in India, China, Japan, and elsewhere.

## PERSIA

Persia is the European name for the region that is now Iran. This area has been the site of a number of vibrant cultures. The **Medes** were the first to develop there, lasting from approximately 700 to 549 BC, when they were expelled by the army of Cyrus. This great king then established the **Achaemenid dynasty**, which itself was destroyed by Alexander the Great in 330 BC. After this, a succession of peoples including the **Parthians**—rivals to Rome—inhabited the region, until a durable **Sasanian dynasty** was established in AD 224. Persia was in constant conflict with the **Byzantine Empire**, and would eventually be overtaken by the **Arabs** in the 7th century AD.

## ZOROASTRIANISM

Zoroastrianism was the state religion of Persia during the **Sasanian dynasty** between the years AD 224 and 651. It is based upon the prophecies of **Zoroaster** (also known as Zarathustra, c. 628-551 BC), a Persian who claimed to have encountered the divine being Ahura Mazda. Zoroastrians believed that the world was composed of good and evil spirits, who are in constant conflict. Fire was sacred to the Zoroastrians. Many of the concepts of Zoroastrianism would be included in Christianity, especially by the Manichean sect, who also saw the world as a struggle between absolute good and absolute evil. Zoroastrianism receded in popularity with the rise of Islam.

## CITY-STATE OF ATHENS IN ANCIENT GREECE

Ancient Greece was dominated by two city-states, **Athens** and **Sparta**. These two had very distinct cultures. Athens was a coastal city with a democratic form of government which amassed wealth by trading overseas. Athens is also known as the city that gave life to philosophy and the arts. **Socrates** engaged in his famous dialogues in the streets of Athens, and though he was eventually executed by the Athenian government for supposedly corrupting the youth, his thoughts achieved immortality in the writings of his student **Plato**. In turn, Plato's student **Aristotle** developed a strict form of reasoning that has formed the basis of much subsequent Western thought. Athens is also renowned for the architectural marvel that is the **Parthenon**.

## SPARTA IN ANCIENT GREECE

While Athens was known for its devotion to the arts and its democratic form of government, its rival city-state **Sparta** was devoted to agriculture and the military. Sparta was not located on the coast, and therefore the Spartans had little contact with distant peoples. Spartan society was governed by a strict class system. Most people (**helots**) worked the land of other people as virtual serfs. In the upper classes, participation in **military training** was compulsory. Indeed, Spartan youths left their families to begin military training at a young age. The Spartans did not produce any noteworthy philosophers, but as a culture, they stressed the good of the group over that of the individual. This is in stark contrast to most Athenian thought, which celebrates the achievements of the individual.

**Review Video: Ancient Greece**
Visit mometrix.com/academy and enter code: 800829

## GREECE IN THE PERICLEAN AND HELLENISTIC AGES

The **Periclean Age** in Greece, so named because Pericles was the leader of Athens during the period, took place in the 5th century BC. It was during this period that most of the great contributions to Western culture were made, including the philosophy of Socrates, the medical work of Hippocrates, and the great dramatic works of Aeschylus, Sophocles, and Euripides. The **Hellenistic Age** (4th century BC), on the other hand, is more commonly known for the military conquests made by **Alexander the Great**. If it were not for the conquests of Alexander during the Hellenistic Age, many of the innovations and achievements of the Periclean Age may not have had such a great influence on the West. It should be noted that the Hellenistic Age was not without its own great thinkers; in fact, Alexander studied as a boy under Aristotle.

### MAJOR WARS OF GREECE IN THE PERICLEAN AND HELLENISTIC AGES

During the **Age of Pericles**, an alliance of Greek city-states was challenged by the mighty Persians. Miraculously, the outnumbered Greeks were able to defeat the Persians at Thermopylae and Marathon, and staved off conquest. The war with the Persians impoverished the Greeks, however, and increased rivalries among the city-states. In Athens, the requirements for citizenship were loosened, though slavery remained. Conflict between Sparta and Athens culminated in the **Peloponnesian War**, won by Sparta. Eventually, the whole of Greece would be conquered by **Philip of Macedon**, who allowed the Greeks to maintain their culture and traditions. **Alexander the Great** was the son of Philip and became the master of an empire larger than any the world had ever seen. During his reign, he united many disparate peoples through a common law and exchange policy. He died at the age of 33, and his empire was divided into three parts amongst his generals.

### ROMAN REPUBLIC

Roman civilization dates from the founding of the city in 753 BC until the defeat of the last Emperor, **Romulus Augustus**, in AD 476. The republic itself lasted from the overthrow of the monarchy in 509 BC until the empowering of the first Emperor, **Octavian Augustus**, in 27 BC. The area along the Tiber River where Rome would be built was previously inhabited by a group known as the **Etruscans**. Rome took its name from the legendary **Romulus**, who is said to have founded it after triumphing over his brother Remus. The basic structure of Roman society consisted of **patricians** at the top of the social hierarchy, who were descendants of the founders of the republic and often wealthy. Beneath the patricians were the **plebeians**, which consisted of all other freemen. Finally, at the bottom of the social hierarchy were **slaves**. Women were not included in most social or economic business, although a Roman woman's rights were often significantly preferable to her contemporaries in other civilizations. The **Roman Republic**, which was the first political arrangement of Rome, was led by two consuls who were chosen annually. The **consuls** presided over the **Senate**, made up of a permanent group of those who had been previously elected to a high-ranking magistracy (originally primarily patrician in composition), and the **Assembly**, which was solely for the plebeians. Rome had extensive laws covering individual and property rights.

**Review Video: Roman Republic Part One**
Visit mometrix.com/academy and enter code: 360192

**Review Video: Roman Republic Part Two**
Visit mometrix.com/academy and enter code: 881514

### EXPANSION OF ROME

#### *PUNIC WARS*

The first real challenge to the territorial expansion of Rome was the city of **Carthage**, located across the Mediterranean in North Africa. Carthage was founded by the Phoenicians. There were three major conflicts, known as the **Punic Wars**, fought between Rome and Carthage. Rome won the **First Punic War** and acquired Sicily in the process. The Carthaginian effort in the **Second Punic War** was led by Hannibal and included his famous crossing of the Alps. Hannibal was quite successful in Italy, but a combination of a war of attrition throughout Italy and the counterattacks on

Carthaginian holdings in Spain and the city of Carthage itself by the Romans forced Hannibal to retreat to North Africa to defend Carthage. In the **Third Punic War**, Rome finally destroyed Carthage; in fact, it is often rumored that the victorious Romans burned Carthage to the ground and then salted the fields of their vanquished foe, a tribute to the Senator Cato the Elder's repeated cry at the end of various speeches of "*Ceterum censeo Carthaginem esse delendam*" ("Moreover, I have determined that Carthage must be destroyed").

**Review Video: The Punic Wars**
Visit mometrix.com/academy and enter code: 879745

### *Greece, Gaul, and Spain*

After defeating Carthage once and for all, Rome met little resistance as it continued to acquire more territory. This was partly due to the superiority of Roman weaponry, and in part because the Romans were good at bringing conquered peoples into the fold. Rome typically allowed conquered people to maintain their native cultures, so long as they paid tribute to Rome. Rome defeated the Macedonians and took **Greece**, then conquered large portions of **Gaul** (France) and **Spain**. The vastness of the Roman Empire necessitated some advances in infrastructure technology. Romans are justly famous for their solid and durable **roads** and **aqueducts** (systems for delivering water), many of which survive today.

### Grand Alliance of Julius Caesar in Rome

As Rome continued to expand, class conflicts developed between the nobility and the poor. In this era of unrest, it became possible for individual leaders to claim more power than the law had allowed previously. In 60 B.C., the famous general Julius Caesar formed the three-person alliance known as the First Triumvirate to govern Rome. The other two members were **Gnaeus Pompey Magnus** and **Marcus Licinius Crassus**. During this period, Caesar led a successful campaign against the Gauls (a people in modern-day France) and made himself richer than the entire Roman State on the proceeds from his conquest. After Crassus was killed in battle, Caesar pushed Pompey out and assumed total control of Rome, crowning himself dictator-for-life. Though Caesar was very popular with the mob, his decision to claim lifelong power alienated him from the nobility in the Senate. He was assassinated by a group of senators, led by **Marcus Iunius Brutus**, in 44 B.C.

### Second Roman Triumvirate

After the assassination of Caesar in 44 B.C., Rome was mired in chaos. Those who had conspired to kill Caesar had hoped to return to the republican form of government, but instead another trio of leaders came to the fore, this time as a governmental commission of "three men for reconstituting the Republic," known as the **Triumvirate**. The Triumvirate was composed of **Marc Antony**, one of Caesar's greatest generals and a Consul at the time; **Octavius**, the nephew and testamentary heir of Caesar; and **Marcus Aemilius Lepidus**, a third wheel who was quickly made a non-entity. While Octavius stayed in Rome, Antony left for Egypt, where he stayed for a time as the guest and lover of **Cleopatra**. Eventually, infighting between Octavius and Antony led the former to mount a campaign against Egypt. When they realized that they were defeated, Antony and Cleopatra committed suicide to avoid the shame of being paraded in Octavian's triumph. Lepidus having been marginalized, Octavius (now known as Augustus) became the first **Emperor**.

### Pax Romana

After the ascension of Augustus, Rome entered a period of relative tranquility. Augustus dubbed this era, which lasted about forty years, the **Pax Romana**. Rome remained an empire, although the conquered peoples were able to obtain Roman citizenship without having to forfeit their native customs. It was at this period that Rome reached its greatest geographic proportions, stretching all the way up to present-day Scotland. This was also the greatest period for **Roman artistic achievement**; both Virgil and Ovid were active during the Pax Romana, and, indeed, the Aeneid of Virgil was written in part to glorify Augustus. It was at this time that the polytheist religion of Rome was challenged first by the **Judaism** of the conquered Hebrews, and later by the early **Christians**.

## Constantine and the Christians

The Roman Emperor **Constantine**, in response to the inconvenient vastness of his dominion, established an eastern capital: **Constantinople**, in AD 330. Having received a sign in the heavens which promised him victory over his rivals for the office of Emperor should he convert to Christianity, Constantine famously issued the **Edict of Milan**, in which he called for the end of the persecution of Christians, after a sound victory as promised. After this act, Christianity flourished in the Roman Empire and became the official religion of the state. A movement called **monasticism** developed within the religion, advocating the renunciation of worldly goods in favor of contemplation and prayer. After the death of Constantine, the empire once again proved unwieldy for one man, and therefore it split as it had previously, with the western half being governed from Rome and the eastern half from Constantinople. This arrangement would prove untenable, however; a Germanic tribe of **barbarians** eventually sacked Rome, and the western Roman capital fell in AD 476.

## Byzantine Empire

The eastern half of the Roman Empire became known as the **Byzantine Empire**. After the fall of Rome, **Emperor Justinian** led successfully from Constantinople for a number of years. The Justinian era is especially remembered for the contributions to law and religious artwork, in particular the development of mosaics. In the years after the fall of Rome, the **Catholic Christian Church** gradually rose to fill the power vacuum. In what had been the Western Roman Empire, the Church acted completely independent of any political body, while even in the Byzantine Empire the Church was increasing in power. Only the influence of the Byzantine Emperor kept the Church from being the most powerful group in all of Europe.

## Rise of Christianity

**Early Christianity** was a mass of competing doctrines, including various groups such as the Gnostics and Arians who all sought to have their view legitimized as the truth. Eventually, the **orthodox church**, through an ecumenical council of bishops, created in the 4th century AD the canon of New Testament texts which exists today. The apostles had created a hierarchy of bishops, priests, and deacons who stressed obedience to duly constituted church authority. By the middle of the 2nd century, Christianity began to attract intellectuals in the **Roman Empire**. Although Christians were still liable to be persecuted in the farther reaches of the empire, many turned to the Church as the empire crumbled, as the Church was all that was left of civilization, and would rebuild Europe over the next millennium.

## Kingdom of Kush

Kush was a powerful African kingdom that lasted in some form from 2000 BC until AD 350. For a long time, **Kush** was based around the city of **Kerma**, in what is now Sudan. Kushites became wealthy because of their mineral resources and because of their advantageous location in the northwest corner of Africa, where they were at the crossroads of several intercontinental trade routes. There was a great deal of contact between Kush and **Egypt** in this period. In 767 BC, King Kashta of Kush defeated the Egyptians, and the Kushites had control of the entire Nile Valley. Kush would soon be weakened by the Assyrians, however, and would eventually fall prey to the **Romans**; in AD 350, the new capital of Kush, Meroe, was sacked.

## Aksum (Axum)

Aksum, a town in what is now northern Ethiopia, was the capital city of one of Africa's most powerful kingdoms between the 1st and 6th centuries AD. The kings of **Aksum** were said to have descended from **Menelik**, one of the sons of the famous King Solomon. These people controlled almost all of the trade on the **Red Sea** and made a tremendous profit on the exchange of ivory. In the 4th century AD, Aksum eliminated the kingdom of **Kush** and became the predominant power in Africa. It was also during this century that Aksum was **Christianized**; it remains a hub of Ethiopian Christianity to this day. In its later stages, Aksum's control extended into southern Arabia and would eventually give way to the Persians and the Arabs.

## Nok Culture

One of the most successful cultures of the African Iron Age was the **Nok culture**. The Nok developed **ironworking** technology before anyone else, and also created a rich artistic culture that spread throughout the West African forest region. The Nok were mainly active between the 5th and the 1st centuries BC. Their creation of iron farm implements made it possible for farmers to develop surplus crops, and thus urban centers could develop. This increase in agricultural productivity also made it possible for there to be more specialization of labor. Therefore, not only were civilizations more stable, but they were also better able to protect themselves, as they now had both better weapons made of iron and more time to train warriors.

## Ancient Ghana

Beginning in the 7th century AD, **Ghana** was a major trading power in west Africa. It was mainly located in the areas that are now known as Mali and Mauritania. The people of Ghana grew rich by exchanging ivory and gold from the south and salt from the north. Eventually, Ghana would become an empire and would collect lavish tributes from all of the lands within its control. In the 11th century, the capital of Ghana was **Kumbi**. In 1076, however, Kumbi fell to the Almoravids, a Muslim tribe. The whole of Ghana would eventually be subsumed into the burgeoning empire of **Mali**.

## Ancient Mali

Today, Mali is the largest nation in West Africa. Indeed, throughout African history, **Mali** has been a major power. Until the 11th century, it was a part of the empire of Ghana, a wealthy trading nation. Mali would eventually rise to prominence in its own right. The economy of Mali was based upon the rich mineral resources (especially gold) of the region. Mali reached its highest prominence during the reign of **Mansa Musa** (AD 1312-7). This ruler introduced Islam to his people, which at this time lived as far north as Morocco. The city of **Timbuktu** became a cultural center for the region, as well as a crossroads for trade routes that stretched across the Sahara. Over time, internal disputes would divide Mali into several smaller kingdoms.

## Songhai Empire

The Songhai empire flourished in West Africa between the 14th and 16th centuries. Centered in the valley of the Niger River, the **Songhai** were first organized by Christian **Berbers** in the 7th century. Four hundred years later, they established their capital at **Gao** and became an Islamic nation. Except for a brief period in which they were ruled by the empire of Mali, the Songhai controlled over a thousand miles along the Niger. Like most of the African powers, the Songhai made their money through trade. **Muhammad I**, who ruled from 1493 to 1528, expanded the empire to its greatest area. One of the weaknesses of the Songhai, however, was that they did not have a traditional means of succession, and thus frequent infighting among the powerful eventually led to the empire's demise.

## The Huns

The Huns were a nomadic people who moved east across central Asia during the 4th century AD. The **Huns** were divided into several branches. The **White Huns** overran the Sasanian Empire and conquered many cities in the northern part of the Indian subcontinent. Another group roamed eastern Europe and established a strong empire on the Hungarian Plain around AD 400. The Huns were known for their amazing horsemanship and for being aggressive on the battlefield. It was under the guidance of **Attila** (440s) that the Huns reached their highest level of prominence. During this period, they collected tribute from many of the areas within the Roman Empire. Soon after the death of Attila, however, the Huns became complacent and lost most of their territory.

## The Mongols

The Mongols, who descended from the Huns, were a nomadic group that roamed east-central Asia. Around the year AD 1206, the various **Mongol** tribes were united under **Genghis Khan**, whose empire then stretched from the Black Sea to the Pacific Ocean, and from Tibet to Siberia. After the death of Genghis, the Mongol lands were divided up. This did not, however, slow expansion; Mongols eventually controlled parts of Iran as well. **Kublai Khan** was another prominent Mongol leader; he destroyed the Song dynasty in China and replaced it with the Yuan. By the 14th century, the Mongol Empire was beginning to disintegrate. Like many of its kind, it proved too large to govern. The Ming and subsequently the Qing dynasties put the remaining Mongols under Chinese control.

## Emergence of Russia

In the Middle Ages, Russia had a complicated and inefficient system of succession, which meant that the various lands were constantly being fought over, and authority was often dubious. For a long time, **Russia** was dominated by the **Mongols** (Tatars), who kept the local governments weak in order to continue receiving tributes. Moscow was able to parlay loyalty to the Tatars and colonization of other feudal estates into a great deal of power during this period. Supported by their Tatar overlords, the **Muscovite princes** were able to partition off their new lands in such a way that it became very difficult for nobles to consolidate their landholdings, which prevented any wealthy lords from ever challenging the princes of Moscow.

## Steppe Peoples and Seljuk Turks

Between the years AD 1000 and 1450, invaders from the **steppes** conquered parts of Asia, the Middle East, and Europe. These people had originally been nomads, but in this period, they began to settle and become tradesmen. The clans that made up this group were loosely based on family ties; once they became stationary, they began to appoint powerful chiefs for leadership support. Near AD 1000, the **Seljuk Turks** moved from Central Asia into the Middle East. This group then controlled the trade routes between Asia, Africa, and Europe, and charged tolls on these routes, building an empire with their wealth. In 1071, the Seljuk Turks defeated the Byzantines at the **Battle of Manzikert**; a Christian defeat which would be part of the motivation for the **First Crusade**. The Seljuk Turks were known as excellent fighters and mediocre rulers; local leaders frequently ignored the central government and fought one another for control of land. This infighting weakened the group until they became prey to new nomadic invaders from Central Asia.

## Poland and Hungary in Eastern Europe During the Middle Ages

During the Middle Ages, a number of different leaders tried to unite the various lands of **Poland**. These attempts were always defeated by the nobility, who preferred the country to be an oligarchy rather than a monarchy. Poland was also much involved during this period in a battle with the **Teutonic knights** over the Baltic coastline. **Hungary** was a feudal state by the beginning of the

14th century, and the various patches of land which constituted the country were ruled as if they were independent. Bishops in the **Eastern Orthodox Church** were among the largest landholders. Ostensibly, the nobility was in charge of the defense of the Hungarian people, though they rarely supplied the money and material for war.

## Origins and Expansion of Islam

The religion of Islam was founded by the prophet **Muhammad** in AD 610. **Islam** is a monotheistic religion based on the **Koran**, a book of scripture according to the Muslim god, **Allah**. The practice of Islam is based on "**Five Pillars**": faith in Allah, a pilgrimage to the city of Mecca, a yearly fast during the month of Ramadan, the giving of alms, and prayer five times a day. Muhammad also asserted that Islam should be spread throughout the world. Indeed, as the Christian Church was becoming the dominant factor in Europe, Islam was spreading throughout North Africa, the Middle East, parts of Asia, and even Spain. The simultaneous ascensions of Christianity and Islam inevitably led to conflict, most notably in the **Crusades**.

**Review Video: Islam**
Visit mometrix.com/academy and enter code: 359164

## Islamic Civilization

After the formation of Islam in the 7th century AD, it took 3 or 4 centuries to develop the institutional structures of the religion. **Islamic law** was created, and a new class of Muslim religious leaders and scholars emerged who took a prominent place in society. The Islamic civilization drew elements from its surroundings, namely the culture of the Greeks, Iranians, Christians, Jews, and Zoroastrians. At first, the Islamic Empire was ruled by a single **caliph** and a small Arab elite. As the empire expanded, however, this became untenable, and the lands were divided into a number of independent political entities. Also, factions began to emerge among Muslims, most notably between the **Sunnis** and **Shiites**, who rivaled over the true successor to Muhammad, among other issues. Because the entire Islamic world operated with a common system of trade, it quickly became very wealthy.

**Review Video: The Islamic Empire**
Visit mometrix.com/academy and enter code: 511181

## Feudalism in Western Europe

Feudalism was the system of social and economic organization that developed in Europe in the Middle Ages (roughly AD 750 to 1300). **Feudalism** is characterized by rigid hierarchies among the various classes. At the top of the hierarchy was the **king**, and below him **lords**, who oversaw a smaller area of land. Below the lords were **noblemen** who had been granted control over farmland in exchange for their pledge of allegiance to the king. These noblemen were known as **vassals** and **subvassals**. The land managed by each vassal was known as a **fief**, and the home of the vassal was known as the **manor**. Each manor and the community surrounding it comprised a self-sufficient unit. The laws of **primogeniture** were enforced at this time, meaning that the ownership of the fief would descend to the firstborn son of the lord. Finally, the land was cultivated either by **peasants** or **serfs**; peasants were free farmers, while serfs were basically slaves who were forced to work for the lord and were bound to their lands.

## Charlemagne

The emergence of the feudal system in Western Europe meant that instead of a centralized power, there were many local authorities. **Charlemagne** (AD 742-814) was a Germanic leader who tried to unify the former Western Roman Empire. In AD 800, **Pope St. Leo III** crowned Charlemagne

Emperor of Rome during Christmas Mass at St. Peter's Basilica in Rome, establishing a political relationship with the **Church** that would last throughout the Middle Ages. Charlemagne allocated a great deal of power to regional leaders and did not tax his subjects. For this reason, he was unable to make many internal improvements during his reign. Nevertheless, Charlemagne is credited with promoting the arts, especially within the thriving monasteries, without which much of antiquity would not have been transcribed and thus preserved. After the death of Charlemagne, his lands were divided up among his three grandsons according to the **Treaty of Verdun**.

### HOLY ROMAN EMPIRE

The Holy Roman Empire was the name given to the holdings of **Otto the Great** in 962, who had unified the central area of Charlemagne's empire. As in Charlemagne's day, this was a disparate group of territories, and proved difficult to govern. Otto incorporated the **Church** into his government, though he continually sought to minimize its power. One of the legacies of Otto's reign would be the rivalry between the Church and state. Gradually, the Church leaders acquired power, until they were exercising great control over the day-to-day activities of most citizens. Perhaps inevitably, this great power began to corrupt many of the Church's leaders. Indicative of the state of the Church was the often unpunished offense of **simony**, in which prestigious and important offices were bought and sold.

**Review Video: The Middle Ages: The Holy Roman Empire**
Visit mometrix.com/academy and enter code: 137655

### WESTERN EUROPE IN THE 12TH AND 13TH CENTURIES

In the 12th century AD, the various **fiefs** in Western Europe increasingly came into contact with one another. As advances in transportation technology made trade with distant neighbors possible, there developed more necessity for specialization. Rather than be entirely self-sufficient, lords found it was more economically advantageous to perfect the cultivation of one crop and exchange that for everything else. As **trade** became more important, so did the merchants in towns, known as burghers, who wielded considerable political power. Trade arrangements led to alliances between various towns, and the whole of Western Europe became more homogenous. The distinction between **classes** also became much less pronounced during this period. There were drawbacks, however: the increasing number of people in towns, as well as the more frequent travel between towns, contributed, no doubt, to the **bubonic plague epidemic** of the mid-14th century.

### FAITH AND LEARNING IN WESTERN EUROPE DURING THE LATE MIDDLE AGES

Surprising though it may seem, one of the best things that happened to Christian thought during the Middle Ages was its contact with **Islam**. The complex philosophies of Muslim scholars helped spur the evolution of **Christian theology**. These, in addition to the rediscovery of ancient philosophers such as Aristotle, led Christians to begin to glorify **reason** as the God-given tool for investigating religious faith. Many assertions made by the new rational theologians, however, were dubbed **heresy** by many Church leaders, as more and more Christian thinkers were bemoaning the materialistic ways of the Church leaders. One of the leading Christian thinkers of the Middle Ages was **St. Thomas Aquinas**, whose *Summa Theologica* outlined rational explanations for the belief in God and in the miracles of Christianity.

### FORMATION OF UNIVERSITIES IN THE MIDDLE AGES

The rapid evolution in Christian thought that took place during the Middle Ages gave rise to the formation of the first **universities**. For the first time in Western Europe, young men would move to large cities to study theology, law, and medicine at formal institutions. In addition to this trend, the academic method known as **scholasticism** was developed, in which scholars would use logic and deductive reasoning in order to analyze a work or determine something of an abstract nature. Among the so-called scholastics, two schools of thought developed: those scholars who adhered to the ideas of Plato were known as **realists**, and those who followed Aristotle were known as **nominalists**. The word *realist* is somewhat confusing when used to refer to the work of Plato, who believed that our perceptions of objects were merely perceptions of the barest shadows of their reality. Another development of Christianity in this period was **mysticism**; Christian mystics believed that they could achieve union with God through self-denial, contemplative prayer, and alms-giving.

## Germany, Italy, and France in the 13th Century

During the 13th century, France was transformed from a group of disparate fiefs into a centralized monarchy by **Philip Augustus** (Philip II). His heir, Philip IV, would establish the **Estates General**, a governing body composed of representatives from each province. The Estates General contained noblemen as well as wealthy commoners. Meanwhile, Germany endured an **interregnum**, or period between kings, after the ruler died without a clear successor. Italy, as well, spent this period as a collection of strong and independent townships. In a decentralized state, it became easier for wealthy merchants to wield power. In Germany, the **Hanseatic League**, an association of merchants, set regional trade policy.

## Magna Carta

**England**, unlike many of the other regions of Western Europe, had been accustomed to a strong monarchy. This tradition was challenged in AD 1215, when noblemen forced King John to sign the **Magna Carta**, a document which gave feudal rights back to the nobles and extended the rule of law to the middle-class burghers. The Magna Carta made the formation of the **Houses of Parliament** possible. Over time, Parliament would evolve into a two-house structure: the **House of Lords**, which contained nobles and clergy, and the **House of Commons,** which contained knights and burghers. The House of Lords was mainly occupied with legal questions, while the House of Commons dealt mainly in economic issues.

## Feudalism End in Western Europe

In the late 13th century, increased contact between regions and greater representation in government culminated in a number of **peasant revolts** and **serf uprisings**. During this period, members of the clergy became even more secular and open in their greed for fame and power. This alienated many common citizens from the Church. The invention of **gunpowder** also changed the social arrangements in Western Europe; fewer noblemen were willing to participate in combat, and so the code of chivalry gave way to **mercenary soldiers**. Noblemen largely turned their attention to acquiring some of the fantastic wealth available in trade. The quality that men strived for in these days was called **virtue**, meaning a solemn dedication to the arts and sciences.

## Papal Bull "Unam Sanctam" and the Crisis in the Western Church

Around the year 1300, the power of the Pope in political affairs was weakening because of the rise of strong monarchs and a spirit of nationalism. **Pope Boniface VIII** attempted to force kings to obey him but was unsuccessful. In response, Boniface issued a papal bull in 1296 that instructed **King Philip IV** of France to not tax the church; Philip ignored this command. Boniface would not relent, and issued the bull "**Unam Sanctam**," in which he declared that there are two powers on the earth, the temporal and the spiritual, with the latter always superior, and that there is no salvation outside of loyalty to the Roman Pontiff. Once again, Philip refused the claims of the Pope and decided to silence him by having him kidnapped and brought to France. Boniface was able to escape captivity but died soon afterward. This significantly weakened the political authority of the papacy.

## Babylon Captivity and Schism and the Crisis in the Western Church

After the death of Pope Boniface VIII, King Philip IV of France persuaded the College of Cardinals to select a French archbishop as the next pope. This pope, **Clement V**, moved the papacy to Avignon, France, where it would remain for 67 years. Debate raged during this period as to whether a pope could be legitimate in any city other than Rome. Also, Clement's court became notorious for its extravagance. In 1378, a new pope was chosen; an Italian, who chose the name **Urban VI** to indicate that he planned on keeping the papacy in Rome. Upset with Urban's policy, 13 French cardinals selected a new pope, the French-speaking **Clement VII**. Now, there were two popes, and each one declared the other illegitimate. This confusion lasted from 1378 until 1417, with the Pope in Rome and an antipope in Avignon.

## Hundred Years' War

England made a claim on the French throne in 1337, and the result was a **war** (or series of wars) that lasted for 116 years. France was angry, in return, that England had not upheld its feudal obligations to the French throne, to whom the English king was technically a distant vassal. France had the support of the Pope, but England used the innovation of the longbow to score some significant victories. It was during this war that the charismatic figure **Joan of Arc** emerged. Joan was a French peasant who led troops to several unlikely victories after being visited by God. Her deeds rallied the spirits of the French, and France eventually won. The catastrophic losses suffered by both sides had major consequences: England withdrew from contention as a land power, electing instead to develop a **navy**; in France, **Louis IX**—St. Louis—took advantage of the chaos to consolidate power in the monarchy.

## Effects of the Black Death and Johannes Gutenberg

Toward the end of the Middle Ages, two events greatly shaped future events. The **bubonic plague**, also known as the Black Death, killed between 30% and 60% of the European population. The influx of people to squalid cities made the rapid spread of this disease possible. The seemingly random devastation caused by the disease caused many people to question their faith, and the power of the Church suffered as a result. The other monumental event was the invention of the **printing press** by Johannes Gutenberg in about 1436. This invention was used first to produce a cheap copy of the Bible. Soon, though, printing presses with movable type were being used to print all sorts of things, and the literacy rate in Europe rose dramatically. It immediately became possible to disseminate ideas quickly.

**Review Video: An Overview of the Black Death**
Visit mometrix.com/academy and enter code: 431857

## Feudalism in Japan

Feudalism developed in Japan after wars in the 11th century left much of the land in the control of military leaders. These men did not actually own the land, but a complex set of rights were given to them, whereby they had the exclusive right to cultivate and profit from the land. Many Japanese were disenchanted with the central government at this time, so the idea of powerful regional leaders appealed to them. A code of ethics specific to feudalism emerged, and Japanese peasants were required to pledge loyalty to a particular lord rather than to a political ideal. One particular feudal administration, the **Minamoto**, acquired almost the entirety of Japan and replaced the central government for most people.

## Mayas

The Mayas were based in Mexico's Yucatan Peninsula, Tabasco, and Chiapas, as well as in what is now Guatemala and Honduras. Between the years AD 200 and 950, they developed a sophisticated civilization, with complex religions, architecture, arts, engineering, and astronomy. The **Mayas** did have a form of hieroglyphic writing, but most of their history and folklore was preserved orally. The Mayas are responsible for creating an extremely accurate **calendar** and for first conceiving the number **zero**. The Maya civilization was supported by agriculture, but it was run by a class of priests and warriors. In the 9th century, the Mayas were overrun by Toltecs from the north, who created the legend of the feathered serpent **Quetzalcoatl**.

### *Maya Religion*

The Mayas conceived of the universe as a flat, square earth, whose four corners and center were dominated by a god. Above the sky, there were 13 levels, and below were 9 underworlds, each dominated by a god. The sun and moon, deities in their own right, passed through all of these levels every day. Each male god had a female goddess counterpart. The Mayas also had patron gods and goddesses for various occupations and classes. Maya rulers had religious powers. Religious rituals often entailed human sacrifice and self-mutilation. The Mayas also played a ritual ball game that had religious importance; the losers of this game stood to lose their lives. Mayas developed their cities as tributes to the gods.

## Aztecs

When the **Toltec empire** had been eradicated around the year 1150, the power in Mesoamerica shifted to the valley of Mexico, around three lakes. By about 1325, the **Aztecs** had seized control of this area. The Aztec civilization was organized into **city-states**, much like early medieval Europe; political intrigue and state marriages were as common among the Aztecs as among the French. The Aztecs were known as fierce warriors and were hated by their neighbors because of their brutality. According to legend, the Aztecs settled in **Tenochtitlan** after a scout saw an eagle with a serpent in its beak perched on a cactus there. The Aztecs formed alliances based on threats and forced tributes.

## Incas

The Incas inhabited a huge area, from present-day Ecuador to central Chile to the eastern side of the Andes Mountains. The **Incas'** territory expanded especially after the 14th century AD. The Incas were engaged in frequent conflicts with rival groups, and they frequently enslaved the groups that they defeated. They eventually formed a permanent underclass of **serfs** in order to ensure that the lands of the military leaders would be cultivated. Incas typically dispersed rival groups in order to prevent being attacked. The Incan religion contained a god in heaven, a cult of ancestors, and a number of sacred objects and places. The Incas called themselves the **children of the Sun**.

## Tang Dynasty

The Tang dynasty was in control of China from AD 618 to 907. One of the main projects pursued by the **Tang** rulers was the **unification** of the far-flung and diverse Chinese states. The early portion of the Tang dynasty is considered one of the high points in Chinese history; the economy and the arts both flourished. Under the leadership of Tang generals, Chinese soldiers would claim parts of Afghanistan, Tibet, and Korea. The Tang were also somewhat unique as Chinese leaders in that they encouraged the introduction of foreign ideas into Chinese culture. **Printing** was invented in China during this period, and thus ideas could be disseminated much more easily. The end of the Tang dynasty came after a period of internal governmental conflict.

### Song Dynasty

The Song dynasty of China lasted between the years AD 960 and 1279. The **Song** rulers are credited with reuniting many portions of China that had become disjointed. Historians usually distinguish between the Northern and the Southern Song. The leaders of the Song dynasty made a deliberate effort to reduce the emphasis on military conquest; instead, they focused on developing China's **civil service**. The Song dynasty saw a rejuvenation of **Confucian philosophy** in China, as well as a renewed interest in the **arts**. Some people compare the Song dynasty with the European Renaissance. The Song was the only dynasty in China not to be ended by internal conflict; the Song were ousted by a rebel leader instead.

### Mauryan Empire

The Mauryan Empire lasted approximately between the years 321 and 185 BC. in India. It was established by the powerful leader **Chandragupta Maurya** and featured a strong military and an efficient bureaucracy. The **Mauryan empire** eventually spread as far west of the Indus River as present-day Afghanistan. At its greatest expansion, the Mauryan empire comprised almost the entirety of what is now India. The leader **Ashoka** (c. 272-232 BC) converted to Buddhism, and his rule was prosperous for rich and poor alike. After the death of Ashoka, however, the Mauryan Empire splintered, as the southern lands sought autonomy and the northern lands were subject to constant foreign invasions.

## World History 1400 to 1914

### Beginning of the Renaissance

In the 14th century, the turmoil caused by war and plague weakened the power of Christian theology. In its place came the philosophy of **humanism**, in which the emphasis is placed on individual potential and determination while detracting from one's attention to the realm of the divine. Humanist thought contributed to a resurgence in the arts and sciences, which eventually came to be known as the **Renaissance**. In the 14th and 15th centuries, the center of this resurgence was in **Northern Italy**, in large part because this was the crossroads of several important trade routes. Specifically, the city-states of Milan, Florence, and Venice cultivated excellent artists. Talented youths typically studied in these cities with their expenses paid by a wealthy patron; the most famous patrons were the **Medici** family in Florence.

**Review Video: The Renaissance**
Visit mometrix.com/academy and enter code: 123100

#### *Italian Artists of the Renaissance*

The early part of the Renaissance was dominated by the artists congregated in Northern Italy. Among them were several immortal talents. **Donatello** (1386-1466) sculpted a marvelous statue of David and was the first artist in this period to depict the naked human body (religious concerns had kept recent artists from doing so). **Botticelli** (1444-1510) is the painter of the famous Birth of Venus. **Leonardo da Vinci** (1452-1519) excelled in a number of different fields, but he is perhaps best known for painting the Mona Lisa and the Last Supper. **Michelangelo** (1475-1563), though, was probably the most famous painter and sculptor of the time; he painted the ceiling in the Sistine Chapel and sculpted the most famous statue of David.

#### *Literature and Science in the Renaissance*

Although the Renaissance is typically associated with achievements in visual art, the period also saw a magnificent outpouring of literary and scientific talent. One of the most significant works to emerge from this period was *The Prince*, by the Florentine **Niccolo Macchiavelli**. This book outlined a practical plan for political management, one that would be emulated by ruthless leaders in the future. Some of the other noteworthy authors were **Erasmus** (*In Praise of Folly*), **Sir Thomas More** (*Utopia*), **Montaigne**, **Cervantes** (*Don Quixote*), **Ben Johnson**, **Christopher Marlowe**, and, of course, **William Shakespeare**. At the same time, remarkable advances were being made in the sciences. **Copernicus** incited controversy by suggesting that the Earth revolved around the Sun; **Kepler** and **Galileo** would acquire hard data to support this claim.

## Age of Exploration

The Age of Exploration is also called the **Age of Discovery**. It is generally considered to have begun in the early 15th century and continued into the 17th century. Major developments of the Age of Exploration included **technological advances** in navigation, mapmaking, and shipbuilding. These advances led to expanded European exploration of the rest of the world. **Explorers** set out from several European countries, including Portugal, Spain, France, and England, seeking new routes to Asia. These efforts led to the discovery of new lands, as well as **colonization** in India, Asia, Africa, and North America.

**Review Video: Age of Exploration**
Visit mometrix.com/academy and enter code: 612972

## Role of Economics in the Age of Exploration

At the same time that the Renaissance was reinvigorating European cultural life, a desire to explore the world abroad was growing. Indeed, the ability to make long voyages was facilitated by the advances in **navigational technology** made around this time. The main reason for exploration, though, was **economic**. Europeans had first been introduced to eastern goods during the Crusades, and the exploits of Marco Polo in the 13th century had further whetted the western appetite for contact with distant lands. This increasing focus on exploration and trade caused a general shift in the balance of power in Europe. Landlocked countries, like Germany, found that they were excluded from participating in the lucrative new economy. On the other hand, those countries which bordered the **Atlantic** (England, France, Spain, and Portugal) were the most powerful players.

## Obstacles to Exploration by Europe Before 1400

Before 1400, few Europeans knew anything about the world. When **Christopher Columbus** read of the exploits of the Italian Marco Polo, however, he was inspired to seek out new trade routes. Also, **Prince Henry** of Portugal established a navigation institute that encouraged sailors to explore. For a long time, extended sea voyages were restricted by a lack of navigational and seafaring technology; the inventions of the compass, astrolabe, and caravel remedied this situation. There was also a high cost associated with long travels (around 1400); however, new monarchs in France, England, Spain, and Portugal decided that they were willing to pay a high price to get a piece of the spice trade. Finally, the question of a motive for exploration was answered by the increasing fervor for missionary work, as well as the economic necessity of developing new trade routes.

## Major European Explorers

**Vasco da Gama** was the first European to sail around the Cape of Good Hope, on the southern tip of what is now South Africa. This made it possible to reach Asia by boat. **Balboa** explored Central America and was the first European to view the Pacific Ocean. **Magellan** is remembered as the first to circumnavigate the globe. **Cortes** was a powerful commander who subjugated the Aztecs in what is now Mexico; he used great brutality to achieve his ends. **Pizarro**, like Cortes, was a conquistador; he conquered the Incas in what is now Peru. **Amerigo Vespucci**, from whose name the word

*America* was derived, mapped the Atlantic coast of South America and was able to convince stubborn Europeans that these lands were not a part of India.

## Joint-Stock Companies at the Time of the Age of Exploration

As exploration created new opportunities for amassing wealth, **Portugal** enjoyed special favor because of its excellent location and cordial relations with many of the Muslim nations of North Africa. The ruler of Portugal at this time was even known as Prince Henry "the Navigator" (1394-1460). In order to solidify trade arrangements, European rulers began to think about colonizing foreign lands. In order to fund these expensive trips, a new kind of business known as the **joint-stock company** was developed. In a joint-stock company, a group of merchants would combine their resources to pay for the passage of a vessel. These groups would later be influential in securing colonial charters for many of their agents. One of the most powerful examples was the **Muscovy Company of England**, which controlled almost all trade with Russia.

## Mercantilism at the Time of the Age of Exploration

As foreign trade became the most important part of every nation's economy, the economic theory of **mercantilism** became popular. According to mercantilism, a nation should never import more than it exports. Of course, it is impossible for every country to achieve this goal at the same time, so European countries were in fierce competition at all times. The solution that most nations pursued was to establish **colonies**, because these could supply resources for export by the mother country without really being considered imports. This rush to colonize had disastrous consequences for the indigenous peoples of the Americas and Africa. Europeans often looted the Native Americans for anything of value, and their need for cheap labor to cultivate the land there spawned the **African slave trade**.

## Reformation

A response to corruption in the Catholic Church and lapses in enforcement of the basic tenets of the faith, such as those against simony, the **Reformation** was a movement that called for a return to what many believed to be a simpler message of salvation that they felt to be more scripturally accurate. Many people in this time were outraged by the vast landholdings and stuffed coffers of the Church, which they felt should be concerned with tending to the spiritual health of its members. In 1440, the invention of the **printing press** had made it possible for ideas to be disseminated more widely, and authors of the Renaissance had sharply criticized the greed of the clergy. People were also angered by the selling of **ecclesial offices** and especially the selling of **indulgences**, in which a person would pay money to have one's time in purgatory shortened. Selling salvation was indeed against the tenets of the Church, but was often largely unenforced. The general distrust of the Church in this period is known as **anticlericalism**.

## Martin Luther

Martin Luther was a German friar who first became famous for criticizing the Catholic Church's sale of indulgences. In **1517**, in accordance with the tradition of theological debate, **Luther** posted his critique of this practice on the door of his local church; the document known as the "**Ninety-five Theses**" won him immediate fame. Luther then set about undermining the institution of the Church, arguing that individuals did not need the help of clergy to establish a strong relationship with God. Luther went even further, stating that faith, rather than obedience to arbitrary Church rules, would be what got individuals into heaven. The final straw for the Church came when Luther directly challenged the Pope, declaring that no one man could be the perfect interpreter of Scripture. Luther was excommunicated but continued to spread his message. Germany was then wracked by a war between the Lutherans of the north and the Catholics of the south. The **Peace of Augsburg** in 1555 was the resolution to this conflict, in which the subjects of a prince would follow that prince's faith, a practice referred to as *cuius regio, cuius religio*—literally, "whose jurisdiction, whose religion."

**Review Video: Martin Luther and the Reformation**
Visit mometrix.com/academy and enter code: 691828

## Protestants

Inspired by Luther, many other critics of Catholic excess joined together throughout Europe. These groups were known collectively as **Protestants**. One of the largest sects of Protestants was the **Calvinists**, named after founder John Calvin. This group believed in the idea of predestination, or that God had already fixed each person's eternal destiny, and that only the Elect would join Him in heaven. Naturally, most people believed themselves to be among the Elect. In England, **King Henry VIII** split from the Catholic Church after his request for an annulment from Catherine of Aragon was denied by the Pope. Henry established the **Church of England** with himself as leader, and had five more wives before his death.

**Review Video: The Protestants**
Visit mometrix.com/academy and enter code: 583582

## Counter-Reformation

After being bombarded by Protestant attacks for years, the **Catholic Church** finally began to make some positive changes. This program was known as the **Counter-Reformation**, and it was aimed at stopping the spread of Protestantism. For instance, the sale of indulgences was halted, and more authority was given to local bishops. The Church reaffirmed many of its core teachings (such as the earning of indulgences, transubstantiation, veneration of the Virgin Mary, the necessity of works, etc.) yet admitted its errors with regard to simony and abuses of clerical power, which were quickly remedied. One of the most influential men of this movement was **Sir Ignatius Loyola**, a Spaniard who founded the **Society of Jesus (the Jesuits)** to promote the Catholic interpretation of Scripture. The **Council of Trent** was a 20-year meeting that determined the official Catholic interpretation on all matters of theology. The Counter-Reformation also saw the re-emergence of the **Inquisition**, in which heretics were sought out and punished.

**Review Video: The Counter-Reformation**
Visit mometrix.com/academy and enter code: 950498

## Introduction of the Era of European Monarchies (1500-1650)

Between the years 1500 and 1650, most of the major European powers were led by **absolute monarchs**, who claimed a divine right to rule. These European monarchies often consolidated their power by marrying into one another. The strength of the monarchies fostered a resurgent spirit of **nationalism** and consequently led to more frequent conflicts between nations. In 1500, **Spain** was probably the most powerful nation in Europe, because of her lucrative colonies and impressive Armada. Over the next century and a half, however, **France** and **England** would emerge as the dominant powers in the region. **Germany** and **Russia**, though largely excluded from shipping, were still powerful during this period.

**Review Video: Absolute Monarchs: An Overview**
Visit mometrix.com/academy and enter code: 678546

**Review Video: Absolute Monarchs: France**
Visit mometrix.com/academy and enter code: 953883

**Review Video: Absolute Monarchs: Germany**
Visit mometrix.com/academy and enter code: 562601

**Review Video: Absolute Monarchs: Russia**
Visit mometrix.com/academy and enter code: 974242

**Review Video: Spanish Government in the 1500s**
Visit mometrix.com/academy and enter code: 735727

## Powers of Spain Between 1500 and 1650

The height of Spanish power began with the reign of **King Ferdinand** and **Queen Isabella**; these monarchs promoted exploration and became fantastically rich as a result. The Hapsburg **King Charles V** would increase Spain's prominence and territory, because he had acquired lands in France, Austria, and Germany through inheritance. Spain was drawn into a number of conflicts over these new possessions, however: France disputed his claim to parts of Italy, and the Ottoman Turks challenged his Armada in the Mediterranean. Charles V would finally be forced to abdicate the throne, leaving his brother **Ferdinand I** in control of Austria and Germany, and his son **Philip II** in control of Spain and some western lands. During Philip's reign, most of these possessions would be lost; particularly bitter was the loss of the Netherlands, which quickly became a trading power in their own right.

## Pizarro and the Incas

Francisco Pizarro (c. 1478-1541) was a Spanish explorer. He lived for a time in what is now Panama, where he heard tales of the fabulous wealth enjoyed by the **Incas** in the Andes Mountains. **Pizarro** was determined to conquer this empire, and with 168 men he reached the Incan city of Tumbes in 1532. At this time, the Incas were in the middle of a civil war. Pizarro used this to his advantage; he massacred one side and took their leader prisoner. In order to free himself, the leader arranged a huge ransom, which Pizarro collected and then ignored, killing the leader anyway. Soon, Spaniards conquered the Incan city of **Cuzco** and installed a puppet regime. After some turmoil, Pizarro took over the leadership of **Peru** until his assassination in 1541.

## Cortez and His Relationship with the Aztecs

Hernán Cortez (1485-1547) was a Spanish conquistador. He assisted in the conquest of **Cuba** and lived there until 1518, when he was assigned to lead an expedition into **Mexico**. He and 700 men landed on the Mexican shore, and he promptly had his ships burnt in order to indicate his sincerity about establishing a foothold in the country. **Cortez** then led his troops into **Tenochtitlan**, the capital of the **Aztec Empire**. They were received graciously by the Aztec ruler, **Montezuma**, whom they immediately enslaved. The Aztecs tried to revolt against the Spanish influence, but Cortez formed a coalition with other anti-Aztec groups and brutally eliminated the Aztec uprising. Cortez went on to rule "New Spain" for a number of years.

## Government of France Between 1500 and 1650

While England was undergoing a turbulent transition from an absolute to a limited monarchy, **France** was governed by a succession of powerful and talented Bourbon monarchs. The **Estates General**, the French counterpart to the British Parliament, was not especially powerful. During a period in which the Bourbon heir was too young to govern himself, the charismatic **Cardinal Richelieu** governed France. Cardinal Richelieu was a Catholic, of course, but he did not persecute the French protestant Huguenot sect. Rather, he compromised with his enemies in an attempt to consolidate the power of the French crown. Cardinal Richelieu also established a strong bureaucracy, known as the ***noblesse de la robe***.

## Government of Germany Between 1500 and 1650

Unlike many of the other Western European powers in 1500, **Germany** was still essentially just a collection of disjointed city-states. The **Hapsburg** family was powerful there, but the lands they called their **Holy Roman Empire** were not well organized, and the Hapsburgs were weak compared to other European leaders. The **Peace of Augsburg**, which had quelled disputes between Lutherans and Catholics, was destroyed by the **Thirty Years' War** (1618-48), which began when Protestants challenged the authority of the Hapsburg emperor. Germany would become so chaotic and disjointed during this period that other nations would step in, whether to seize some land or to help out one side or the other. The brutality of this war left Germany in a state of turmoil.

## Russian Rule Between 1500 and 1650

As the nations of Western Europe were beginning to rely on foreign trade almost exclusively to support themselves, **Russia** remained a feudal nation. After the Mongols were overthrown, Russia was ruled by a succession of **Czars**, and Russia was largely excluded from the cultural rejuvenation of the Renaissance period. Instead, Russians suffered through the reign of **Ivan the Terrible** (1530-84), a fierce ruler who pushed the borders out in the east with horrible brutality and suffocated any rivals or critics. Ivan's reign was so oppressive that Russia could not develop a merchant class to rival those of the Western European powers, despite having some impressive natural resources.

## Scientific Revolution

The rapid advance in learning known as the **Scientific Revolution** was a product of the systematic form of inquiry known as the **scientific method**. With the scientific method, learning is incremental: a question is posed, a hypothetical solution is offered, observations are made, and the hypothesis is either supported or refuted. The consistency of the method made it easy for scientific discoveries to be transferred from one country to another. Along with a standardized form of **measurement**, the development of the scientific method gave scientists a common language. Scientists also benefited from the development of powerful **telescopes** and **microscopes**.

### *Major Figures*

After **Copernicus** startled the world by challenging the geocentric (that is, earth-centered) model for the universe, Italian **Galileo Galilei** supplied scientific experiments that proved the accuracy of Copernicus' theory. One of the philosophical heroes of the Scientific Revolution was Frenchman **Rene Descartes**, who attempted to base his beliefs about the world upon empirical and provable facts: most famously, "I think, therefore I am." **Francis Bacon** was an English intellectual who wrote copiously on the possibilities for science to improve the human condition. **Sir Isaac Newton** excelled in many fields but is best known for his theories of motion and gravitation. Newton helped create the general idea that objects in the world behave in regular and predictable ways.

**Review Video: The Scientific Revolution**
Visit mometrix.com/academy and enter code: 974600

## England During the Tudor and Stuart Rulings

For many years, England was ruled by the **Tudor** family. **Henry VIII**, the founder of the Anglican Church, had been a Tudor, and his daughter **Elizabeth** continued his policies. During the Elizabethan age in England, trading and exploration increased, and the Spanish Armada, sent to overthrow Elizabeth as a protestant heretic, was defeated. After Elizabeth died in 1603, the **Stuart** family ascended to the throne. The Stuart period would be marked by conflict. Both **James I** and **Charles I** butted heads with Parliament over the issue of taxation, and there were also continual conflicts between **Puritans** (followers of John Calvin) and **Anglicans** (adherents of the Church of England). The Puritans joined with Parliament in opposition to the monarchy.

## Cromwell and William and Mary

The alliance of Parliament and the Puritans was led by **Oliver Cromwell**. His army was successful in deposing and executing **King Charles I**, and Cromwell was subsequently installed as **Protector of England**. Cromwell's rule was undermined by Anglican nobles and clergy who disliked his Puritanism. After the death of Cromwell, England was ruled by the two sons of Charles I, **Charles II** and **James II**, the latter of which was forced to abdicate by Parliament. After this period of relative chaos, **William and Mary** of the Netherlands were asked to rule England in a limited monarchy. This shift in power was known as the **Glorious Revolution**. The **Declaration of Rights** that limited the power of the monarchy gave Parliament more power and made possible a long period of tranquility.

## The Enlightenment

Between the years 1600 and 1770, political and social philosophy in Europe underwent a tremendous change, known collectively as the **Enlightenment**. Just as Northern Italy had been the center of the Renaissance, so now **Paris** was the hub of progressive thought. The collection of philosophers, who sought to bring every subject under the authority of reason, included both **deists** (those who believed in God) and **atheists** (those who did not). The study known as **political science** first emerged during this period. Intellectuals began to question the divine right that had been claimed by absolute monarchs in the past; they sought to determine which was the best form of government for all the citizens of the country.

**Review Video: Age of Enlightenment**
Visit mometrix.com/academy and enter code: 143022

### *Major Figures*

One of the most sparkling wits of the Enlightenment period belonged to the Frenchman **Voltaire** (1694-1778). He challenged the authority of the Church, declaring that people should tolerate the views of others and that no one man or group had a monopoly on absolute truth. **Thomas Hobbes** (1598-1679) was one of the most influential political theorists of the period. In his masterpiece "Leviathan," he declared that the base impulses of the people had to be restrained by a powerful and just monarch. **John Locke** (1632-1704), on the other hand, declared that men were born with natural rights which could not be justly denied them. **Rousseau** (1712-78), a Swiss philosopher, asserted that the government only ruled so long as it did so to the satisfaction of the general will of the people.

## Peace of Westphalia and Louis XIV

The monarchs of the Enlightenment period found themselves under increasing pressure to be tolerant and benevolent. In Western Europe, so-called "enlightened despots" governed in order to promote the best interests of their subjects; this was probably done more to retain power than to express any profound solidarity with the commoners. France had become the central power on the European continent after the **Peace of Westphalia** (1648), which ended the **Thirty Years' War** and weakened Germany. The long reign of **Louis XIV** of France was characterized by grandiosity and the cultivation of the arts. Louis spent considerable effort trying to acquire new territories for France and glory for himself, and so alarmed the other European powers with his swiftness from victory to victory that many former enemies allied against France.

## Creation of Prussia and Contributions of Frederick the Great

The **Peace of Westphalia** (1648) established the independence of several small sections of Germany; chief among these new states was Prussia. **Frederick the Great** (1712-86) became the ruler of **Prussia** in 1740 and displayed marvelous efficiency and benevolence. He made a genuine effort to allow for the coexistence of all the religious groups in Prussia, and also worked to improve the lives of the serfs. Frederick also encouraged immigration to Prussia, which brought in new ideas and technological advances. Prussia, which had long suffered economically because of its lack of a coastline, now became a producer of luxury goods like porcelain and silk.

## Russia During the Rule of Peter the Great and Catherine the Great

**Peter the Great** (1672-1725) was responsible for the transformation of Russia from an impoverished agricultural nation to a strong commercial nation. Peter was enamored of the ways of the western European nations and made several trips to other capitals to learn the intricacies of Enlightenment politics and trade. **St. Petersburg** was intended to be a Russian city in the style of Paris or Berlin. Peter's innovations revitalized the economy, but they also set a standard for decadence that would be carried on by future czars. **Catherine II**, otherwise known as Catherine the Great, ruled from 1762 to 1796 and implemented many Enlightenment policies in education and the arts. Nevertheless, in the remote provinces of Russia, the **feudal system** endured, and the economy remained stunted.

## French Revolution

### *Causes*

Before the revolution, France was governed by an absolute monarch and, with regard to matters of taxation, the **Estates General**, which had been formed in order to represent the common people. The Estates General was composed of three estates: the clergy (**First Estate**), nobility (**Second Estate**), and everyone else (**Third Estate**). Unfortunately, this body had been marginalized by a series of powerful monarchs, and it was arranged such that the largest group by far, the Third Estate, only had one-third of the vote. In any case, the Third Estate usually found its desires opposed by the other estates. Another source of anger for the middle class and peasants was the **tax structure**; the nobles and clergy were not forced to pay taxes, and thus the burden of France's depressed economy fell upon the Third Estate.

### *King Louis XVI and National Assembly*

Aware of the injustice of the French tax policy, **King Louis XVI** tried to pass some reforms but was repeatedly thwarted by the greedy nobles and clergy. The **Third Estate** was infuriated and refused to vote in the Estates General anymore. Instead, prominent members of the middle class banded together to form the **National Assembly**, which purported to represent the interests of common Frenchmen. At the same time, the peasants were in full revolt. On July 14, 1789, they stormed the

Parisian prison known as the **Bastille**. The success of this riot inspired more peasants to clamor for representation, and the diversion it caused kept the government from dealing with the National Assembly.

### *Declaration of the Rights of Man*

After the storming of the Bastille and the formation of the National Assembly in 1789, the French middle and lower classes joined together and established a new government with the slogan "**Liberty, Equality, Fraternity**." This government quickly reformed the tax code and declared that government offices would henceforth be filled on the basis of merit. The National Assembly also eliminated serfdom and drafted a **Declaration of the Rights of Man**, which was similar to the American Bill of Rights. The National Assembly then seized the lands that belonged to the Church and eliminated the feudal rights of the aristocracy. Soon, there was dissension within the Third Estate, and the revolution became more radical and violent.

## French Revolution and the Reign of Terror

As the government established by the Third Estate descended into chaos, the radical Jacobin leader **Robespierre** took charge. He had an idealistic vision of what France could become, and he was willing to kill thousands in order to see it realized. The **guillotine** provided a swift way to execute scores of opponents, a group that included anyone who dared challenge the Jacobin party line or was suspected of retaining their Catholic faith in the new culture of state-mandated atheism. Among those executed were **King Louis XVI** and his wife, **Marie Antoinette**. After a while, the French tired of the violence and turmoil of the **Reign of Terror**, and Robespierre himself fell victim to the guillotine. A group of five prominent men, known as the **Directory**, was established to restore calm. This group would last until 1799, when it was overthrown in a coup that would eventually bring **Napoleon Bonaparte** to power.

## Rise of Napoleon Bonaparte

Napoleon Bonaparte (1769-1821) began his career as a French military commander, scoring major victories in Austria and England. Upon his return to the chaos of France, he led a coup and was installed as the leader of France. He was subsequently elected by a popular vote. Almost immediately, **Napoleon** reformed French education, agriculture, and infrastructure. The main object of Napoleon's rule, however, was the acquisition of territory both in Europe and in the New World. Napoleon's troops quickly conquered Austria, Portugal, Spain, and Prussia. Napoleon, who modeled himself after Charlemagne in many ways, then crowned himself **emperor**. The French empire proved too large to manage, however, and Napoleon further weakened himself with a disastrous campaign against Russia.

**Review Video: The French Revolution: Napoleon Bonaparte**
Visit mometrix.com/academy and enter code: 876330

## Independence Struggle in Latin America

When Spain fell to Napoleon's forces in 1809, the provinces of **Chile** and **Buenos Aires** both declared themselves independent. At this time, **Peru** was the stronghold of Spanish power in the New World, and therefore the rebels attacked the government there. Led by the Argentinean **Jose San Martin**, rebels entered Lima and declared Peru an independent state in 1821. The greatest military leader of the independence movement, however, was **Simon Bolivar**. He had traveled extensively in Europe and used his knowledge of the enemy to run the Spaniards out of Colombia, Venezuela, and Central America. Bolivar eventually seized control of Peru and hoped to form a great union of South American nations, but this alliance was eventually torn asunder by internal feuds.

## FALL OF NAPOLEON

After Napoleon's debacle in Russia debilitated his military, revolts sprung up in many of the nations that he had conquered, and Napoleon was overthrown. The leaders of the countries that had overthrown Napoleon met in Vienna to decide how to respond to him. These three men, **Prince von Metternich** of Austria, the English **Duke of Wellington**, and **Alexander I** of Russia, were constantly in disagreement, however, and Napoleon used this opportunity to return from his exile on the Isle of Elba in the Mediterranean and reclaim power. Finally, Napoleon was defeated at **Waterloo** and sent into permanent exile. The allies met again at the **Congress of Vienna** in 1815 where France was not treated too harshly, and it was determined that a balance of power should be maintained in Europe to ensure that no one in the future tried to dominate the continent.

## OPIUM WAR

The Opium War lasted between the years 1839 and 1842. It began because the British kept trafficking **opium** from India into China because they wanted to trade with the Chinese, and opium was the only product that China could not produce for itself. The Chinese government, however, was appalled by the effect that the drug had on its citizens and mounted a serious anti-opium campaign. When British merchants appealed to their leaders, the British navy was sent in order to force the Chinese to accept the opium. The British ended up seizing several Chinese cities, including Shanghai and Nanking. The war ended with the **Treaty of Nanking** in 1842; China was forced to cede Hong Kong to the British, and several Chinese ports had to be left open for trade.

**Review Video: Anti-Colonial Struggles: The Opium War**
Visit mometrix.com/academy and enter code: 111806

## TAIPING REBELLION

The Taiping Rebellion lasted in China between the years 1850 and 1864. It was a religious and political rebellion against the government of the **Manchus**, led by the Christian **Hung Hsiu-ch'uan**. The rebels advocated the public ownership of land and a self-sufficient economy. They wanted to rid China of the encroaching influences of foreign merchants. Hung's troops were able to conquer Nanking and make it the capital of their "Great Peaceful Heavenly Dynasty." Internal feuds weakened the Taiping, however, and the western powers (concerned that they would lose the Chinese market) helped to oust them in 1864. The **Taiping Rebellion** was by far the bloodiest war of the 19th century.

## MEIJI REFORM

In 1854, an American group led by **Commodore Matthew Perry** forced Japan to open its ports to foreign merchants. Japan had been closed to the West for 200 years. The Japanese people were not pleased with this development, and they blamed the **Tokugawa shogun** (the military leader of the period). In 1867, the shogun resigned and **Emperor Matsuhito** declared that he was now in charge. The Japanese capital was moved from Kyoto to Edo (which was renamed Tokyo). The ensuing period in Japanese history is known as the **Meiji Period**. During it, the feudal system was abolished, and Western ideas became popular. The samurai had their land right revoked and were eventually eliminated altogether. In the late 19th century, Japanese leaders began to turn their attentions to expansion onto the Asian continent; in the Sino-Japanese war, they conquered parts of China and Korea.

## BOXER REBELLION

The Boxer Rebellion was a peasant uprising in China around the turn of the 20th century. The rebels aimed to overthrow the **Manchu government** and to cast all foreigners out of China. The rebels were known as the **Boxers** because they practiced certain mystical boxing rituals. After Japan had defeated China in 1895, the Japanese had exercised a great deal of influence on the Chinese economy. Around 1900, Boxers began to kill foreign merchants and diplomats. An international force was assembled to defeat the Boxers. During the ensuing fight, the city of **Peking** was almost entirely destroyed. Eventually, the western powers prevailed and forced the Boxer leaders to sign an incredibly unfavorable treaty.

**Review Video: Anti-Colonial Struggles: The Boxer Rebellion**
Visit mometrix.com/academy and enter code: 352161

## Industrial Revolution

### *English Textile Industry*

The **Industrial Revolution** in Europe in the 19th century produced immediate and far-reaching changes in the social structure. **England** was perhaps the first to feel the effects of rapid industrialization; the factory system for manufacturing textiles was implemented, meaning that individuals were only required to do one in the series of tasks required to prepare a piece of cloth. This division of labor increased productivity. New energy sources, such as the steam engine, also made fabulous increases in productivity possible. Coal was introduced as an aid to the iron-smelting process, and the mass production of cotton textiles was soon propelling the English economy.

### *Social Changes*

With the success of the textile industry, more and more workers were needed in the European cities, and therefore people began to abandon their country lives and take factory jobs in town. This rapid **urbanization** created a new **middle class** in Europe, and it also created a number of problems. Most cities did not have the infrastructure to support such an explosion in population, and as such, disease, crime, and poverty were common. The booming success of industry made many people rich as investors and merchants, and therefore the middle class assumed even more political power in Europe. **Social mobility** was infinitely more possible in this economic environment, encouraging many people to stick with jobs that were demeaning and not especially lucrative.

### *Working Class and Luddites*

As people flooded the cities to work in the booming factories, large landowners consolidated the farmlands they left behind. **Working-class** individuals were probably not pleased with their new lives; 18-hour days, low wages, and dangerous machinery were among the problems faced by this new underclass. Oftentimes, women and children were employed for the most menial jobs, and they were paid less than men. A small rebellion, led by a group called the **Luddites**, tried to resist the tide of industrialization and were known for vandalizing factory equipment. Still, most individuals were enticed by the prospect of upward mobility that the new, fluid class system offered, and were willing to endure hardship in exchange for hope.

**Review Video: The Industrial Revolution**
Visit mometrix.com/academy and enter code: 372796

**Review Video: Industrialization**
Visit mometrix.com/academy and enter code: 893924

## Nationalism in 19th-Century Europe

In the 19th century, the spirit of nationalism that had been building in Europe since the Middle Ages reached a critical mass. **Nationalism** refers to pride in the traditions, culture, language, and past of a certain nation of people, and not necessarily to pride in one's country. This is important to note, because in the 19th century, there were many nations of people thrown together as parts of a larger kingdom. The rising tide of nationalism, then, was a concern to the ruling **monarchs**, who hoped to hold together disparate nations under their control. Russia, for instance, contained a wide variety of cultures and languages under one leadership.

**Review Video: Historical Nationalism**
Visit mometrix.com/academy and enter code: 510185

## Classical Liberalism in 19th-Century Europe

The political and economic philosophies of the Enlightenment laid the foundation for 19th-century **classical liberalism**. **Adam Smith's** "The Wealth of Nations," written in 1776, introduced the concept of the "invisible hand," suggesting that market forces, if left largely to operate freely, could lead to economic prosperity. Although Smith's work preceded the Industrial Revolution, his ideas influenced later classical liberals who championed free-market policies. Another influential thinker, **Thomas Malthus**, in "An Essay on the Principle of Population" (1798), wrote that unchecked population growth would outstrip food supply, leading to famine and disease. While his work was later used to justify laissez-faire economic policies, Malthus himself advocated for population control measures rather than the outright suffering of the poor.

## Social Liberalism in 19th-Century Europe

Social liberalism developed in the late 19th century as an alternative to classical liberalism. **Social liberalism** declares that political problems can be solved by the work of liberal institutions in the government. Unlike the classical liberals, social liberals believe that the government should exercise some influence on the **economy** and should extend some basic **welfare services** to the people. Social liberalism aimed to improve life for the poor and disadvantaged. Social liberals were also very outspoken on issues of civil rights and individual liberties. Some of the most famous social liberals are **Jeremy Bentham**, **John Stuart Mill**, and **John Dewey**.

## Emergence of Socialism in 19th-Century Europe

Socialism is a political philosophy which declares that the economic means of production should be owned by the workers. This control may either be exercised directly by the workers through local councils or by the state with the consent of the workers. Socialists hope thereby to create a state of **social equality** and an even **distribution of wealth**. Not surprisingly, this movement was most popular among the working classes in 19th-century Europe. Socialists at this time declared that capitalism served only the interests of the very wealthy and exploited everyone else. In their view, a socialist society would provide a greater reward for hard work and would create harmonious societies. Socialism and communism come from the same ideological lineage, but they differ in some ways. Generally speaking, socialism and communism both hope to have the means of production controlled by a collective or governing organization and not owned privately. **Socialism** would allow for individuals to continue to have private property, whereas **communism** would eliminate private property and have the collective or state regulate the distribution of wealth.

**Review Video: Communism vs. Socialism**
Visit mometrix.com/academy and enter code: 917677

## EMERGENCE OF MARXISM IN 19TH-CENTURY EUROPE

The political theories of socialism and communism both take their inspiration from the works of **Karl Marx** (1818-83). Marx declared that economics has been the primary determinant in history and that the history of society is nothing more than a "history of class struggle." Marx asserted that problems have been created in situations where the material that a worker produces is worth more than the compensation he receives for his work. The surplus goes to the capitalist owner, and the worker is caught in a situation where he can never get ahead. The inevitable result, according to Marx, is a revolution of the working class (which he called the **proletariat**) and the installation of an economic system similar to socialism or communism.

**Review Video: Karl Marx**
Visit mometrix.com/academy and enter code: 362061

## 19TH-CENTURY BRITISH POLITICS

During the 19th century, the memory of Napoleon and the balance of power established by the **Congress of Vienna** prevented any large conflicts. The **Industrial Revolution** had made Britain the wealthiest and most powerful nation in Europe. The rise of a rich middle class caused the British Parliament to alter voting laws so that more of the wealthy would have influence. This was done with the **Reform Act of 1832**; in 1833, Britain abolished slavery in its colonies. This was not enough for the many working-class Britons, however, and they lobbied long and hard for universal suffrage until it was finally granted in the 1880s. The British movement for universal suffrage was known as **Chartism**.

**Review Video: 19th Century Politics: Britain**
Visit mometrix.com/academy and enter code: 266214

## 19TH-CENTURY FRENCH POLITICS

Internal turmoil caused France to miss out on much of the wealth of the Industrial Revolution. After the demise of Napoleon, **Louis XVII** had been restored to the throne by the **Congress of Vienna**. He was succeeded by the archconservative **Charles X**, who was quite unpopular and was chased off the throne in the **July Revolution of 1830**. In his place came **Louis Philippe**, who administered over a fairly stable country for eighteen years until he was deposed in the revolution of 1848. Next came **Napoleon III**. Elected the emperor of France in 1851, he remained in power until the French defeat in the **Franco-Prussian War of 1870**. From 1870 until 1940, France would be governed by a constitutional and democratic government that was, for the most part, conservative.

## 19TH-CENTURY GERMAN POLITICAL SYSTEM

Ever since the end of Charlemagne's empire, Austria and Germany had not been unified as a single nation. This was finally achieved by the Prussian **Otto von Bismarck** after a long period of suppression of German nationalists. Bismarck's unification of **Prussia** was mainly aimed at defeating the rival Hapsburgs, who controlled Austria. When Prussia won the **Austro-Prussian** and **Franco-Prussian wars** in quick succession, Bismarck declared that he had achieved his ends and unified the German empire. He oversaw the creation of the **Reichstag**, a legislative body that would provide representation to the middle and lower classes. Germany threw itself into the project of industrialization.

## 19TH-CENTURY ITALIAN POLITICAL SYSTEM

Italy, like Germany, had really been more of a disjointed collection of independent city-states than a nation in its own right. In the 19th century, however, there was a drive to unify the region. A leader from the Piedmont region, **Camillo Cavour**, tried to bring the various city-states together through diplomacy rather than combat. This process took a very long time but was eventually completed in the 1870s. **Northern Italy**, which had intimate contact with Germany, became industrialized during this period, and the city of Milan enjoyed immense growth. **Southern Italy**, on the other hand, remained largely rural. This distinction between the two halves of Italy would be a source of conflict in the future.

### 19TH-CENTURY RUSSIAN POLITICAL SYSTEM

At the beginning of the 19th century, much of Russia was still mired in an impoverished, quasi-feudal state. After the death of **Alexander** in 1825, the **Decembrists** tried to force the incoming Czar to adopt a constitution allocating some power to the people. The next czar was **Nicholas I**, who used secret police to try to eliminate the roots of the popular insurrection. This policy of suppression only further isolated Russia from the rest of Europe, which was at that time reducing the power of the monarch. Russia later lost the **Crimean War** to Britain, France, and the Ottoman Empire, and many Russians bemoaned the backward state of their country. Finally, a new czar, **Alexander II**, freed the serfs and tried to industrialize. This happened slowly.

### RUSSIAN REVOLUTION OF 1905

At the turn of the 20th century, **Russia** was torn by the trends of industrialism and imperialism. The country was still being operated as an absolute monarchy, and was behind on social reforms common to the rest of Europe. Russia was trying to undergo rapid industrial expansion in the cities. Russia experienced a humiliating defeat of their navy in the **Russo-Japanese War,** causing increased labor unrest and dissatisfaction with the strong monarchy. The socialist party in Russia split into the **Bolsheviks,**who favored immediate socialist reform, and the **Mensheviks,** who favored gradual reforms and cooperation. When a peaceful demonstration against the czar was brutally suppressed, rebel forces made up of political activists, peasants, and workers became energized, leading to the **Russian Revolution of 1905.** This revolution continued with revolts by peasants and soldiers, until the czar promised to create a constitutional monarchy with a powerful legislative body, known as the **Duma**. These changes promised civil liberties and a parliamentary process, but the Tsar soon after went back on his word and limited the power of the Duma, leading to increased civil unreast.

## World History 1914 to Present

### ENTANGLING ALLIANCES PRIOR TO WWI

In the early years of the 20th century, relations among the various European powers were complex. Ever since the **Franco-Prussian War**, won by Prussia, the two sides had been enemies. At the center of their conflict was the territory of **Alsace-Lorraine**, which each side claimed as its own. In order to bolster their position in the region, each side entered into networks of alliances. After years of negotiations, two main alliances contained the major European powers: the **Triple Alliance** (Germany, Austria, Italy) and the **Triple Entente** (France, Britain, Russia). These two alliances would end up being the opposing sides in the great war of the ensuing years.

### THE BALKANS AND BEGINNING OF WWI

In the years before the First World War, the **Balkans** were attempting to gain independence from the Hapsburg empire of Austria. This insurrection culminated in the assassination of Austrian **Archduke Franz Ferdinand** in 1914 by **Gavrilo Princip**, a member of a Serbian nationalist group. At this point, a chain reaction of war declarations (spurred by the comprehensive alliances of the time) ensued. Austria declared war against Serbia, Germany and Turkey joined with the Austrians,

Russia declared war on these countries in support of Serbia, France joined with Russia, and Britain and Italy joined forces with France, even though Italy had been a member of the Triple Alliance.

### Combat and Exit of Russia During WWI

Despite the fact that almost every nation in Europe had entered into World War I, most Europeans thought the conflict would be brief. Instead, advances in **weapons technology** made the war bloody and excruciatingly slow. Much of the fighting was done from **trenches**, and some battles would see the deaths of thousands of soldiers at a time. The war was also slow because the sides were very evenly matched; that is, until 1917, when the United States entered on the side of Britain. Also, in 1917, the Russians exited the war via the **Brest-Litovsk Treaty**. Russia was basically exhausted after suffering through a Revolution in 1917 in which the **Bolsheviks** came to power. The entry of the US provided the British and French with supplies and troops, and Germany was soon forced to call for a truce.

### Treaty of Versailles

As the First World War wound down, a disgruntled German populace ousted the emperor and installed a moderate socialist government. This government, known as the **Weimar Republic**, would last until 1933. At the **Paris Peace Conference**, the victors of the war (the US, Britain, France, and Italy) exacted some revenge on Germany. The **Treaty of Versailles** penalized Germany economically and territorially; Alsace-Lorraine became independent, and the German military was dismantled. The Treaty of Versailles would need to be modified by two subsequent agreements: the **Treaty of Locarno,** which outlined a more reasonable reparations plan for Germany, and the **Kellogg-Briand Pact,** which asserted that diplomacy rather than force would be used to resolve conflicts.

### Western Europe and Italy After the First World War

In the years after the First World War, the general mood in Europe was one of wariness. Most nations were exhausted by the conflict, and few felt that the signing of the **Treaty of Versailles** and the formation of the **League of Nations** had created a permanent peace. In the 1920s, Britain, Germany, France, and the United States were all liberal democracies without a strong executive. Unlike the United States, however, the European nations suffered a profound economic depression. One nation that saw no diminution in nationalism was **Italy**. In part out of a fear of communism, Italians supported the rise of the fascist dictator **Benito Mussolini**. **Fascism** is defined as an extreme-right movement characterized by totalitarian rule with an emphasis on national unity and identity. Fascism generally manifests in dictatorial rule and suppression of the free speech and rights of dissenters. It originated in Italy and promised to the Italians a return to the glory days of Rome, when they were a mighty power ruled by a dominating executive. Of course, in order to maintain his authority, Mussolini had to brutally suppress any opposition.

### Russian Revolution of 1917

After the **Revolution of 1905**, Russia had enjoyed a few years of relative peace. After a while, however, the peasants became dissatisfied with the weakness of the Duma, and after strikes and protests, **Czar Nicholas II** was forced to abdicate the throne. In place of the monarchy, a **provisional government** was set up to work alongside more progressive local councils, known as **Soviets**. These two groups were constantly at odds, however, especially during Russia's participation in the **First World War** (the Soviets wanted to withdraw and focus on national issues, while the Provisional Government felt obliged to fight). During this period, **Vladimir Lenin** rose to prominence as the Marxist leader of the **Bolshevik Party**. In the **Russian Revolution of 1917**, Lenin and his supporters ousted the provisional government and exited the war. Lenin then began the immense project of nationalizing the Soviet economy.

## Lenin and Stalin

After his success in the Revolution of 1917, **Lenin** began to advocate the revolt of the working class in other nations. Naturally, this did not endear the new Russian government to the leaders of other nations. Russia became increasingly isolated both economically and politically from the rest of the world. Domestically, Lenin established the **New Economic Policy**, which blended capitalism and communism. This plan worked well enough in agriculture, but it never achieved much success in industry. After Lenin's death, **Joseph Stalin** came to power and began an ambitious plan of collectivizing farms and nationalizing factories (known as the **Five Year Plans**). Stalin was ruthless in the pursuit of his goals; he established labor camps to house his opponents. It is estimated that 20 million people were killed by Stalin's regime during the period now known as the **Great Terror**.

## China in the Early 20h Century

In 1911, the **Manchu dynasty**, which had been significantly weakened by the **Boxer Rebellion**, was finally overthrown. A period of instability followed, in which **Sun Yat-sen** declared the creation of a republic with its headquarters in Nanking. Sun Yat-sen began a political party aimed at improving life for the common people; it was known as the **Kuomintang**. During this period, both Mongolia and Tibet declared their independence from China. The Chinese people became disenchanted with the Kuomintang government after what they saw as unfavorable agreements following World War I. After the death of Sun Yat-sen in 1925, a national government was established at Canton; the **communist party** was a major participant in this government.

## Rule of the Kuomintang and the Sino-Japanese War in 20th-Century China

In 1926, the military leader **Chiang Kai-shek** led campaigns in central and northern China, in the hopes of unifying the country. During this period, Chiang broke with the **communist party**, and Communists were persecuted in Shanghai. In 1927, a national government led by the **Kuomintang**, who had previously fallen out of favor, was established in Nanking. The peasants were not pleased with this leadership, and they were organized as the **Red Army** under **Mao Tse-tung** in the south. In what is known as the **Long March**, Mao led his army north to Yenan, where they would gather strength. The situation in China was made even more volatile by the Japanese invasion in 1937. In what is known as the "**Rape of Nanking**," Japanese troops killed over 200,000 Chinese. The people were outraged, and the partisan splits between Mao's communists and Chiang's government only widened.

## Japan in the Years Before WWII

In 1926, amid growing nationalism, **Hirohito** became the Emperor of Japan. The next year, the Japanese prime minister declared that Japan should dominate Asia, and four years later, Japanese forces invaded **Manchuria**. Some historians consider this to be the beginning of the Second World War. After establishing a puppet regime in Manchuria, the Japanese withdrew from the League of Nations and attacked China. The **Sino-Japanese War** ensued. In 1938, Japan outlined its new vision of **Co-Prosperity Spheres**; Japan would be the industrial center of Asia and would acquire its raw materials from its colonies in the rest of Asia. Japan promoted this idea as an opportunity to break from European imperialism, but it was really just the substitution of one master for another. In 1940, Japan would complete its transformation into a **fascist state** by dissolving all political parties.

## Events Leading to World War II in Europe

Still shell-shocked from the First World War, the nations of western Europe were slow to respond to the growing menace of **Nazi Germany**. In general, they pursued a policy of appeasement and isolation. The British prime minister **Neville Chamberlain** was especially committed to using diplomacy over war. Then, in 1936, Hitler sent troops to occupy the **Rhineland**, a strip of territory on the German border. At around the same time, **Mussolini** invaded Ethiopia; the two aggressors, Germany and Italy, entered into an agreement making them the **Axis Powers**. In 1938, Germany annexed Austria and indicated that it was about to attack Czechoslovakia. In response to these actions, Chamberlain brought together Mussolini and Hitler for the **Munich Conference of 1938**. These talks would only briefly suspend German aggression.

### Weimar Republic and the Rise of Hitler

After the abdication of the emperor, Germany was ruled by a legislative body known as the **Weimar Republic**. Most Germans felt that this group had been too willing to accept punishment in the treaties that followed the war. Germans also thought that this government was responsible for the **inflation** which crippled the German economy in the post-war period. Germany, then, was vulnerable to the charms of a leader who told them they had nothing about which to be ashamed. This leader was **Adolf Hitler** (1889-1945). A failed artist, Hitler became the head of the **National Socialist**, or **Nazi**, party. His speeches were expressions of ardent nationalism, although often Hitler seemed to be calling for a return to an ideal German state that had never actually existed.

### Belief System of the Nazi Party

Led by **Adolf Hitler**, the Nazi party championed the **Aryan race** as superior to all others, especially the "insidious" Jews. Hitler suggested that the noble ambitions of the true German people required ***lebensraum***, or living space. In other words, Germany needed more territory. In its early days, the Nazi party was part of the German republican system; Nazi candidates ran for office and served in the **Reichstag** (German parliament). As Germany suffered through a terrible economic depression in the early 1930s, however, the people became impatient. In 1933, the Reichstag was set on fire, and the Nazis used the opportunity to claim total control of the government. Hitler had already been appointed Chancellor in January 1933. He was able to quickly improve the German economy, mostly through the expansion of the weapon-building industry. At the same time, the new government began to quietly round up Jews, Gypsies, and homosexuals.

### Holocaust

As **Germany** sank deeper and deeper into dire economic straits, the tendency was to look for a person or group of people to blame for the problems of the country. With distrust of the **Jewish people** already ingrained, it was easy for German authorities to set up the Jews as scapegoats for Germany's problems.

The Holocaust is the name given to the systematic killing of Jews, Gypsies, homosexuals, and others by the Nazis. **Anti-Semitism** had existed in Europe for millennia, but the Nazis gave it renewed emphasis and, after making numerous false claims about Jews, began persecuting them upon Hitler's rise to power in 1933. Jews were disenfranchised, forced into ghettos, had their property taken, and were finally sent to work and be killed in **concentration camps**. Approximately 6 million Jews were killed during the **Holocaust**. As the situation for the Germans became more dire in the Second World War, Hitler sought to implement what he called the "final solution," in which hundreds of thousands were killed just before the fall of Nazi Germany.

The Allies were aware of rumors of mass slaughter throughout the war, but many discounted the reports. Only when troops went in to liberate the prisoners was the true horror of the concentration camps brought to light.

**Review Video: The Holocaust**
Visit mometrix.com/academy and enter code: 350695

### *Consequences of the Holocaust*

Many of the Nazi leaders were tried and convicted at the **Nuremberg trials** for their roles in the Holocaust. West Germany would later issue a **Federal Compensation Law**, through which billions of dollars were paid to survivors. During and after the Holocaust, Zionist Jews fled to **Palestine**. Public sympathy with their plight would be one of the main reasons for the creation of **Israel** in 1948. The total destruction of the Jewish community in Europe caused many Jews to question their faith, and those that remained in Europe are markedly more secular than their ancestors. The shock of the Holocaust has also caused many institutions, including the Roman Catholic Church, to consider their own latent anti-Semitism. Unfortunately, the anti-genocide legislation created in response to the Holocaust was not strict enough to rally international support against the **Rwandans** (who slaughtered hundreds of thousands of Tutsis in 1994) or the **Bosnian Serbs and Croats** (who killed thousands of Muslims in the early 1990s).

## Pacific Arena in WWII

The **Japanese**, like the Germans, became seduced by the notion of their own racial superiority during the 1930s. As in Germany, this inevitably led to a lust for territorial expansion. By 1941, Japan had conquered Korea, Manchuria, and parts of China. Japan was also threatening to invade American interests in the Philippines. The United States imposed **economic sanctions** on Japan, making it difficult for the Japanese war industry to function. In response, the Japanese launched a surprise attack on the United States by bombing the US naval base of **Pearl Harbor**. After the attack on Pearl Harbor, the United States declared war upon Japan (and Germany, in turn, declared war on the United States). The Japanese made huge territorial gains before the US turned the tide at the **Battles of Midway and Guadalcanal**. The war in the Pacific would take much longer than the war in Europe due to the island-hopping nature of the fight. The unwillingness of the Japanese to surrender made it almost impossible for America to entirely vanquish them without enormous loss of life. So, the United States decided to drop atomic bombs on **Hiroshima** and **Nagasaki** to force Japan to surrender and finally end the war in the Pacific in August 1945.

## Beginning and Initial Years of World War II in Europe

After **Chamberlain** had tried to forestall German aggression at the **Munich Conference of 1938**, Germany nevertheless invaded Czechoslovakia in 1939. It was also during this year that Hitler signed a secret agreement with **Stalin** pledging not to attack Russia so long as Russia stayed out of German affairs. Hitler then declared war on and conquered Poland. At this step, Great Britain and France were finally forced to declare war upon Germany. Germany at this point was a dominating military adversary. New advances in motorized military vehicles made it possible for Germany to conquer large areas of land quickly in a new form of warfare called **Blitzkrieg** (lightning war). The **Axis powers** conquered almost the entire European continent, including France, over the course of 1940. Only Great Britain remained in opposition, and the Nazis undertook a ferocious aerial assault on the British, who were by then led by **Winston Churchill**, but failed to do enough damage to make an invasion of the island country practical. Instead, Hitler turned east and decided to violate his truce with Stalin, invading **Russia** in 1941. The Germans overwhelmed much of the Soviet military and advanced deep into Russian territory in a huge surprise offensive.

## Middle Years and Conclusion of World War II in Europe

The tide turned against Hitler once the United States entered the war. The harsh Russian winter halted the German advance into Russia short of Moscow in 1941. The Germans made further gains in the summer of 1942 but were decisively beaten at the **Battle of Stalingrad** and were slowly pushed back out of Russia from then on. American and British troops landed in North Africa in 1942 and used that as a springboard to invade Italy in 1943. In 1944, the Americans and British opened yet another front with a massive invasion of northern France in the **D-Day landings**. Fighting numerically superior forces on multiple fronts, the Germans steadily lost ground and the Allies pushed into Germany from both East and West in 1945. Surrounded and with the war lost, Hitler committed **suicide** in his bunker in Berlin in April 1945, and the remaining German forces **surrendered** shortly afterward.

### India and Pakistan After WWII

In 1947, after years of peaceful protests led by **Mahatma Gandhi**, India was given its independence and partitioned into two states, **India** and **Pakistan**. The following year, Gandhi would be assassinated in India. In 1965, border disputes would flare into the **Indo-Pakistani War**. In 1971, Pakistan would fend off attacks from Bengali rebels, who sought to achieve independence. The next year, however, **Bangladesh** would be established as an independent state. In 1984, India had its own internal problems; after the Indian army occupied the **Golden Temple** sacred to the Sikhs, the Indian leader **Indira Gandhi** was assassinated by her Sikh bodyguards. **Anti-Sikh riots** resulted, and much blood was shed.

### Beginnings of The Cold War

After the defeat of the Axis powers in WWII, the United States and Russia entered into a long and often secret conflict, in which each side used diplomatic, economic, and occasionally military forces to try to assert itself as the dominant world power. The first issue on which these nations butted heads was the **rebuilding of Europe**. Germany was divided into an eastern and western section; the western half was democratic and looked to the US for guidance, while Eastern Germany became a communist nation in the USSR's sphere of influence. Russia worked to bring all of its neighbors (including Poland, Czechoslovakia, Hungary, Romania, and Bulgaria) under its control. The western borders of these nations formed what Churchill referred to as the **iron curtain**, dividing communist Eastern Europe from democratic Western Europe.

### Truman Doctrine, Marshall Plan, NATO, and Warsaw Pact

In order to stop the spread of communism in Europe and elsewhere, President Truman asserted his policy of "containment" in the so-called **Truman Doctrine**. This meant that the US would support the anticommunist governments throughout the world. The **Marshall Plan** advanced this policy by supplying aid to war-ravaged countries in Western Europe. When the **Eastern Bloc countries** prevented aid from reaching West Berlin, the US, England, and France organized the **Berlin Airlift** to overcome this obstacle. In 1949, the Western European and North American nations entered into a mutual defense treaty, NATO (North Atlantic Treaty Organization). As a response, the Eastern Bloc nations joined with the Soviet Union in the **Warsaw Pact**.

### Communist Revolution in China

China was torn by civil strife all throughout the Second World War. At one point, the American government had to renounce its trade rights in **China** in order to persuade China not to sign a peace treaty with Japan while the US still needed Chinese support. Once Japan had been defeated, the **Red Army** under Mao moved into **Manchuria** (which had recently been vacated by the Soviets). The major cities were still occupied by Nationalist forces, supported by the Americans. In 1946, fighting resumed between the opposing factions, and the **Nationalists** under Chiang were eventually forced to abandon central China. In 1949, the Red Army forced Chiang Kai-shek to leave the mainland and find refuge in Taiwan. On October 1, 1949, the communists declared the official creation of the **People's Republic of China**.

## ARMS RACE, CUBAN MISSILE CRISIS, AND BAY OF PIGS IN THE COLD WAR

During the **Cold War**, the United States and the Soviet Union each tried to deter an attack by the other by building up fantastic arsenals of **nuclear missiles**. The two nations would also expend considerable effort trying to be the first in space. Finally, in the late 60s and early 70s, the two nations would begin talks aimed at mutual disarmament. This occurred in part because relations between China and the USSR had cooled. Before this period of détente, however, there had been a couple of serious threats to global peace. In 1961, the US had financed an unsuccessful invasion of Cuba at the **Bay of Pigs**. This led the Soviet Union to establish missile bases on communist Cuba; the US and USSR almost declared war on one another during the **Cuban Missile Crisis of 1962**.

## END OF THE COLD WAR

Over time, the leaders of the Soviet Union and United States began to realize the total annihilation that would ensue if nuclear war was declared, and it was agreed that both sides would **disarm**. The two treaties that were signed during the 1970s are known as the **Strategic Arms Limitation Talks (SALT) I and II**. When **Mikhail Gorbachev** came into power in the USSR in 1985, he established a policy of **glasnost**, or "openness." In response to US President Ronald Reagan's military build-up using the might of the US economy, Gorbachev understood that the Soviet Union could not economically compete militarily under a communist system and overcome the military might of the United States. He thus advocated **perestroika**, a gradual metamorphosis of the Soviet economy. In 1991, these reforms culminated in the disintegration of the ruling Communist party, and the **disbanding of the Soviet Union**. This occurred two years after the **Berlin Wall**, which for more than forty years had separated communist and anticommunist Germany, was finally torn down.

**Review Video: The End of the Cold War**
Visit mometrix.com/academy and enter code: 278032

## MIDDLE EAST FROM 1947 TO 1977

After WWII, the United Nations announced that **Palestine** would be partitioned in order to make room for a new Jewish state. **Israel** was created in 1948. In 1951, the Iranian leader **Mossadegh** nationalized the oil interests, making his government extremely wealthy and powerful. This move would be emulated by future leaders. In 1967, in the **Six-Day War**, Israel routed a coalition of Arab nations, seizing the West Bank, Sinai, and Jerusalem. In 1972, Palestinian terrorists murdered 12 Israeli athletes at the Olympics in Munich. In 1973, the oil-producing Arab nations placed an embargo on shipments to the West, causing major energy crises in the US and Europe. Also, in 1973, Israelis and Arabs battled again in the **Yom Kippur War**. In 1977, Egyptian leader **Anwar Sadat** became the first Arab leader to visit Israel.

## MIDDLE EAST FROM 1978 TO 1985

In 1978, American President **Jimmy Carter** hosted successful peace talks between Egypt and Israel at **Camp David**. The next year, however, a fundamentalist Islamist regime would take power in Iran, and many Americans would be taken hostage, only released upon the election of **Ronald Reagan**. Between 1980 and 1988, Iran and Iraq engaged in a bloody and brutal war, begun when the Iraqi leader **Saddam Hussein** seized territory in eastern Iran. Also, during this period, Afghan rebels were engaged in a prolonged, ultimately successful fight for independence from the Soviets. In 1982, Israel attacked Lebanon, which was harboring the Palestinian leader **Yasser Arafat**. Lebanon would be forced to oust Arafat the next year. Israel would continue attacking Arafat and the **Palestinian Liberation Organization**, and the PLO would continue to sponsor terrorist activities against Israel.

## MIDDLE EAST FROM 1987 TO 2003

In 1987, Syrian troops entered Lebanon and stopped the civil war. Also, during this year, 402 pilgrims died during riots in the Saudi Arabian sacred city of Mecca. In 1988, the Palestinian resistance (known as the Intifada) began in earnest against Israel. Iraq invaded Kuwait in 1990, and after UN sanctions were levied, the US invaded in 1991. The Iraqi soldiers set fire to thousands of Kuwaiti oil wells while retreating. In 1992, Arafat and Israeli PM Yitzhak Rabin shook hands in Washington, and Arafat would soon return to Gaza after years of exile. In 1995, the Israelis and Palestinians signed an agreement giving the Palestinians autonomy in the West Bank and Gaza areas. Despite continuing violence, another agreement was reached in 1998, this one stating that the Palestinians would be granted land in exchange for keeping the peace. Violence continued, however, and in 2003, Israel began construction of a barrier between itself and the Palestinian territories.

## NEW EUROPE AFTER 1991 THROUGH 1998

In 1991, **Gorbachev** resigned as the last president of the USSR, and a number of the Soviet provinces, including Lithuania and Latvia, declared independence. The **Maastricht Treaty**, formally announcing the creation of the European Union, was signed in 1992, and the next year a unified European stock market opened. In the **"Velvet" Revolution of 1993**, Slovakia separated from Czechoslovakia, which became the Czech Republic. Meanwhile, the former USSR was enduring civil strife until **Boris Yeltsin** seized power in 1993. In 1994, Russian troops attacked **Chechnya**, which was trying to achieve independence. In 1998, President Clinton helped broker a peace agreement between the **British** and **North Irish rebels**.

## NEW EUROPE AFTER 1999

In 1999, the Czech Republic, Poland, and Hungary all joined **NATO**, further eliminating the old divides between western and eastern Europe. The conflict in Chechnya increased during this year, and Yeltsin was succeeded as Russian leader by the former KGB agent Vladimir Putin. An **International Criminal Court** was created in the Hague (Netherlands) in 2002, despite the vehement opposition of the United States. In the late '90s, many of the western European governments had become quasi-socialist, and they spent much of their time debating the immense increase in **immigration**. Meanwhile, the former Soviet states have had a rough transition from command to market economies, and are still somewhat economically depressed.

## EMERGENCE OF THE PACIFIC RIM AFTER 1991

In the 1990s and early years of the 21st century, Japan and China emerged as two major economic powers. Despite suffering a prolonged recession, **Japan** continued to be one of the world's manufacturing leaders. However, several internal scandals have shaken Japanese confidence and have caused many to question the close relations between corporations and government. In **China**, the suffocating communist regime has relaxed its economic strictures somewhat, and the result has been an economic boom. China created several **special economic zones** along its eastern coast to lure foreign business. Now however, Chinese firms are control a sizable portion of the market in their own right.

## FIRST WORLD, SECOND WORLD, AND THIRD WORLD

**First-world nations** are those that have advanced capitalist economies and are fully industrialized. The former Soviet states, which are slowly developing capitalist economies after having inefficient socialist economies for so long, are classified as **second-world nations**. This term has fallen out of general use, as these nations have slowly become more similar to first-world nations. The relatively poor and non-industrialized nations of Latin America, Africa, and Asia, most of which were colonized or involved in other exploitative trade arrangements with the Western empires at one time, are known as the **third-world nations**. Although these nations are far more numerous than those of the first or second world, they wield much less political power.Underdevelopment

Third-world countries that do not have the modern economic conditions possessed by the wealthier nations are said to suffer from **underdevelopment**. That is, they do not have the industrial, social, or political strength that is required to be a self-sustaining party in the global economy. In some countries, underdevelopment is clearly the result of **dysfunctional politics**; third-world nations are more likely to be ruled by a small group or by a dictator. Underdeveloped nations are typically those that were colonized at one time. Because their economy during the colonial period was so heavily based upon exporting raw materials, they never created a manufacturing base and found themselves unequipped for independence. Experts are at odds as to whether first-world nations should aid underdeveloped countries by funneling money to them or by helping them to develop modern economies.

## Specific Technological Advances Since 1991

In 1993, the first **web browser** was developed, beginning the era of internet communications that has revolutionized every area of human life. The internet did not become widely used, however, until 1997 and 1998. In 1997, a Scottish lab successfully **cloned** a lamb from adult sheep DNA, opening the door to the cloning of other animals, or human organs for medical purposes, and even for the cloning of entire human beings. This last possibility was strengthened in 2001, when the work of **sequencing the DNA** of the human genome was finally finished. Although **embryonic stem-cell research** has been limited in the US (other sources than embryos remain legal), other countries are using cells from human embryos to search for cures for disease. Another leap in genetic technology came in 2012 with the advent of CRISPR, a tool for directly editing the genes of any organism. In 2008, a new technology was used to implement Bitcoin called blockchain. This is a powerful method for sharing and storing information in an incredibly secure way, among many other uses. One of the most astonishing acheivements in science in recent history was in 2016 when the LIGO observatory used incredibly sensitive detectors to sense gravitational waves from distant colliding black holes.

## Modernization

Modernization is the process by which societies develop sophisticated industrial technology, as well as the political, cultural, and social systems that are most effective in sustaining and advancing that technology. For a long time, sociologists noted that the most modernized countries, namely the Western empires, were the most successful, and that other societies should strive to emulate them. In recent decades, however, more sensitive sociologists have declared that **modernization** need not be equated with Westernization, and that the indigenous cultures of South America and Africa, for example, need not be cast off for these places to enjoy prosperity. One way sociologists can assess the relative modernization of a society is by comparing the **gross national product** (GNP), which is the total value of all economic activity within a society. Often, GNP is divided by total population to determine a society's **per capita gross national product**.

## State Theory of Modernization and World System Theory of Modernization

The state theory of modernization supports the ideals of **capitalism** by maintaining that whenever the government is restricted from seizing private property, capitalism will develop and free markets will arise as people modernize and strive to become more productive. The **world system theory of modernization**, also known as the **dependency theory**, states that some nations modernize at the expense of less-developed nations, and that so long as this exploitation continues, the less-developed nations will be unable to improve their lot. This theory essentially takes the

**Marxist** view of the capitalist society, in which those who own the means of production are able to maintain dominance over the workers, and applies it to the interactions of nations.

### Globalization

Globalization is the process whereby all the social groups in the world are being brought into closer connection with one another. This has occurred mainly through the advances in transportation and communication technology, although the era of colonialism also had the effect of shrinking the world. This phenomenon has, in some cases, made it more difficult for repressive regimes to isolate themselves; during the Tiananmen Square uprising in China, for instance, Western media was able to communicate with the student rebels and present their story to the rest of the world. Many observers lament **globalization**, however, because they feel it will homogenize culture and crowd out fascinating, but not economically successful, societies.

**Review Video: Globalization**
Visit mometrix.com/academy and enter code: 551962

### Automation

Automation is when machines are employed to do work formerly done by humans. This is typically done when an industry seeks to have greater worker productivity, but it may have some costly side effects. The work that remains for people after automation is frequently repetitive and mindless. Sociologists studying the phenomenon have observed increased alienation and lowered self-esteem among workers whose jobs have been automated. Also, automation reduces the need for specialization by driving employees out of their previously unique fields; this creates both unhealthy competition for menial jobs and confusion over social roles among the workers. Unfortunately, the pressures of the **capitalist market** make it impossible for most businesses to avoid automation.

### Hyperurbanization

Hyperurbanization has occurred when the development of population growth in urban areas has moved too quickly and has outpaced the necessary accompanying growths in industry and business. The inevitable result of **hyperurbanization** is unemployment and inadequate public services. This has been a particular problem in **third-world countries**, which are experiencing mass internal migration from the countryside to the cities. In fact, the urbanization currently taking place in China may be the largest movement of people in the history of the world. It is impossible for any society, no matter how wealthy, to keep up with such a migration and provide adequate roads, health care, education, water, food, and electricity.

## Chapter Quiz

Ready to see how well you retained what you just read? Scan the QR code to go directly to the chapter quiz interface for this study guide. If you're using a computer, simply visit the online resources page at **mometrix.com/resources719/texeshist7-12** and click the Chapter Quizzes link.

# U.S. History

## American History Pre-Columbian to 1789

### First European Explorers in America

Although **Christopher Columbus** frequently gets credit for "discovering" America in 1492 (even though people were already living on the continent), **Vikings** from Scandinavia actually arrived in about AD 1000. These explorers constructed no permanent settlements, however, and did not remain for long. It was not until economic expansion in Europe made exploration worthwhile that explorers returned. Columbus and the explorers who would come later were looking for the **Northwest Passage** that would take them directly to Asia and were annoyed by the new land that kept getting in the way. Columbus died believing that he had landed in some outpost of India (hence, calling the natives "Indians").

> **Review Video: Christopher Columbus**
> Visit mometrix.com/academy and enter code: 496598

### English Interest in the New World

The English lagged somewhat behind other European nations in exploration of the New World. Finally, however, a combination of economic and social incentives convinced them to look west. For one thing, the **enclosure movement** in England had made land very scarce, and the practice of **primogeniture** meant that only the eldest son could inherit the land. For these reasons, many Englishmen moved to the New World for the promise of cheap land. England also had a large population at this time, so the government viewed the New World as a good place to send criminals and beggars. Another reason for the increase in interest in America was the **Protestant Reformation**. Many English Catholics and Protestants felt alienated by the new Church of England and wanted to find a place in which they could worship more freely.

### Settling of North America by the English

The first English attempt to found a colony in the New World was made by Sir Humphrey Gilbert in **Newfoundland** in 1583 and was a complete failure. Sir Walter Raleigh would lead two more failed attempts at founding a colony on **Roanoke Island** in 1586 and 1588. The second of these colonies is known as the **Lost Colony**, because it disappeared without a trace while Raleigh was gone. Finally, the British were able to establish a permanent colony at **Jamestown**, Virginia in 1607. The settlers in Jamestown came for gold and to convert the Natives to Christianity. One of the important events of the early years of Jamestown was the issuing of the Virginia Charter, which declared that English settlers in the New World would be treated as Englishmen with full English rights.

> **Review Video: Founding of Jamestown**
> Visit mometrix.com/academy and enter code: 881040

### Virginia Colony

#### *Beginnings*

The English colony of **Virginia**, which began at Jamestown, was at first plagued by a poor location and a scarcity of skilled laborers. Captain **John Smith** was elected leader in 1608, and he proved to be the strict leader the colony needed to survive. A large proportion of the settlers would die during the winter of 1609-10. What finally saved the Virginia colony was the wild popularity of **tobacco**. In

1619, the **House of Burgesses** met, becoming the first legislative body to be formed in the New World. King James I of England correctly predicted that this would only lead to trouble for his nation. Later that year, 20 African indentured servants arrived on an English privateer with a Dutch letter of marque; Virginia would become the first colony to legalize **slavery**, in 1660.

**Review Video: The English Colony of Virginia**
Visit mometrix.com/academy and enter code: 537399

#### *Royal Colony*

Virginia officially became a **Royal Colony** in 1624. This was in part because the Virginia Company (the joint-stock company that had previously administered affairs) had gone bankrupt, and partly because King James I wanted to exercise more control. After the English Civil War of the 1640s, many of the supporters of the king, known as **cavaliers**, settled in Virginia. During this period, the wealthy colonists began claiming the coastal land and pushing the poor people farther inland, where they were prey to Native American attacks and were underrepresented in the House of Burgesses. Frustrated, a group of settlers led by **Nathaniel Bacon** burned Jamestown to the ground. **Bacon's Rebellion**, as it came to be known, was thought of by some as a harbinger of things to come.

### New Netherland Colony

The Dutch East India Company hired the English explorer **Henry Hudson** to search for the Northwest Passage to Asia. Instead, he journeyed up the Hudson River and claimed the area now known as **New York** for the Dutch. The Dutch purchased **Manhattan Island** from the Lenape Native Americans for $24 and established a town called **New Amsterdam** there, an aristocratic town, in which everyone had to be a member of the Dutch Reformed Church. Eventually, in 1664, this Dutch settlement would be overwhelmed by the British colonies surrounding it. King Charles II gave the area to his successor, James, Duke of York, who quickly gave the town and colony the name it bears today.

### Beginnings of English Colonies of Maryland, the Carolinas, and Georgia

**Maryland** was established in 1634 as a **proprietary colony**, meaning it was exclusively owned by one person. The owner, Lord Baltimore, ran his colony like a feudal estate. Maryland prospered because of tobacco and became a haven for persecuted Catholics. **North Carolina** was originally settled by Virginians and quickly acquired a reputation as independent and democratic. Many English colonists avoided North Carolina because they felt it was overrun by pirates. **South Carolina**, meanwhile, was a proprietary colony established in 1670. South Carolina hosted a large number of religious groups. **Georgia**, meanwhile, was a proprietary colony established in 1733. Its namesake, George II, hoped that it would be a buffer zone between the colonists and the Native Americans and populated it almost exclusively with criminals and debtors.

### Southern Colonies

#### *Economic Life*

In the early days of the Southern colonies, most people lived on **small farms**. Although they made up a tiny part of the population, the owners of the **coastal plantations** wielded enormous power. These aristocrats typically grew a single crop on their lands; in North Carolina, Virginia, and Maryland, **tobacco** was the cash crop, while the large growers in South Carolina and Georgia favored **rice** and **indigo**. Plantations, like the feudal manors of the past, were almost totally self-sufficient units, although the owners imported most of their luxury items from England. The Southern colonies had the closest ties with England, mainly because England provided the market for their tobacco; crops grown in the colonies were sold back in England by agents (known as factors).

**Review Video: The Southern Colonies**
Visit mometrix.com/academy and enter code: 703830

### Social Life

The social lives of the Southern colonists were filled with dancing, card-playing, cotillions, hunts, and large community dinners. Southerners were considered to be very optimistic in temperament, in contrast to their more dour Northern counterparts. It was extremely difficult to move up in the **social hierarchy** in the South; the richer colonists generally took the best land and thus were able to maintain their position in the economy and in the government, as the poor had to move away from the towns to find farmland. Because farming was the only available occupation, there were not any venues for ambitious men to distinguish themselves. North Carolina was generally considered to be the state with the least **social stratification**.

### Life Expectancy and Education

The average man in the Southern colonies could expect to live **35 years**. This was in part due to disease; stagnant water and unfamiliar heat helped the spread of many contagions throughout the population, and malaria was a constant danger. In response to the high mortality rate, families tended to have lots of children. Also, **education** was not a high priority in the colonies in those days. One problem was that the population was too scattered for a central public school to be possible. Wealthy plantation owners would hire a **tutor** for their children, who might later be sent off to the College of William & Mary or one of the new schools up North: Harvard, Yale, or Princeton. For the less affluent, however, it was more likely that any education would be received as an **apprentice** of an experienced craftsman.

### Religious and Political Life

In all of the Southern colonies, the **Anglican Church** was supported by taxes. Anyone who wanted to enter politics would have to be a member of the Church, though the majority of the colonists were not. In general, the Southern colonies had the greatest degree of **religious toleration**. Politics during this period were largely controlled by the planter aristocracy. Each Southern colony had a **governor** (chosen by the colony's English sponsor), a **governor's council**, and an **assembly** to represent the people. During the 1700s, these assemblies took more and more power away from the governors. In order to run for office, a man had to be a member of the Anglican Church; many people, including Thomas Jefferson, would acquire membership in the Church and then never set foot inside it again.

### Beginning of Slave Trade

After periods in which Native Americans or indentured servants from England were used as laborers, most of the labor in the Southern British North American colonies was performed by **African slaves**. These slaves were taken in wars between African chieftains and then sold to European traders. Oftentimes, the African leaders would trade slaves for guns in order to protect themselves from other slave traders. Several African states, most notably the Yoruba and the Dahomey, became wealthy from this trade. The journey from West Africa to the West Indies was dangerous and depressing, and many slaves died en route. Before they were sold into the American colonies, slaves first worked in the brutal heat of the sugar plantations of the British West Indies. Only about half would survive long enough to see America.

### *Legalization of Slavery*

Between 1640 and 1660, the Southern colonies slowly evolved from a system of servitude to one of **slavery**. In 1661, Virginia became the first colony to legalize **chattel slavery for life**, and made it such that the children of slaves would be slaves as well. The number of slaves increased dramatically in the 1680s after the **Royal African Company** lost its monopoly and the industry was thrown open to anyone. Virginia established **slave codes** to keep revolts down: slaves could not be taught to read, could not gather together, could not have weapons, and could not leave the plantation without written permission. Naturally, slaves often rebelled against their treatment, but they were outnumbered and overpowered.

### Early Resistance to Slavery

Many slaves resisted submission, and many died as a result. For any serious offense, a slave would be executed in front of his or her peers as a deterrent. From its inception, there was **resistance** to slavery. In 1688, the **Quakers** declared that slavery was inhuman and a violation of the Bible. Many felt that slavery degraded both master and slave. In order to justify the hateful institution, slave owners declared that black people were less than human, or that, as descendants of the Biblical figure Ham, they were ordered by God to serve white people. The hymn "Amazing Grace" was written by guilt-wracked former slave trader **John Newton**. Slaves could only become free by proving mulatto (half white) status or by buying their freedom (some masters would allow their slaves to work for pay on the weekends).

### Puritanism and the Pilgrims in Massachusetts Colony

Puritans believed in the idea of predestination, meaning that God has already chosen which people will get into heaven. In order to suggest to others (and to themselves) that they were among the elect, **Puritans** were obsessed with maintaining proper decorum in public. Those Puritans who wanted to fully separate from the Church of England were known as **Pilgrims** (or Separatists). The Pilgrims originally went to Holland, but after determining that they would be unable to make a good life there, they got permission from the Virginia Company to settle in the northern part of the Virginia colony in 1620. The **Plymouth Company** was commissioned, and the **Mayflower** set sail. Because of storms and poor navigation, however, they ended up in the area that would come to be known as Massachusetts. One of the early moves of the group was to agree to the **Mayflower Compact**, whereby all members of the group would be bound to the will of the majority.

**Review Video: The Mayflower Compact**
Visit mometrix.com/academy and enter code: 275859

### *Puritans*

The Puritans established the colony of **Massachusetts Bay** in 1630. They hoped to purify the **Church of England** and then return to Europe with a new and improved religion. The Massachusetts Bay Puritans were more immediately successful than other fledgling colonies because they brought enough supplies, arrived in the springtime, and had good leadership (including **John Winthrop**). Puritans fished, cut timber for ships, and trapped fur. The local government was inextricably bound with the Church; only Church members were allowed to vote for the **General Court** (similar to the House of Burgesses), although everyone was required to pay taxes. The Puritans established a **Bible Commonwealth** that would last 50 years. During this time, Old Testament law was the law of the community.

## Political and Social Life in the Early Massachusetts Colonies

The **Massachusetts Bay Puritans** were known for religious intolerance and a general suspicion of democracy. Even though they had left England because of religious persecution, they did not set up their colony as a safe haven for others. One of the people who was kicked out of the colony for blasphemy was **Roger Williams**, who went on to found a colony at **Providence**. Williams taught that the colonists should be fair to the Native Americans and that political leaders should stay out of religion. Roger Williams eventually founded the **Baptist Church**. The Puritans generally felt that the common people were incapable of governing themselves and should be looked after by their government. Also, many Puritans objected to democracy because they felt it was inefficient.

## English Civil War and the New England Confederation

During the English Civil War, the Puritans tried to separate from the Church of England; they issued the **Body of Liberties**, which stated that the Massachusetts Bay was independent of England and was therefore no longer bound by English Civil Law, that there could be no arbitrary governors appointed to dissolve a local legislature, and that town meetings of qualified voters would be held to discuss local issues. Later, in 1643, a **New England Confederation** was formed, consisting of Massachusetts Bay, New Plymouth, Connecticut River Valley, and New Haven. The goals of this confederation were to protect the colonists from the French (in Canada) and the Native Americans, to safeguard their commercial interests from the Dutch in New Netherland (later New York), and to return runaway slaves.

## Dominion of New England

The impertinence of the **Massachusetts Bay colony** was a constant annoyance to **King Charles II** and he thus punished them by granting charters to rival colonies in Connecticut and Rhode Island and by creating the **Dominion of New England**. The purpose of this organization was to boost trade by enforcing the **Navigation Acts** of 1660 and 1663, which stated that all trade had to be done on English ships and had to pass through England before it could go anywhere else. The English, of course, made the colonists pay a tax on any exports that were not bound for England. The colonists loathed the Dominion government, not only because of its economic penalties but because it tried to promote the Anglican Church in America. A rebellion against the Dominion probably would have occurred if the **Glorious Revolution** in England had not ended it prematurely.

**Review Video: The Massachusetts Bay Colony**
Visit mometrix.com/academy and enter code: 407058

## Land, Demography, Climate, Economics, and Slavery in Puritan Life

The **land** settled by the Puritans was rocky and bare, and it took tremendous labor to subsist off of its products. Massachusetts had an extremely homogenous **population**, mainly because there was little reason to stay there other than to be among people of the same faith. Non-Puritan immigrants usually moved south, where the soil was better and the population was more tolerant. Because agriculture was so tricky, a more diverse **economy** developed in New England than existed in the South. Puritans engaged in fishing and trapping, and there were a number of craftsmen in each town. There were **slaves** in New England, though not nearly as many as in the South. Furthermore, slaves in New England were more commonly used as household servants than hard laborers.

## Social and Religious Life of the Puritans

There was more chance for **social mobility** in Massachusetts than in any other colony in America. This was mainly due to the diverse economy. As for religion, it dominated every area of an individual's life. The Puritan Church was known as the **Congregational Church**; at first, this was an exclusive group, but it gradually became easier to become a member. Indeed, by the mid-1600s, religious fervor seemed to be waning in Massachusetts. A group called the **Jeremiads** warned the people that they were in danger of lapsing into atheism, but many people did not mind. Around this time, ministers began to offer **half-way covenants**, which gave church members partial privileges.

### Salem Witch Trials

During the 1690s in New England, there was still a strong belief in **Christian mysticism**. Many people were paranoid about spiritualists and mediums. This, combined with perhaps some local feuds, led to 19 women and one man being executed for **witchcraft** in 1692. Most likely, however, the accused individuals were only suffering from delusions caused by a kind of hallucinogenic bread mold (ergot). The witch trials only stopped when people in high places began being accused. The **Salem witch trials** tarnished the image of the clergy for a long time and further contributed to a general relaxation of religious fervor in this period.

### Pennsylvania Colony, Quakers, and The Charter of Liberties

The Pennsylvania (literally "Penn's woods") colony was established by **William Penn** in 1681. Penn declared that the colony would provide religious and political freedom for all. The main religious group to settle in the area was the **Society of Friends** (Quakers). Quakers believed that every person could communicate with the divine, that the church should not be supported by tax dollars, and that all men are equal. The Quakers have always been pacifists, and they were the first group to oppose slavery. In Pennsylvania, voting rights were extended only to landholders or large taxpayers. The **Charter of Liberties** (1701) established a unicameral legislature working alongside a governor.

### The Great Awakening

The Great Awakening was a religious revival in New England in the 1730s and 40s. It began in response to the growing secularism and was aided by the recent migrations into the cities, where it was easier for large crowds to form. **Jonathan Edwards** was one of the most famous preachers of this time. The **Great Awakening** was the first mass movement in America; it helped break down the divides between the various regions of the British colonies and led to the formation of some new Protestant denominations. Though the Revivalists did not directly advocate the abolition of slavery, they did suggest that there was divinity in all creation and that, therefore, black people were worthy of being converted to Christianity.

### Bible Commonwealth and Political and Intellectual Life in New England

The New England colonies started out as **Bible Commonwealths**, where Biblical law was local law, and a man's standing in the church determined his political power. Over time, however, New England became more liberal, and politics came to be dominated by the **wealthy men** rather than by the church leaders. Life expectancy in the New England colonies became roughly what it is today. **Education** was valued greatly in New England, and the fact that most people lived close to a town made it possible for more people to receive inexpensive training. Puritans believed that ignorance of God's word could lead one to be tricked by the devil, and thus they made sure that all of their children learned to read.

### Middle Colonies

#### *Economic Life, Slavery, and Society*

The **Middle Colonies** (New York, Pennsylvania, Delaware, East and West New Jersey) shared characteristics with both New England and the Southern colonies. The **economy** was diverse, though less so than in New England. Shipping and commerce would gradually become crucial in the port cities of Philadelphia and New York. There were plenty of **slaves** in the Middle Colonies, most of whom served as laborers on ships. The Dutch treated their slaves well; the English did not. People in these colonies tended to have a healthier lifestyle than their neighbors to the south, and therefore they tended to live longer. The diverse economy made **social mobility** possible, though large landowners were for the most part entrenched in positions of power.

### *Education, Religion, and Politics*

Most education in the Middle Colonies was received as an **apprentice** to a successful craftsman. Often, local churches would maintain schools during the week. The two main religious organizations in this region were the **Anglican Church** and the **Dutch Reformed Church**, often at each other's throats because they were competing for members and tax dollars. A typical government in the Middle Colonies had a **governor**, a governor's council, and a **representative assembly**. Men were only allowed to vote if they owned property. The Middle Colonies had the most diverse population, mainly because they had available land and promised religious freedom (at least in Pennsylvania).

## George Grenville and the Proclamation of 1763

George Grenville became the prime minister of Britain in 1763, and immediately abandoned the policy of "salutary neglect" that had been upheld by the former prime minister Robert Walpole. On the contrary, he asserted that the American colonists should have to pay for British military protection, even though the Americans claimed not to need it. According to the **Proclamation of 1763**, all American colonists were to stay east of the Appalachian Mountains. This policy was ostensibly created in order to protect the colonists in the wake of **Chief Pontiac's Rebellion** in 1763, in which Native Americans attacked colonists and were subsequently slaughtered by the British. Many colonists, however, felt that the Proclamation was a transparent attempt to maintain British control of the fur trade.

## Sugar (Revenue) Act, Currency Act, and the Quartering Act

The Sugar (Revenue) Act of 1764 established a duty on basically any products that were not British in origin (e.g., molasses, indigo, and sugar). Unlike the Molasses Act, the **Sugar Act** was fully enforced. Most colonists resented this taxation, which they felt was used to fund the French and Indian War. The **Currency Act of 1764** forbade colonists from issuing paper money and stated that all taxes paid to England must be paid in gold and silver rather than paper. This act eliminated the worthless Continental Dollar. The **Quartering Act of 1765** required colonists to provide bedding and food to the regiments of British soldiers in America. This regulation increased paranoia amongst the colonists, who began to wonder exactly why the British soldiers were there in the first place.

## Stamp Act of 1765

The Stamp Act of 1765 was levied without the consent of the colonists. It specified that a stamp must be applied to all legal documents (there was considerable debate over the definition of this phrase) indicating that a tax had been paid for the defense of the colonies. This act was extremely unpopular, perhaps mostly because its presence was so visible; its implementation generated loud cries of "**taxation without representation.**" The British responded by claiming that the colonists had "virtual representation" by members of Parliament. The colonists continued to claim that they needed direct and actual representation, although many feared that even if they were to get it, they would probably lose most votes anyway.

## Stamp Act Congress, the Sons of Liberty, and the Declaratory Act

In 1765, the colonists created the Stamp Act Congress in New York in order to peacefully resolve the conflicts created by the Stamp Act. This group established the **Non-importation Agreements**, which amounted to a boycott of English products. At the same time, the **Sons of Liberty** in Boston were running amok: vandalizing British goods, tarring and feathering stamp collectors, and erecting so-called "liberty poles," from which collectors would be hung by their pants. In 1766, the new British prime minister **Rockingham** repealed the Stamp Act because the boycotts were damaging the British economy. In part to punish the colonists for their insubordination, in 1766 the British Parliament issued the **Declaratory Act**, which asserted that they had the right to legislate on behalf of the colonists at any time.

## Townshend Acts

The Townshend Acts, named after Charles "Champagne Charlie" Townshend, the prime minister of Britain from 1766-72, placed an indirect tax on household items coming into the colonies and tightened the customs duties. The Acts also called for stricter vice-admiralty courts and established the **Writs of Assistance**, which were essentially blank search warrants. The colonists' response to the Townshend Acts was twofold: a **pamphlet war** was waged by men like John Dickinson, James Otis, and Samuel Adams, and there were also more violent protests, as for instance the **Boston Massacre**, in which a mob in the Boston Common was fired on by the British, perhaps accidentally. Colonists used the "Massacre" as a rallying cry, and the Townshend Acts were repealed (with the notable exception of the tax on tea).

## Lord North, the Gaspee, the Committees of Correspondence, and John Wilkes

Lord North succeeded Townshend as British prime minister in 1772. In this year, the Sons of Liberty set fire to the **Gaspee**, a British revenue ship, off the coast of Rhode Island. The Sons of Liberty were driven to further violence by Massachusetts governor Tom Hutchinson's announcement that his salary would be paid by the British. The **Committees of Correspondence** were subsequently formed to organize the protest against the British and to keep colonists informed on British matters. At around this time, the British MP **John Wilkes** became a folk hero in the colonies because of his impassioned speeches in defense of liberty. Although Wilkes never spoke directly on behalf of the colonists, he was jailed for his speeches.

## Coercive (Intolerable) Acts

The Coercive Acts, known as the **Intolerable Acts** in America, were issued in response to the Boston Tea Party and had several parts. The **Boston Port Act** closed the port down, supposedly until the destroyed tea was paid for, although this never happened. The **Massachusetts Government Act** put the colony under martial law. A military governor, Thomas Gage, was placed in charge of the colony. The **Administration of Justice Act** required that all judges, soldiers, and tax agents be English and that all crimes be tried in England. The **New Quartering Act** asserted that British soldiers were allowed to enter private homes and demand lodging. The **Quebec Act of 1774** declared that everything west of the Appalachians was Quebec; although this was basically done so that Britain could govern more effectively, it caused speculation among the colonists that the British were going to sell America to the French.

## First Continental Congress

The First Continental Congress was held September 5, 1774, and was attended by a representative of every colony except Georgia. This Congress issued the **Suffolk Resolves**, stating that they would give Boston aid in the form of food and clothing, but would not take up arms on behalf of Boston. The **Continental Association**, an agreement not to buy or sell English goods, was formed. A conservative named Joseph Galloway advocated the creation of a **Council of All Colonies**, a legislative body which would share power with Parliament. The **Galloway Plan** was nixed by Massachusetts, however, because that colony refused to share power with any British authority. Massachusetts at this time was in a highly volatile state.

## Thomas Gage and Paul Revere

Thomas Gage, the military governor of Massachusetts, was under increasing duress at the beginning of 1775 and asked the British government for either 20,000 more troops or a repeal of the Coercive Acts. Instead, Britain sent 2,000 troops, which **Gage** used to collect guns, gunpowder, and shot. On April 18 of 1775, the British troops sailed across Boston Harbor toward the large stockpile at Concord. **Paul Revere** then took his famous ride to warn the other colonists about the approach of the British. Although Revere was captured, his ride was finished by Samuel Prescott and William Dawes. On the way to Concord, in Lexington, shots were fired and 8 colonial militiamen were killed. The British then moved on to Concord, where the real fighting began.

## Second Continental Congress

The Second Continental Congress was held May 10, 1775, in Philadelphia. **George Washington** became the commander of the Americans, mainly because it was felt that he would be able to bring the Southern colonies into the fold. This Congress also drew up the **Olive Branch petition**, a peace offering made to the King of England. The **Articles of Confederation** were drawn up here; their emphasis on states' rights proved to be a poor setup for organizing a comprehensive military strategy. This Congress created the **Committees of Safety**, a system for training community militias. This Congress created a bureaucracy for the purpose of organizing a navy and raising money. Finally, it was here that the colonists formally declared **independence**.

**Review Video: The First and Second Continental Congress**
Visit mometrix.com/academy and enter code: 835211

## Reasons for Declaring Independence

At the time that the Declaration of Independence was issued, many colonists were opposed to complete separation from England. Many of them still considered themselves Englishmen and were afraid to be branded as traitors. They also realized that they were in uncharted waters; no revolt had ever been successful in winning independence. Finally, many colonists feared that even if they were successful in winning independence, the result would be chaos in America. The minds of many of these reluctant colonists were changed, however, by the **Battle of Bunker Hill**, which was won by the British. After this battle, King George II declared that the colonists were in a state of rebellion. Furthermore, the British labeled the members of the **Second Continental Congress** as traitors and ignored the **Olive Branch petition**. Confused colonists were further inflamed by the British use of Hessian mercenary soldiers. The writings of **Thomas Paine** also converted many colonists to the revolutionary cause.

## Declaration of Independence

The Declaration of Independence was proposed at the **Second Continental Congress** by Richard Henry Lee, and was composed by a committee of Franklin, Jefferson, John Adams, Robert Livingston, and Roger Sherman. The document has three parts: a **preamble** and reasons for separation; a **theory of government**; and a formal **declaration of war**. Jefferson attempted to have it include a condemnation of slavery, but was rebuffed. The Declaration had many aims: to enlist help from other British colonies; to create a cause for which to fight; to motivate reluctant colonists; to ensure that captured Americans would be treated as prisoners of war; and to establish an American theory of government. In fulfilling this last purpose, Jefferson borrowed heavily from

Enlightenment thinkers like Montesquieu, Rousseau, and Locke, asserting famously that "all men are created equal."

**Review Video: Declaration of Independence**
Visit mometrix.com/academy and enter code: 256838

### *SIGNIFICANCE*

The issuing of the Declaration of Independence had effects both on the Revolutionary War and on world history at large. As far as its immediate effects, it changed the war in America from a war for liberty to a war for independence, by rhetorically **emancipating** America from Britain. It also opened a path for the **French Revolution** a few years later, one motivated by the principles expressed in the Declaration. Revolutions in South America, Africa, and Asia have also used the Declaration of Independence as inspiration. In the subsequent history of the United States, the document would be used by **abolitionists** as an argument against slavery and by **suffragists** as an argument for the right of women to vote.

## SARATOGA CAMPAIGN

The British military plan during the early stages of the Revolutionary War was known as the **Saratoga campaign** (or the Germain Plan). It called for a three-pronged attack aimed at capturing New York and thus separating the Northeast from the Southern colonies. This plan broke down because of the following reasons: One of the generals, Howe, was supposed to go up the Hudson River to Albany, but instead decided to go after Philadelphia. Another general, Burgoyne, was able to conquer Fort Ticonderoga, but then languished without supplies for months, and eventually had to surrender to colonial troops. The third general, St. Leger, made considerable progress across New York from Lake Ontario but lost steam after a series of small battles.

## BATTLE OF SARATOGA

The colonial General Gates defeated the British General Burgoyne at the **Battle of Saratoga** in 1777. This defeat confirmed the failure of the British Saratoga Campaign. More importantly, perhaps, it convinced the French that the Americans could win the war. The French then signed the **Treaty of Alliance** in 1778, which supplied the Americans with money, men, and ships. This treaty was in part negotiated by Benjamin Franklin. The French were not necessarily motivated by a spirit of goodwill towards the Americans; they hoped to gain back the territory they had lost in the French and Indian War. Moreover, the French believed that by aiding the Americans in the Revolutionary War they could position themselves to colonize parts of North America as yet unclaimed.

## SOUTHERN CAMPAIGN IN THE REVOLUTIONARY WAR

The British military campaign in the **Southern colonies** was planned by Sir Henry Clinton and implemented by General Cornwallis in the years 1778 to 1781. Cornwallis quickly took **Savannah** and **Charleston** and then moved into the interior of South Carolina. Here and in North Carolina, a series of bloody battles (many of them against the great American general Nathanael Greene) weakened Cornwallis and forced him to make a supply run to **Yorktown** on the Virginia coast. There, the British suffered a naval defeat at the hands of the French and then were routed by Washington-led troops. During their retreat, the British naval forces were further weakened by a violent storm, and Cornwallis was forced to **surrender** on October 17, 1781.

## LEGACY OF THE REVOLUTIONARY WAR

After the conclusion of the Revolutionary War, neither the Proclamation of 1763 nor the Quebec Act applied, and thus colonists could **move west** across the Appalachians. A few British loyalists lost their land. After the war, many states moved to separate the church and state; in Virginia, for instance, Thomas Jefferson wrote the **Virginia Statute of Religious Freedom**, creating total separation in that state. States also revised the **Criminal Codes**, in an effort to make the punishment more closely fit the crime. Finally, whereas in 1750 most citizens did not question the institution of slavery, by 1780 many states began to examine this policy. Vermont was the first state to **abolish slavery**. Meanwhile, Southern states argued that the war would not have been won without slave labor.

**Review Video: The American Revolutionary War**
Visit mometrix.com/academy and enter code: 935282

## Articles of Confederation

The Articles of Confederation were largely ineffective because they gave too much power to the states and too little to a central government. Many historians now say that the best thing about the **Articles** was that they showed the authors of the Constitution what to avoid. Part of the Articles was the **Land Ordinance of 1785**, a plan created by Jefferson for dividing the Western land into organized townships. The sale of land in these territories helped generate money for the new government. The **Northwest Ordinance of 1787** divided the land above the Ohio River into five territories, which would soon become states. This ordinance would become the model for how all future states would be formed.

### *Foreign Affairs*

Both the Americans and the British violated the terms of the **Treaty of Paris**, which had ended the Revolutionary War in 1783. The British, for instance, never fully abandoned their lucrative fur trade in the Ohio Valley. Americans, on the other hand, never paid back their pre-war debts. Meanwhile, the Spanish (who controlled Louisiana and Florida) openly challenged American borders in the South, at times encouraging Native Americans to make war on the fledgling nation. Americans sought the right of deposit on the Mississippi; that is, the right to load material from a boat to a dock. The Spanish were not quick to grant this right. Meanwhile, American ships were forced to pay tribute to the Barbary states in order to trade in the Mediterranean.

### *Debt, Passing Legislation, Law Enforcement, and the Court System*

After the Revolutionary War, the United States found itself in a massive and troubling **debt**. Meanwhile, Congress was having great difficulty passing any **legislation** because in order to be made into law, a bill had to receive 9 of 13 votes, and there were often fewer than 10 representatives present. The government had no **chief executive** and thus law enforcement was left to the states. Another major problem was that the lack of a **central court system** made it hard to resolve disputes between citizens from different states, or between the states themselves. Congress did not have the power to **tax** the people directly, and could only request funds. Furthermore, although Congress could issue **currency**, it had no authority to keep the states from issuing currency of their own, so wild inflation and depreciation were common.

### *Competing Currencies and Legislative Troubles*

Under the Articles of Confederation, Congress did not have the power to raise an **army** directly; it could only ask for troops from the states. The problems with this arrangement were amply demonstrated by **Shays' Rebellion** in Massachusetts in 1786 and 1787. This rebellion was in part a response to the economic uncertainty caused by competing currencies. Under the Articles, Congress did not have the power to regulate interstate or foreign commerce. Each state in the confederation had different tariffs and trade regulations, and no foreign countries would enter into trade agreements with a nation so disorganized. In short, the **Articles of Confederation** left America unable to maintain order at home, unable to gain respect abroad, and unable to improve its economy.

## PHILADELPHIA CONVENTION OF 1787

Although 55 delegates attended the **Philadelphia Convention of 1787**, only 39 signed the Constitution that emerged from this gathering. The attendees at the convention were exclusively rich men, but were all well-qualified to construct a new government. George Washington presided over the convention, and James Madison (the "father of the Constitution") served as secretary. The **representation** afforded to the people, as well as to states of different sizes, was a contentious issue throughout. Finally, in what is known as the **Great Compromise**, it was decided that the **lower house** (House of Representatives) would be chosen by the people, and the **upper house** (Senate) would be chosen by the state legislature. This convention also produced the **3/5 compromise**, whereby each slave was to be counted as 3/5 of a person. A 20-year moratorium was placed on the slave trade as well. Finally, it was decided at the convention that Congress should have control of commerce and tariffs.

## CONSTITUTION

On September 17, 1787, the **Constitution** was presented to the people of the states. This document has three parts: a **preamble**, 7 **articles** outlining the powers and responsibilities of the 3 branches of government, and a section of **amendments**, the first ten of which are known as the **Bill of Rights**. The Constitution contains no bills of attainder, meaning that individuals cannot be denied life, liberty, and property without a trial. It does contain the concept of habeas corpus, meaning that arrested individuals must be charged with a crime within 72 hours. Federal judges are to be chosen for life, and there is an electoral college to select the president. In order to be in the House of Representatives, individuals had to be land-owning white males. The Constitution is famous for its system of **checks and balances** whereby the president can veto Congress, but Congress can override the veto with a 2/3 vote, and the courts can call the acts of either body "unconstitutional."

### *RATIFICATION PROCESS, FEDERALISTS, AND ANTI-FEDERALISTS*

In order for the Constitution to take effect, it had to be **ratified** by ¾ of the states. The **Federalists** were those in favor of the Constitution. They were primarily wealthy men who lived along the coast and wanted the commercial protection afforded by a strong federal government. **Anti-Federalists,** on the other hand, were mainly small farmers and artisans who felt that the Constitution was not truly democratic and would erode the power both of the states and of individuals. The Anti-Federalists wanted a Constitution that allowed for annual elections, a standing army, and a Federal fortress. They also disapproved of the atheism of the document. Unfortunately for the Anti-Federalists, the superior organization of the Federalists helped the Constitution become ratified, despite the fact that most Americans were opposed to it.

# American History 1790 to 1864

## Beginning of the Federalist Period and the Judiciary Act of 1789

After the ratification of the Constitution, **George Washington** was inaugurated as the first **president** in New York City. He immediately went outside the Constitution to form the first **Cabinet**: Thomas Jefferson, Secretary of State; Alexander Hamilton, Secretary of the Treasury; Henry Knox, Secretary of War; Edmund Randolph, Attorney General; and Samuel Osgood, Postmaster General. With the **Judiciary Act of 1789**, it was decided that there would be six justices and one chief justice on the Supreme Court. This act also established the federal court system and gave the Supreme Court original jurisdiction to issue writs of mandamus. The clause allowing the Supreme Court to issue writs of mandamus was later ruled unconstitutional in the case of ***Marbury v. Madison*** (1803), thereby establishing the doctrine of judicial review. **Judicial review** gives federal courts the authority to ensure state or national legislation does not violate the Constitution.

## Hamilton's Funding and Economic Plan for the Financial System

The United States was born with $80 million in debt. **Alexander Hamilton**, however, was not terribly concerned by this; on the contrary, he encouraged **credit** as a means of financing the rapid capital improvements that would aid economic expansion. Hamilton introduced a **funding process**, whereby the government would buy back government bonds at full price in order to place money into the economy. Unfortunately, word of this plan leaked to some speculators, who bought the bonds at reduced rates and made huge profits. This led to accusations of a conspiracy. Another aspect of Hamilton's economic plan was for the federal government to **assume state debts**. This was done in part to tie state governments to the national government.

### *Custom Duties, Excise Taxes, and Federal Banks*

In order to pay off the national debt, Hamilton promoted the **Revenue Act of 1789**, which was ostensibly a tax on imports, though it amounted to very little. Hamilton hoped to appease American industry with this measure without alienating foreign interests. The **Whiskey Tax**, instituted in 1791, was another attempt to generate revenue. This tax was wildly unpopular, however, and Washington was forced to call in several state militias to deal with various uprisings. At this time, Hamilton was also trying to establish a national bank, based upon the Bank of England. The **Bank of America** was established with $10 million in capital and aimed to repay foreign debts, provide a uniform national currency, aid in the collection of taxes, make loans, and act as a federal depository.

## Foreign Diplomacy Under Washington

The United States stayed **neutral** during the wars of the French Revolution, even issuing a proclamation to that effect in 1793. Meanwhile, the British were constantly testing this neutrality: they did not leave their posts in the Northwest, they seized American ships and forced American sailors into service, and they frequently aided the Native Americans in their conflicts with the United States. This conflict eventually led to the **Jay Treaty** in 1794, which made the Spanish fear an Anglo-American alliance, causing them to become more willing to discuss American use of the Mississippi River. **Pinckney's Treaty**, also known as the **Treaty of San Lorenzo** (1795), gave the United States free use of both the Mississippi and the city of New Orleans.

## Jay Treaty

The Jay Treaty of 1794 aimed to calm the post-revolution conflicts between Britain and the United States. In it, the British promised to leave their forts in the Northwest and to pay for all the recent damages to ships. The British also allowed the US to form a limited commercial treaty with the British West Indies. The **Jay Treaty** asserted that the rivers and lakes of North America could be used by both Britain and the United States. However, the treaty made no provisions for any future seizures of American ships and made no mention of Native American attacks on the American frontier. The Southern states were annoyed that the treaty won no compensation for slaves freed during the Revolutionary War, and, moreover, stipulated that Southerners had to repay their pre-war debts. The controversy surrounding the Jay Treaty led to the formation of the first **political parties**.

## Rise of the First Political Parties

Unlike a faction, which exists in order to achieve a single goal, a **political party** endures beyond the accomplishment of a specific goal. The first two political parties in the United States were the **Federalists** and the **Democratic-Republicans**. **Hamilton** is the primary figure associated with the Federalists, who were wealthy northeasterners in support of a strong central government and a loose interpretation of the Constitution. The Federalists advocated a strong president, the economic policies implemented by Hamilton, and a strong relationship with the British. The Democratic-Republicans, on the other hand, were associated with the so-called "common man" of the South and West. Led by **Jefferson** and **Madison**, they advocated a limited central government, a strict interpretation of the Constitution, a close relationship with France, and closely restricted government spending.

## Washington's Farewell Address and Presidential Accomplishments

In 1796, Washington decided he was too tired to continue as president. In his famous **Farewell Address**, he implored the United States to avoid three things: permanent alliances, political factions, and sectionalism. Washington felt that the nation could only be successful if people placed the nation ahead of their own region. For his own part, Washington made some significant improvements during his presidency. He avoided war at a time when the nation was vulnerable. He also avoided political alliances and promoted the national government without alienating great numbers of people. Washington oversaw Hamilton's creation of the economic system and guided expansion to the west (as well as the creation of three new states: Vermont, Kentucky, and Tennessee).

## Election of Adams and Conflict with the French

**John Adams** became the second president of the United States in the election of 1796; his opponent, **Thomas Jefferson**, became vice president because he received the second-most electoral votes. Adams was immediately confronted by the French, who were angry about the **Jay Treaty** and the broken **Treaty of Alliance of 1778**. After the French began destroying American ships, Adams sent American diplomats to meet with the French ambassador **Talleyrand**, who demanded tribute and then snubbed the Americans. There followed an undeclared naval war between 1798 and 1800, during which, the American military grew rapidly, warships were built, and the Department of the Navy was established. Finally, at the **Convention of 1800**, the Treaty of Alliance of 1778 was torn up and it was agreed in this new **Treaty of Mortefontaine** that the Americans would pay for damages done to their ships by the French, among a host of other clauses, including each country giving the other Most Favored Nation trade status.

## Domestic Events Under Adams

The Alien and Sedition Acts were established in 1798, in part because of xenophobia arising from conflict with the French. The **Alien Act** increased the number of years before one could obtain citizenship, gave the president the power to deport anyone, and allowed the president to jail dangerous aliens during times of war. The **Sedition Act** made it a crime to libel or slander US officials or policies; many people believed this policy was a violation of First Amendment rights. The **Virginia and Kentucky Resolves**, promoted by Jefferson and Madison, stated that a contract exists between the state and national governments, but that the national government had exceeded its authority and broken the contract. This document advocated that states should have the power of nullification over national policies; only Virginia and Kentucky supported this policy, which had the potential to fatally undermine the Constitution.

**Review Video: The Alien and Sedition Acts**
Visit mometrix.com/academy and enter code: 633780

## FEDERALIST PERIOD

The **Federalist period** had some remarkable successes and some bitter failures. It saw the establishment of the national bank and the Treasury system under Hamilton. The United States, amazingly, was able to pay off all of its debt during this period. The **Federalist administration** can also be credited with maintaining international neutrality, establishing the Pinckney Treaty, crushing the Whiskey Rebellion, and getting the British out of their northwest posts. On the other hand, over time, the Federalists became known as an elitist party, and the Alien and Sedition Acts were very unpopular. The Jay Treaty was seen as a diplomatic failure by most Americans, and in general, the Federalists were not able to maintain very cordial relations with Europe (especially France).

## ELECTION OF 1800

In the election of 1800, the **Federalists** were represented by John Adams and C. C. Pinckney, and the **Democratic-Republicans** by Thomas Jefferson and Aaron Burr. The Federalists had been weakened both by the unpopularity of the Alien and Sedition Acts and the internal feud between Adams and Hamilton. They therefore focused their campaign on Jefferson, accusing him of being an atheist, of stealing money from the poor, and of having an affair with a slave. In the election, Jefferson finished with the same number of electoral votes as his supposed running mate, Burr, who surprisingly refused to concede. This situation led to the **12th amendment**, which states that a candidate must stipulate his desired office. **Jefferson** finally won the tie-breaking vote in the House of Representatives, sweeping the Federalists out of office.

## AARON BURR

After losing his challenge for the presidency in 1800, **Aaron Burr** was left out of the 1804 election and became embittered. He then lost a bid for the governorship of New York, in part because of the mudslinging of **Alexander Hamilton**. At this point, Burr began to toy with the idea of forming a new country in the West. Hamilton, hearing of this plan, informed Jefferson. Burr promptly challenged Hamilton to a **duel**, and in 1806 killed him at Weehawken, NJ. Burr headed west and planned to start a new country in Louisiana and the areas controlled by Spain. Jefferson formally charged Burr with treason, but, citing executive privilege, refused to attend the trial. Burr was eventually found not guilty, in part because he had only planned a new country, and in part because the US was unable to find any reliable witnesses.

## THE MARSHALL COURT (1801-1835)

The Supreme Court led by **John Marshall** is credited with increasing the power of the national government over that of the states. This court also gave the judicial branch more power and prestige, notably in the case of **Marbury v. Madison** (1803). Marshall was known as an arch-Federalist and as a loose interpreter of the Constitution. In the case of **McCulloch v. Maryland** (1819), the court ruled that a national bank is allowed by the Constitution and that states cannot tax a federal agency. In the case of **Gibbons v. Ogden** (1824), the right of Congress to regulate interstate commerce was reaffirmed, and indeed federal regulation of just about anything was made possible. In **Fletcher v. Peck** (1810), the sanctity of contracts was asserted; this case also established the right of the Supreme Court to declare state laws unconstitutional.

## Marbury v. Madison

Right before President **John Adams** left office after **Thomas Jefferson** won the presidency in the election of 1800, he passed the **Judiciary Act of 1801**. This act eliminated one seat on the Supreme Court, eliminated circuit duties for members of the Supreme Court, and created 16 federal circuit court judgeships. This allowed President John Adams to pack the federal court system with his fellow Federalists before Thomas Jefferson, a Democratic-Republican, took office. **William Marbury** was one of these individuals promised a position by John Adams. However, Adams's Secretary of State, **John Marshall**, did not have time to deliver Marbury's commission (which was the formal job offer for Marbury's position as Justice of the Peace for D.C.) before the Jefferson administration took over. The new Secretary of State, **James Madison**, refused to deliver Marbury's commission after he took office. This led to Marbury suing Madison for his commission, and the issue was brought before the Supreme Court in the case of ***Marbury v. Madison*** (1803).

Although Section XIII of the Judiciary Act of 1789 had a **Writ of Mandamus** which required Madison to honor the appointment, Chief Justice **John Marshall**, whom Adams appointed to the Supreme Court before leaving office, declared this section unconstitutional. This historic act established the doctrine of **judicial review**, which allows the Supreme Court to declare a legislative or executive act unconstitutional. Marshall thereby established an independent judiciary; he is quoted as saying, "The Constitution is the supreme Law of the Land, with the Supreme Court as the final interpreter."

> **Review Video: Marbury v. Madison**
> Visit mometrix.com/academy and enter code: 573964

## Jeffersonian Republicans

After using his inauguration speech to try to pacify angry Federalists, Thomas Jefferson went on to introduce the "**spoils system**," replacing Federalist office-holders with **Republicans**. He also reversed many of the Federalist policies: the Alien Act was repealed, and the Sedition Act expired in 1801 (everyone arrested under its authority was pardoned andabsolved and had their fines repaid). Jefferson also sought to reform the judiciary. The **Judiciary Act of 1801**, otherwise known as the **Circuit Court Act**, was passed by the Federalists in order to cement some of their judges in place; Jefferson in turn forced through the Judiciary Act of 1802, which effectively removed the judges by abolishing the new courts.

## Foreign Policy Under the Jeffersonian Republicans

The most important event during the dominance of the Jeffersonian Republicans was the **War of 1812**, fought between France and Britain. In the United States, there was much speculation as to whether the young nation would side with the shark (Britain) or the tiger (France). In 1803, Jefferson had declared American ships neutral, an act which annoyed both sides. The British subsequently passed the **Orders-in-Council**, and the French the **Berlin and Milan Decrees**, all of which were designed to weaken American shipping in Europe. The US responded with the **Non-Importation Act of 1806**, though this was largely a failure. In 1807, an American ship called the **Chesapeake** was attacked by a British ship, leading Jefferson to issue the **Embargo Act of 1807**. This act forbade American ships from leaving for foreign ports; it was very unpopular and was repealed in 1809.

## Madison and "Peaceful Coercion," and the Non-Intercourse Act of 1809

In the 1808 election, **James Madison** of the Democrat-Republicans easily defeated C. C. Pinckney. Madison continued Jefferson's policy of "**peaceful coercion**" with respect to France and Britain, but the lack of an organized American military made it difficult for him to get the attention of these major powers. In 1809, Madison convinced Congress to pass the **Non-Intercourse Act of 1809**, which forbade trade with Britain and France until they began treating American business fairly. When the British ambassador **David Erskine** vowed to improve the treatment of American businesses, Madison agreed to trade with England. However, Erskine's superior quickly overruled him, making Madison look ridiculous and souring Anglo-American relations further.

## Yazoo Claims and John Randolph

In 1795, the corrupt Georgia legislature sold some land known as the **Yazoo Claims** for almost nothing to a group of northeastern speculators in exchange for a bribe. When a new group of legislators came into office in 1797, they revoked the land sales, infuriating the speculators. In 1802, the land claims were ceded to the national government and Jefferson decided to grant the speculators a cash settlement. **John Randolph**, however, was the chairman of the House committee responsible for paying this settlement, and he refused to make the payment, stating that the deal was "bathed in corruption." Though the Supreme Court eventually granted the settlements in the case **Fletcher v. Peck** (1810), Randolph was permanently alienated from Jefferson and went on to form a group called the **Tertium Quids**. This group was the ultra-conservative pro-states' rights contingent of the Democratic-Republicans.

## Treaty of Ildefonso and the Louisiana Purchase

In an agreement between the French and Spanish known alternately as the **Treaty of Ildefonso** or the **Retrocession**, Napoleon Bonaparte acquired Louisiana. This, along with Spain's closing of New Orleans to American business, made Jefferson nervous, and he thus sent James Monroe to France in order to purchase New Orleans and West Florida. Bonaparte, himself made anxious by a rebellion in Haiti and a renewal of hostilities with the British, signed over 800,000 square miles to the US, making the **Louisiana Purchase** the largest land acquisition without bloodshed in human history. Napoleon hoped to curry favor with the United States to forestall a possible Anglo-American alliance.

## Perception of the Louisiana Purchase and Acquisition of East and West Florida

The Louisiana Purchase was probably the high point of Jefferson's presidency; it was seen at home as a diplomatic victory that also avoided drawing the United States into conflict with the European powers. It destroyed the Federalist party. After the **Louisiana Purchase** was completed, explorers set out to discover just what had been bought; among these explorers were **Meriwether Lewis** and **William Clark**. Meanwhile, the United States began to make inroads into Spanish-controlled **West Florida**. In 1810, rebels attacked Baton Rouge and James Madison claimed that West Florida was now part of the US. Of course, the Spanish protested, but they were unable to reestablish themselves. In 1818, Andrew Jackson would lead a group of soldiers into **East Florida** under the pretense of taming the Seminoles. In 1819, the Spanish would reluctantly sign the **Treaty of Onis**, in which the US formally acquired East Florida for $5 million, which the Spanish promptly returned to pay off some of their debt to the US.

## Macon's Bill No. 2

Madison replaced the Non-Intercourse Act of 1809 with **Macon's Bill No. 2**, which declared that America would be open to trade with any country. The bill also stipulated that if either Britain or France agreed to neutral trading rights with the US, the US would immediately cease trade with the other. France jumped at this opportunity, and the US cut diplomatic ties with Britain. The British, weakened by the American embargoes and by a bitter winter, rescinded the **Orders-in-council**, although the US had already declared war upon them. After the British Prime Minister was assassinated, the new foreign secretary, **Castlereagh**, tried to mend relations, but the US went to war anyway. The **War of 1812** was very unpopular, especially among Federalists in the Northeast.

Many Americans felt that England could not be beaten, that engaging in a war would damage US business, and that Napoleon was not a very savory ally.

## War of 1812

### Controversy

The conservative members of Madison's party, known as the **Tertium Quids**, opposed the **War of 1812** because they felt it would be too expensive, would result in the perpetuation of a standing army, would damage America economically, and would lead to the acquisition of Canada as a slave state. These critics were opposed in Congress by the **Warhawks**, so-called by the Federalists to imply that they were picking a fight. The Warhawks mainly represented the Southwest and the West, and included luminaries such as Henry Clay, John C. Calhoun, and Felix Grundy. They supported the war because they thought it would bolster foreign trade, would discourage the British from inciting Native Americans along the frontier, and could result in land gain. In selling the war to the American people, Madison stressed the British insult to American honor; he mentioned several stories about impressments of Americans into British military service.

**Review Video: Overview of the War of 1812**
Visit mometrix.com/academy and enter code: 507716

**Review Video: Opinions about the War of 1812**
Visit mometrix.com/academy and enter code: 274558

### Events Leading Up to Combat

Despite a great deal of bloated rhetoric both for and against the war, the US fought against Britain for a few basic reasons, namely to gain more **land** and to destroy **alliances** between the British and Native Americans. Americans had become incensed when, following his defeat to the Americans at Tippecanoe Creek, **Chief Tecumseh** had fled north into British-controlled Canada. This provocation provided enough popular support to declare war. Unfortunately, the American military was both unprepared and overconfident. Most American military strategists thought it would be quite easy to take Canada, but the army had only 35,000 troops at the time. Moreover, the first Bank of the United States had just gone defunct, so there were scarce economic resources to support a war.

### Major Battles

At the **Battle of Lake Erie** in September of 1813, the American Commander Perry secured Detroit for the US. At the **Battle of Lake Champlain**, the American General Thomas McDonough secured northern New York from British invasion. At the **Battle of the Thames**, the American General William Henry Harrison defeated a coalition of British and Native American forces; Tecumseh was killed. Andrew Jackson scored a decisive victory at the **Battle of Horseshoe Bend**. During this war, much of Washington, DC (including the White House) was torched. A crucial point of the war came when the US was able to successfully defend **Fort McHenry**, outside of Baltimore; this conflict inspired Francis Scott Key's composition of "The Star-Spangled Banner." At the **Battle of New Orleans**, Andrew Jackson used a rag-tag collection of soldiers and pirates to defeat the British navy.

### Conclusion of the War

Throughout the War of 1812, there was loud opposition from the **Federalists** in the Northeast. At the **Hartford Convention**, they formally blamed Madison for the war and proposed changes to the Constitution whereby a 2/3 vote would be needed for declaring war and for admitting new states to the Union. The War of 1812 required several agreements to fully restore relations between the US and Britain. The **Treaty of Ghent** returned Anglo-American ties to their pre-war terms, and proposed that commissions be created to settle differences. The **Rush-Bagot Treaty of 1817** formally declared that there would be no naval race between the 2 countries. At the **Convention of 1818**, a line was drawn along the 49th parallel, dividing Canada from Louisiana, and it was declared that the 2 countries would jointly occupy Oregon. In the **Adams-Onis Treaty of 1819**, a western boundary for Louisiana was set, and the Spanish renounced their claims to Oregon.

### *Significance*

The War of 1812 did not really accomplish its supposed goal of establishing neutral trading rights for American ships. The exodus of Napoleon during the war made this a moot point. Nevertheless, from Madison's perspective, the war could only be seen as a major **success**. The United States lost no major territory, and scored enough victories to keep the British from making any extreme demands. More importantly, perhaps, Americans were overjoyed that the US was finally getting respect from the major European powers. **Nationalism** exploded in the US: people forgot the debacle of the failed national bank, and the economy boomed. Finally, the success of the War of 1812 effectively drove the final nail into the coffin of the **Federalist party**.

## Strengthening of American National Identity

The success of the War of 1812 and the prospering economy made Madison extremely popular. In the Northeast, with the implementation of the British factory system, and in the Southeast, with the invention of the cotton gin, manufacturing interests were booming. This sense of **national identity** was strengthened by the emergence of the United States' first generation of **post-colonial artists**. In literature, James Fenimore Cooper and Washington Irving (*The Legend of Sleepy Hollow*) were eminent. A uniquely American style of **architecture** developed, led by Jefferson, among others, emphasizing columns, symmetry, and classical proportions. The **Hudson River school** produced a group of painters influenced by the natural beauty of their region; among them was John James Audubon.

## Triumph of Neo-Federalism

In 1816, Madison declared that the government should increase the army, the national debt, and the banking interests, an agenda oddly reminiscent of Federalism. The **Second Bank of the United States** was shown to be necessary by the War of 1812, but it was poorly organized and came to be known as a "moneyed monster." The **Tariff of 1816** was established to protect fledgling industry; it was as popular in the Northeast as it was unpopular in the South. Much of the tariff money went to developing infrastructure; the new method of **paving** invented by John MacAdam enabled the creation of long thoroughfares, mostly in the North. It was even proposed in the so-called "Bonus Bill" that all of the surplus money from the new bank should go to the roads; Madison vetoed this measure to avoid further alienating the South.

## "The Era of Good Feelings" from 1817 to 1825

In the election of 1816, the Democrat-Republican **James Monroe** defeated the last Federalist candidate, Rufus King, by a landslide. The Federalist opposition to the War of 1812 doomed the party to extinction. Monroe's early term was not without its problems, however. A mild depression caused by over-speculation on western lands led to the **Panic of 1819** and began a 20-year boom-bust cycle. These problems were exacerbated by the **Second Bank of the United States**; the Bank's pressure on the so-called "wildcat" banks to foreclose on properties, as well as the unwillingness of the Bank to loan money, made it very unpopular. The nationalism generated by the War of 1812 was damaged by these economic travails.

## Monroe Doctrine

After a series of revolutions in Latin America, the United States was the first to recognize the **sovereignty** of the new countries. This was in part because the revolutionaries had used the United

States as inspiration; in part because the US preferred to have weak, independent nations nearby; and in part because the US wanted to maintain and expand its lucrative trade with Latin America. The British attempted to persuade the US to sign an agreement preventing foreign intervention in Latin America, but Monroe decided to maintain American independence and issue his own document. This document, known as the **Monroe Doctrine**, had as its two main principles *non-intervention* and *non-colonization*. Many considered it a "paper tiger," because it was really only as effective as the American ability to enforce it. Still, it seemed to encourage foreign nations to come to the bargaining table rather than test the American military.

**Review Video: Monroe Doctrine**
Visit mometrix.com/academy and enter code: 953021

## Election of 1824 and Adams' Administration

All the major candidates in the 1824 election were **Democrat-Republicans**. Although Andrew Jackson received more electoral votes than **John Quincy Adams**, he did not win a majority, and Adams (with the help of Henry Clay) won the run-off in the House of Representatives. Adams was a fierce **nationalist** at a time when many in the country were sectionalist. Although his initiatives for a national university and public funding for the arts were well-meaning, Adams was still believed to be out of touch with the common man. He further alienated the middle and lower classes with the **Tariff of 1828**, known in the South as the "Tariff of Abominations." The South was already on shaky economic ground and the tariff became a scapegoat for its troubles. **John C. Calhoun** was an especially ardent Southern voice; he futilely proposed that states should have the ability to nullify federal regulations.

**Review Video: John Quincy Adams as President**
Visit mometrix.com/academy and enter code: 797549

## 1828

The election of 1828 is considered the first **modern campaign** in American politics. **Andrew Jackson** had the first campaign manager, Amos Kendall, and produced buttons, posters, and slogans to support his candidacy. These men—Jackson, Kendall, John C. Calhoun, and Martin van Buren—formed the beginning of the **Democratic party**. Meanwhile, the incumbent John Quincy Adams ran a very formal campaign, with little of the "flesh-pressing" of Jackson. Adams tried to discredit Jackson as an adulterer and bigamist because Jackson's wife had not been officially divorced at the time of their marriage. When his wife died during the campaign, however, the popular sentiment returned to Jackson, and he won the election by a considerable margin. Jackson's inauguration was an over-crowded, chaotic affair; the president suffered three cracked ribs during the festivities.

## Jacksonian Democracy

The 1820s and 30s are known as the era of **Jacksonian democracy**, which was political rather than economic or social. Jackson was considered to be emblematic of the "common man." In the years after the conclusion of the War of 1812, it was generally considered that America was "safe for democracy," and thus **suffrage** was extended to poor people in many states. As more people became involved in politics, campaigning became more about image and perception than the issues. This change also ended the tradition known as "**King Caucus**," in which candidates were chosen by a small group of powerful men; now, candidates were to be selected by a series of primaries and nominating conventions. Furthermore, the members of the electoral college would be chosen by the voters rather than by the state legislature. The new system maintained the tradition of **patronage** (the spoils system), in which newly-elected officials would fill the government offices with their supporters.

## Jackson as President

Andrew Jackson is often seen as a symbol of the rising power of the New West, or as an embodiment of the "rags to riches" fable. He spent much of his presidency trying to promote the idea of **nationalism** at a time when most of the country was ardently sectionalist. During his presidency, he dominated Congress, vetoing more legislation than all of the previous presidents combined. He was also famous for his so-called "**Kitchen Cabinet**," a group of close advisers without official positions. Many of these men later received formal appointments, including Secretary of State (Martin van Buren), Postmaster General (Amos Kendall), and Secretary of the Treasury (Roger B. Taney).

**Review Video: Andrew Jackson's Presidency**
Visit mometrix.com/academy and enter code: 667792

**Review Video: American Nationalism**
Visit mometrix.com/academy and enter code: 865693

**Review Video: Andrew Jackson - Key Events and Major Issues**
Visit mometrix.com/academy and enter code: 739251

## Major Events of the Jackson Era

### *Raid into Florida and the Webster-Hayne Debate*

One of the least successful events in Jackson's presidency was a **raid into Florida** in 1828, made to subdue the Seminoles. The raid did not go well, and even Jackson's Secretary of War, John C. Calhoun, referred to it as "idiotic." Another major event in Jackson's term was the **Webster-Hayne debate** of 1829-30, held to debate western expansion. The senators of the Northeast were opposed to western migration, mainly because they felt it would weaken manufacturing and create a new political rival. Senator **Robert Hayne** of South Carolina blasted the war record of the Northeast, in the hopes of allying the West and the South. **Daniel Webster** (MA) retorted that the US is not a collection of states but a union that happens to be divided into states; he asserted that if states could nullify federal measures, the only thing holding the Union together was a "rope of sand."

### *Maysville Road Veto and Native American Removal*

In 1830, Jackson set a precedent by **vetoing the funding of a road** that was to be entirely within one state (Kentucky). Many believed that Jackson vetoed this bill to spite Henry Clay, but the move had some positive political consequences as well: the Southerners appreciated the idea that states should tend to their own business, and northerners liked it because the road would have given people easier access to the West. Jackson's attempts at **relocating Native Americans** were less successful. The passage of the **Indian Resettlement Act of 1830** was the first attempt by the national government to force migration. In the case of **Worcester v. Georgia** (1832), the Supreme Court ruled against those who sought to grab Native lands. John Marshall asserted that the **Cherokee nation** was sovereign, but a ward of the US. Despite Marshall's assertion of Native American rights, Jackson supported the slow and steady conquest of land in the South and West.

### *Tariff of 1832 and the Force Act of 1832*

At a feast in celebration of Thomas Jefferson—a man noted for his nationalism—Andrew Jackson promoted the idea of the nation, saying, "Our Union, it must be preserved." John C. Calhoun responded with a speech in which he referred to "Our Union, next to our liberty most dear," indicating that the South was not going to back down. The milder **Tariff of 1832** was then offered by Jackson to appease the South and Calhoun; instead, Southern politicians declared it was not enough, and Calhoun resigned from Congress in order to organize the opposition to all tariffs.

Henry Clay, who realized that Jackson could easily overpower South Carolina, was further disturbed by the **Force Act of 1832**, which stated that the president had the right to use military force to keep a state in the Union. So, Clay proposed an even lower **Compromise Tariff of 1833**: the tariff would be lowered from 35% to 20-25% over the next ten years. Both sides agreed to this compromise.

### *Bank War of 1836*

It had already been arranged that the **renewal of the Second Bank of America** would be discussed in 1836. It was common knowledge that Jackson hated the Bank, and thus Henry Clay and others tried to renew it ahead of time, in 1832. Jackson was then forced to assert his position: he declared that the bank was anti-West, anti-American, unconstitutional, and a "monopoly of money." The unpopularity of Clay's attempt to renew the Bank was one of the main reasons that he was crushed by Jackson in the 1832 election. After making sure that the Bank would not be renewed, Jackson sought to mend fences with the Northeast by avidly promoting the Union. This was Jackson's genius as a politician; he always was careful to get what he wanted without fully alienating any faction.

## Election of 1836 and the Van Buren Presidency

When Jackson decided not to pursue a third term as president, his vice president **Martin Van Buren** ran and won over a group of challengers including the Whig candidate William Henry Harrison. Van Buren's presidency was marked by frequent border disputes with Canada. Also, Van Buren suffered through the **Panic of 1837**; like in 1819, this was caused by over-speculation in the West. In the 1836 "Specie Circular," Jackson had declared that all land bought from the government must be paid for in gold coins. Because gold was hard to come by, many people lost their property. Further economic problems were created by overspending on infrastructure in many states. One of the results of Van Buren's handling of the situation was that it became acceptable for the president to influence the amount of money in circulation. In 1840, a listless Van Buren was defeated by **Harrison**, who promptly died after a month as president. **John Tyler** became the next president.

**Review Video: Martin Van Buren's Presidency**
Visit mometrix.com/academy and enter code: 787203

## Tyler Presidency

**John Tyler**, a Virginia aristocrat, was the first vice president to take over in mid-term. Oddly, even though he was the Whig candidate, he opposed almost all of the Whig agenda. Henry Clay hoped to dominate Tyler, but his attempts to create a third national bank and to improve infrastructure in the West were both vetoed by Tyler. Tyler's presidency was also fraught with conflict with the British; he endured the **Lumberjacks' War of 1842** and the **Hunters' Lodges skirmishes** in 1838, both of which were minor conflicts along the Canadian border. There was also the incident of the ***Caroline***, an American ship sunk by the British for allegedly smuggling supplies to Canadian rebels. In the **Webster-Ashburton Treaty of 1842**, fugitives were exchanged, the border of Maine was set at the St. John River, and it was established that the British could no longer search American ships.

## Expansion and Manifest Destiny

The phrase "**manifest destiny**," meaning the inevitability and righteousness of the American expansion westward, was coined by the editor **John O'Sullivan**. This idea was lent further credence by the work of Horace Greeley, the journalist responsible for the admonition, "Go west, young man!" Besides this mythology, however, there were some sound reasons why the United States expanded westward. For one thing, there was cheap and fertile land in the West, and the more that was claimed by the Americans, the less which could be claimed by the British. Americans also had an eye toward claiming the western ports to begin trading with Asia. Finally, many Americans felt that they would only be benefiting the world by spreading their ideals of liberty and democracy across as much land as possible.

**Review Video: Manifest Destiny**
Visit mometrix.com/academy and enter code: 957409

## Texas' Role in US Expansion

In 1821, **Mexico** received its independence from Spain. Mexico sold Texan lands to Americans, yet these people were still required to live under Mexican civil law (for one thing, people had to convert to Catholicism). In 1832, however, **Santa Anna** led a coup in Mexico and decided to crack down on the Texans. This led to the **Texas Revolution of 1836**, in which Texan General William Travis' men were massacred by the forces of Santa Anna at the **Alamo**, in which both Davy Crockett and Jim Bowie were killed. After suffering some other defeats, the Texans, led by Sam Houston, finally defeated Santa Anna at the **Battle of San Jacinto** in 1836, and he was forced below the Rio Grande. Nevertheless, Texas was not made part of the US, mainly because the issue of slavery was so contentious at the time.

## US Expansion Including Salt Lake City, Oregon, and California

The territory of **Oregon** became more important to the US government as fur-trapping became a lucrative industry. Oregon was also known to contain rich farmland. As for **California**, its natural bounty had been described by whalers since the 1820s. In the 1840s, whole families (including the ill-fated Donner party) began to migrate there. Around this time the **Church of Jesus Christ of Latter-day Saints**, otherwise known as the Mormon Church, was founded by Joseph Smith. Among the beliefs espoused by the Mormons were polygamy, communalism, and the abolition of slavery. After Smith's death, the Mormons were led by Brigham Young and settled in what is now **Salt Lake City**. Meanwhile, in 1848 gold was discovered in a California stream, generating still more excitement over the economic potential of the West.

## Presidency of James K. Polk

The election of 1844 brought to the forefront a number of critical issues; the economy was still hurting from the Panic of 1837, there was growing support for abolitionism and the issue of manifest destiny was gaining steam. Somewhat surprisingly, the bland North Carolinian **James K. Polk** defeated Henry Clay and succeeded John Tyler as president. He instituted the **Walker Tariff**, which lowered the rate at which foreign goods were taxed from 35% to 25%. He also reinstated the **Independent Sub-Treasury system** in 1846. Mainly, however, Polk's presidency is associated with westward expansion; **Texas** was brought into the Union as a slave state in December of 1845. Polk also spent considerable time trying to gain possession of Oregon.

## Mexican War

### *Causes*

The immediate causes of the **Mexican War** were the American annexation of Texas, disputes over the southern border of Texas, and the large amount of money owed to the United States by Mexico. Moreover, it was well known that the Mexicans held the US in contempt, considering them greedy land-grabbers. **Polk** sent an emissary to buy Texas, California, and some Mexican territory for $30 million; he was refused. **Zachary Taylor** then led an American expedition into a disputed area of Texas where some of them were killed. Polk was able to use these deaths as a rationale for war, despite considerable opposition in Congress. Overall, the Democrats supported the war, while the Whigs, led in part by Abraham Lincoln, were opposed.

### *Major Battles and Conclusion of War*

The United States scored major victories over Mexico at **Buena Vista**, where they were led by Zachary Taylor, and **Vera Cruz**, where they were led by Winfield Scott. The American effort in New Mexico was led by Stephen Kearney and in California by John C. Fremont. The **Treaty of Guadalupe-Hidalgo** was signed in 1848 after Polk sent an emissary with cash in an effort to persuade Santa Anna to stop the war. Under the terms of the treaty, the US got California, the rest of Texas, and all of the Mexican territory between Louisiana and California (including what would become Utah and Nevada). In exchange, the US erased a good deal of Mexico's debts. Controversy immediately erupted over whether the new territories would be allowed to have slaves; some abolitionists wanted to cancel the treaty, while some Southern Democrats wanted to claim the entirety of Mexico.

## Road to Civil War

There was immense controversy surrounding the **slavery policy** in the new American territories after the war with Mexico: Polk wanted to simply extend the line of the **Missouri Compromise** out to the Pacific, while abolitionists offered the **Wilmot Proviso**, which declared that none of the territories should have slaves. The Southern states felt slavery should be allowed, and a more moderate view was offered by Stephen Douglas, who declared that the people of the new states should decide whether they wanted slavery or not. In the election of 1848, the war-hero **Zachary Taylor** (Whig) defeated Lewis Cass (Democrat) and the former president Martin Van Buren (Free Soil party, a collection of abolitionist interests).

**Review Video: Missouri Compromise**
Visit mometrix.com/academy and enter code: 848091

## Era of Bonanzas

Between the years 1848 and 1858, the miners known as the "**forty-niners**" dug about $555 million out of the Western soil. In particular, the **Comstock Lode** of Virginia City, Nevada was famous for producing vast amounts of gold and silver. After buffalo were largely eradicated from the Great Plains, there was a "cattleman's bonanza," aided by the invention of barbed wire. The **Cattleman's Association** was a union of cattle dealers joined together to preserve the integrity of the industry, to stop cross-breeding, and to stop cattle thievery. This era marked the end of the open range, mainly because of horrible droughts and bad winters, range wars between the cowboys and sheep farmers, the railroads, and barbed wire.

## Gold Rush and the Compromise of 1850

After **Zachary Taylor** won the election of 1848, he immediately had to deal with the issue of slavery in the new western territories. This issue was magnified by the California gold rush. Taylor declared that all of the lands would be free, enraging the Southerners. Soon after, however, Taylor died of food poisoning and was succeeded by Vice-president **Millard Fillmore**. In order to solve the problem of slavery in the West, Henry Clay proposed the so-called **Compromise of 1850**: California would be a free state, while New Mexico would be allowed to decide for itself; there would be no more slave trading in the District of Columbia; there would be tighter laws regarding fugitive slaves; and Texas would receive $10 million for its lost territories. Fillmore readily signed this agreement, but problems with it arose immediately. One of which was that the **Underground Railroad** of **Harriet Tubman** was already making it very difficult to catch fugitive slaves.

## Election of 1852 and the Growing Crisis of Slavery

In the election of 1852, Democrat **Franklin Pierce** easily defeated the Whig Winfield Scott who was hurt by his association with the abolitionist William H. Seward. At this time, despite the growing crisis of slavery, there were some positive changes in the US. One was that the introduction of **California** as a free state permanently upset the sectional balance. Immigration into the Northeastern cities was bringing a wealth of new ideas. The Northern states resisted the fugitive slave laws by passing initiatives in support of personal liberties and by aiding the Underground Railroad. Harriet Beecher Stowe enraged the South with her novel *Uncle Tom's Cabin* (1852). In 1857, Hinton R. Helper published "The Impending Crisis of the South," an essay that suggested the South was becoming a slave to the North because of its reactionary view on slavery.

## Transcontinental Railroad, Ostend Manifesto, and Kansas-Nebraska Act

The construction of the **Transcontinental Railroad** was begun in 1853 for the purpose of transporting easterners to California. With the **Gadsden Purchase**, the US had purchased some New Mexican lands so the train could avoid the mountains. With the **Ostend Manifesto** in 1854, the US attempted to purchase Cuba from Spain for $120 million; Spain refused, and though the US threatened to take the island by force, they never did (in part because it was believed that the South wanted to make it a slave state). The **Kansas-Nebraska Act** (1854), authored by Stephen Douglas, divided the Nebraska territory into two parts (Kansas and Nebraska) and declared that slavery would be determined by popular sovereignty in those territories. This act drove northerners to the liberal side and caused the creation of the **Republican party**. The opposing factions engaged in violence to try and win the popular vote. Though Kansas worded its constitution in an attempt to have slaves, the document fell apart upon review by Congress, and Kansas entered as a free state.

## Sumner-Brooks Incident, Election of 1856, and the Dred Scott Case

In 1856, Senator **Charles Sumner** (MA) gave an impassioned speech on the "Crime against Kansas," in which he blamed the South for the violence. One of the men whom he singled out for blame was the uncle of Senator **Preston Brooks** (SC); Brooks beat Sumner with his walking stick, and was glorified in the South. In the election of 1856, **James Buchanan** (Democrat) defeated several candidates, including Millard Fillmore (American party; some Southern states had threatened to secede should Fillmore prevail). Next came the **Dred Scott** case. Scott was a slave taken to a free state by his owner and then transported back to a slave state. Abolitionists said he should be a free man. The Supreme Court, however, ruled that slaves are property and can be transported across state lines without being changed. This decision effectively rendered the Kansas-Nebraska Act, the Missouri Compromise, and the whole idea of popular sovereignty being unconstitutional.

## Lincoln-Douglas Debates and John Brown's Raid

During the campaign to become senator of Illinois in 1858, **Abraham Lincoln** and **Stephen Douglas** eloquently debated the issue of slavery. In the so-called **Freeport Doctrine**, Lincoln questioned whether the people of a territory could vote against slavery. The Supreme Court would say no, but Lincoln wondered whether the people should not have the final say. Douglas essentially agreed, stating that the people of the territory should decide. Douglas won the election, though his stance on slavery irritated Southerners. In 1859, the abolitionist **John Brown** led a raid on a federal arsenal at Harper's Ferry, Virginia. Brown's group was only able to take a fire station, and Brown himself was captured and executed by a battalion led by **Robert E. Lee**. Brown became a martyr to the North.

## Election of 1860 and Secession of the South

In the election of 1860, **Abraham Lincoln** defeated three other challengers. Lincoln's platform was anti-slavery, though he vowed to leave it intact where it already existed. He also promised full rights to immigrants, the completion of a Pacific Railroad, free homesteads, and a protective tariff. After the election, South Carolina **seceded**, followed by the rest of the Deep South (Mississippi, Alabama, Georgia, Louisiana, Florida, and Texas). These states established the **Confederate States of America**, with its capital in Montgomery, Alabama. The president of the CSA was **Jefferson Davis**. Outgoing US President Buchanan claimed that he had no constitutional authority to stop the secession, but upon entering office, Lincoln attempted to maintain control of all Southern forts. This led to the firing on **Ft. Sumter** (SC) by the Confederates. As Lincoln called for aid, the Upper South (Virginia, Arkansas, North Carolina, and Tennessee) seceded as well, and the CSA made Richmond, Virginia its new capital.

## Compromises to Save the Union

The US government made a number of compromises in an attempt to preserve the Union after Lincoln's election. The **Crittenden Compromise** extended the line of the Missouri Compromise and promised federal protection of slavery south of that line. The **House of Representatives Compromise** offered an extension of the Missouri Compromise and a Constitutional amendment to protect slavery. The **Virginia Peace Convention** produced an offer to extend the line of the Missouri Compromise and establish that slavery can never be outlawed except by the permission of the owner. Finally, Congress offered $300 for each slave. The South said that this was not enough money, and the North was appalled by the offer, regardless.

## Civil War

The Civil War was fought for a number of reasons, but the most important of these was the controversy regarding **slavery**. The issue of slavery touched on moral, economic, and political themes. Also, the differing geography of the North and South had caused the latter to develop an **economy** that they felt could only survive through slavery. The Civil War also sprang from the ongoing debate over **states' rights**; many in the South felt that states should have the power to nullify federal regulations and believed that the North had too much representation in Congress (and, indeed, the North had received much more federal aid for infrastructure). Finally, there was a general difference in **culture** between the North and South; the North was more of a dynamic and democratic society, while the South was more of a static oligarchy.

**Review Video: Overview of the American Civil War**
Visit mometrix.com/academy and enter code: 239557

### *Advantages of the North*

The **Northern side** in the Civil War contained 22 states with 22 million people. The North also contained most of the US' coal, iron, and copper, as well as 92% of the industry. The Union side had more than twice as much railroad track as the Confederacy and a vastly larger navy. Most importantly, perhaps, the Union had a huge advantage in **troops**. Most of the Northern troops were either volunteers or had been conscripted (starting in 1863). It was permissible to pay someone to take your space in the military. The North generally had between 2 and 3 times as many troops as the South during the war. The South was really only able to survive for so long because it fought a very defensive war.

### *Advantages and Disadvantages of the Confederacy*

The **Confederate States of America** was comprised of 11 states with only 9 million people. When the war began, the South had no organized army or navy. At first, the troops were strictly volunteers, but eventually the CSA established a draft to bolster the ranks. The Confederacy did have some advantages, however. One was that they were fighting on their own soil and thus they already had interior lines of defense as well as knowledge of the terrain. On the whole, the Confederate commanders were more experienced and talented. Finally, the Confederacy had a psychological advantage over the North: they were fighting for a **tangible reason** (namely, to preserve their lives and property), while the North had to motivate its troops with notions of "preserving the Union."

### *Military Strategies of the North and South*

The North began the Civil War by trying to **blockade** the Southern coast and seal off the border states; they hoped to end the war quickly by preventing supplies from reaching the Confederacy. The North also wanted to divide the South into two parts by seizing control of the Mississippi River. This plan would later be adjusted, and **Sherman's March** would try to divide the South into a northern and southern half. The Confederacy, meanwhile, knew that its best chance for success was to fight **defensively** (the South did not want any Northern territory). They also knew that they would need help from European powers. The South hoped to outlast the North's will to fight, to capture Washington, DC, and to receive Maryland into the Confederacy.

> **Review Video: American Civil War: North vs. South Overview**
> Visit mometrix.com/academy and enter code: 370788

## Major Battles

### *First Bull Run, Shiloh, and Second Bull Run*

The **First Battle of Bull Run** was fought in Manassas, VA in July of 1861. The North believed that an easy victory here would allow them to quickly take Richmond. Washingtonians even picnicked around the battlefield, anticipating a pleasant spectacle. It was not to be, however: led by Stonewall Jackson (who actually earned that nickname at this battle), the South won a shocking victory. As a result, the South became somewhat overconfident, and the North realized it was in for a long war. At the **Battle of Shiloh** (TN) in April of 1862, Ulysses S. Grant led the Union to its first major victory. At the **Second Battle of Bull Run** in August of 1862, Stonewall Jackson again defeated a Northern army, this time with the help of Robert E. Lee.

### *Antietam*

At the **Battle of Antietam** (MD) in September of 1862, the Confederate General Robert E. Lee went on the offensive, hoping to bring Maryland into the Confederacy; sever the channels between Washington, DC and the North; and attract the recognition of the European powers. This was the bloodiest battle of the Civil War and ended in a draw. It was after this battle that Lincoln issued his famous **Emancipation Proclamation**. This document freed the slaves in any area that was taken by the Union, or in areas from which slaves could enter the Union. It did not, however, free slaves in the Border States, because Lincoln wanted to maintain loyalty to the Union in these areas. The aims of the Emancipation Proclamation were three: to keep the British from assisting the South, to motivate the Northern troops, and to effect a positive moral change.

> **Review Video: Emancipation Proclamation**
> Visit mometrix.com/academy and enter code: 181778

### *Fredericksburg, Chancellorsville, and Gettysburg*

At the **Battle of Fredericksburg** (VA) in December of 1862, Robert E. Lee successfully repelled the attacks of the Union General Burnside. At the **Battle of Chancellorsville** (VA) in May of 1863, Lee scored his greatest victory of the war; it was during this battle, however, that the Confederate General Stonewall Jackson was mortally wounded by his own troops. At the **Battle of Gettysburg** (PA) in July of 1863, the Confederacy troops led by Lee suffered a damaging defeat. Lee had hoped to take some pressure off the South with a successful surge into the North, but instead got caught in an unfavorable tactical position and endured massive casualties. Most historians believe the Union victory at Gettysburg was the turning point in the war.

### *Vicksburg, Atlanta, and Sherman's March*

The Union General mounted a siege against the crucial Confederate city of **Vicksburg** (MS) in July of 1863. When the Confederates had finally been starved into surrender, the Union had total control of the Mississippi River. Then, between July and October of 1864, the major Southern rail hub of **Atlanta** was conquered and burned by Union troops under General William Sherman. This victory guaranteed that Lincoln would be reelected in the election of 1864. It also marked the beginning of **Sherman's March to the Sea**, a campaign of devastation mounted by the Union in late 1864 and early 1865. Sherman's troops melted Southern rails and destroyed Southern crops and factories, creating a swath of chaos that stretched from Atlanta to Savannah.

## Homestead Act of 1862 and the Transcontinental Railroad

The US government tried many different ways to improve conditions for farmers in the West. Under the **Homestead Act of 1862**, farmers were sold 160 acres for $10, with the proviso that they had to improve the land within 5 years. Between the years 1865 and 1900, only one in six farms began this way. The **Timber Culture Act of 1873** gave more land to farmers, with the proviso that they had to plant some trees on that land.

One thing that helped to populate the West was the completion of the **Transcontinental Railroad** in 1869. The Union Pacific met the Central Pacific railway at Promontory Point, Utah. In 1889, the US government opened Oklahoma for settlement, and by 1893 it was completely settled.

## Lincoln's Reconstruction Plan

According to Lincoln, the relation between the North and the South after the completion of the Civil War would include "malice for none, charity for all." He imagined that the President would lead the **Reconstruction** effort, and, in 1863, he vowed that once 10% of the 1860 voters in a Southern state pledged loyalty to the Union, they could draft a new state constitution and receive "executive recognition." Lincoln was unsure whether black people should be gradually emancipated or relocated, but he knew they should be free. As for his own **Republican party**, Lincoln asserted that it should become a national party and that it should include freed black people, who would receive the right to vote.

## Congress' Reconstruction Plan

With the **Wade-Davis Bill of 1864**, Congress outlined their plan for the rehabilitation of the South after the Civil War. Unlike Lincoln, who had only asked for a 10% (of 1860 voters) loyalty nucleus, Congress wanted a majority before admitting Southern states back into the **Union**. Participants in the state constitutional conventions would be required to sign an "ironclad oath" pledging eternal loyalty to the Union. Ex-Confederate officials would not be allowed to vote or hold office. Slavery, of course, would be **abolished**. Finally, the Confederate debt would be repudiated, and those who loaned money to the Confederacy would be unable to get it back. Lincoln **vetoed** this bill, mainly because he wanted the abolition of slavery to be an amendment rather than a law.

### Second Industrial Revolution

The Second Industrial Revolution was possible in the United States because of the abundance of raw materials and the laissez-faire economic policies of the government. In the space between the years 1860 and 1914, industry grew to about twelve times its original size. This rapid progress was made possible by the rapid growth of the **American railway system**. The railroads were subsidized by the federal government. Around this time, Samuel Morse developed his **telegraph code**, enabling almost instantaneous communication across vast distances. Jay Gould and James J. Hill were among those who made immense fortunes as railroad managers. Cornelius Vanderbilt and his son William were both railroad magnates with a reputation for ignoring the plight of their workers.

**Review Video: Second Industrial Revolution**
Visit mometrix.com/academy and enter code: 608455

**Review Video: The American Railroad System**
Visit mometrix.com/academy and enter code: 843913

## American History 1865 to 1898

### Hampton Roads Peace Conference, Final Battles, and Assassination of Lincoln

At the Hampton Roads Peace Conference in February of 1865, **Lincoln** and Secretary of State **Seward** met with the vice president of the CSA, **Alexander Stephens**. Lincoln made a stern offer: reunion of the states, emancipation of the slaves, and immediate disbanding of the Confederate army. The Confederates, however, were not yet ready to return to the Union. The Northern General US Grant then led troops toward the CSA capital at Richmond. Finally, at **Appomattox** (VA) in April of 1865, Lee surrendered to Grant. Soon after, the Confederate President **Jefferson Davis** would be caught and jailed. Finally, on April 14, 1865, Lincoln was fatally wounded by two shots from the gun of **John Wilkes Booth** in Ford's Theater in Washington.

### Presidential Reconstruction Plan Under Andrew Johnson

Andrew Johnson, a Jacksonian Democrat from Tennessee, became president after the assassination of Lincoln. Though a Southerner, he believed the yeoman farmers of the South had been tricked into war by "cotton snobs." Johnson's plan for reconstruction called for **amnesty** to be granted to all ex-Confederates except for high-ranking officials and wealthy cotton planters, who would be allowed to apply for special pardons. Johnson also called for a **provisional Unionist governor** to be appointed in each Southern state; this leader would hold a constitutional convention at which it would be necessary to disavow secession, repudiate the CSA debt, and accept the 13th amendment. This plan was largely a failure, however, because it infringed on the powers of Congress, was seen as too lenient on the South, threatened the Republicans by giving too much power to Southern Democrats, and ignored freed black people, who were repressed in the South by the so-called **Black Codes**.

### Labor Organizations After the Civil War

#### *National Labor Union and Noble and Holy Orders of the Knights of Labor*

At the end of the Civil War, only about 2% of all US workers were **unionized**; many believed joining a union was an admission that one would never move up. Over time, though, people began to realize that the consolidation of business interests (trusts) had to be met by a consolidation of labor. In 1866, the **National Labor Union** was founded by William H. Sylvis; this idealistic organization advocated an 8-hour workday but disbanded after backing the loser in the 1872 election. In 1869, Uriah Stephens founded the **Noble and Holy Orders of the Knights of Labor**; this group excluded doctors, lawyers, and bankers and supported the end of sexism, the 8-hour workday, paper money, income tax, and the prohibition of alcohol.

### *Haymarket Square and American Federation of Labor*

In 1886, the **Knights of Labor** gathered in **Haymarket Square** in Chicago to protest an attack against another union. During the protest, a bomb was thrown and several people were killed; 7 members of the union were arrested, and some were executed. This incident linked labor unions with violence in the popular imagination. At the same time, less idealistic labor unions like the American Railway Union (led by Eugene V. Debs), the United Mineworkers, and the Molly McGuires were making great inroads in working communities. The **American Federation of Labor** was an alliance of many unions formed in 1881. This group sought a shorter workday, better working conditions, and workman's compensation; they were also not afraid to strike. The AFL frequently engaged in collective bargaining, in which a strike was threatened in order to bring management to the negotiation table.

## Opposition to Organized Labor

The general public **opposed** labor unions because they disliked the idea of closed shops (those places in which one had to be a union member to work) and because they had a reputation for violence. Unions were also fiercely competitive with one another, and there was some animosity between the unions for skilled and unskilled workers. Unions were always at a disadvantage in their dealings with management, in part because management could hire lobbyists (to promote anti-union legislation in Washington) and lawyers and could bribe politicians. Owners often had blacklists of union troublemakers who would not be hired and plenty of "yellow-dog" workers who had signed contracts pledging never to join a union. Owners often hired spies to obtain information among workers, and, in the event of a strike, they could always hire "scabs" to cross the picket lines. It was not unheard of for managers to hire thugs to cause trouble among strikers and perpetuate the rowdy reputation of the unions.

## Agricultural Problems During Populism

In the years following the Civil War, the US heartland suffered from an **overabundance** of wheat and rice; these surpluses, coupled with the advances in transportation and communication, drove prices down. Farmers were forced into high debt which they could never repay, leading to **deflation** and a scarcity of currency. Since many farmers didn't own the land that they worked, the banks often had to **foreclose** when farmers were unable to pay their debts. Farmers blamed their problems on a number of different factors. They blamed the railroads, which usually gave discount rates to bigger shippers. They blamed the banks, which loaned money to the rich but were unforgiving of farmers' economic plight. They also blamed the tax system, claiming that it was easy for businesses to hide their assets and impossible for farmers to do so. Additionally, they blamed the tariff, which discouraged other countries from buying US goods.

## Early Farm Organization During Populism

The **Patron of Husbandry (Grange)** was founded in 1867 by Oliver Kelley to establish cooperatives, in which individuals bought goods directly from the wholesale distributor. His group was also responsible for the **Granger Laws**, which attacked railroad and grain elevator interests. The Grange had basically disappeared by 1875. The **National Farmer's Alliance and Industrial Union** pursued a number of different initiatives: more national banks, cooperatives, a federal storage system for non-perishable items, more currency, free coinage of silver, reduction of tariffs, direct election of senators, an 8-hour workday, government control of railroads and telegraphs, and one term for the president. This group's success led to the formation of the **Populist Party** in 1890.

This party aimed to speak for the farmers and included all of the farmers' unions as well as some labor unions, the Greenbackers, and the Prohibitionists. The party suffered from internal divisions from its inception.

## Radical Republican Reconstruction Plan

By 1867, Johnson's Reconstruction plan had largely failed. His unwillingness to change drove many moderate congressmen to become radicals. Radical Republicans came up with their own Reconstruction plan. First, a "Joint Committee of 15" went south to explore the damage done by the war; while there, they discovered the "Black Codes" repressing freed slaves. With the **Civil Rights Act of 1866**, they provided basic rights for ex-slaves (not including the right to vote). The **14th amendment** then gave black people citizenship and said that state governments could not deny anyone life, liberty, and property without due process. This amendment disqualified ex-Confederates from holding public office and declared that states could lose representation if they infringed on the rights of black people. With the **Congressional Reconstruction Act** (Military Reconstruction Act) of 1867, the South was divided into 5 districts and placed under martial law; Congress forced this bill through, and eventually all of the Southern states capitulated.

**Review Video: The Reconstruction Era**
Visit mometrix.com/academy and enter code: 790561

## Tenure of Office Act and the Supreme Court's Activity

The Tenure of Office Act of 1867 established that in order to fire any Cabinet member, the president had to get the approval of the Senate. Though essentially unconstitutional, this act almost ended the presidency of Johnson when he tried to dismiss **Edwin Stanton**, his Secretary of War. Johnson was charged with a crime, **impeached** by the House of Representatives, and missed being impeached by the Senate by one vote. The Supreme Court, though generally quiet during this period, made a couple of significant rulings. In **ex parte Milligan** (1866), the Supreme Court asserted that it is unconstitutional for military rule to continue after regular courts have been reinstated. In **ex parte McCardle** (1868), a similar case, the Supreme Court was too afraid of Congressional radicals to make a ruling.

## Radical Republican Reconstruction Governments in the South

**Carpetbaggers** were Northerners who, under the guise of reinvesting in the Southern economy, took advantage of the situation by acquiring positions in local governments and raising taxes. **Scalawags** were white Republican Southerners who took similar economic advantage. During the rule of the Reconstruction governments, black people were allowed to hold some public offices, though not if they were freed slaves; the black Senator **Hiram Revels** (MS) served in Jefferson Davis' old seat. Black people had very few economic rights and had no land. **Thaddeus Stevens** declared that black people should receive "40 acres and a mule," but nobody was willing to take this land from its present owners. **Sharecropping** became basically another form of slavery. In short, the Reconstruction governments were corrupt, spent too much, levied too many taxes, and took advantage of newly freed slaves. Still, these governments established state constitutions, built roads and schools, and made education compulsory.

## Election of 1868 and the Grant Administration

After the Civil War, the US was consumed by **materialism**. The election of 1868 pitted **Ulysses S. Grant** (Republican) against Horatio Seymour (Democrat). Grant was a war hero, and Seymour spent much of the campaign defending himself from allegations that he aided the Confederacy. The Democrats proposed that states should decide for themselves the question of black suffrage, and they wanted to give amnesty to former Confederates. Republicans had much more success with their campaign, blaming the Democrats for the war (a strategy known as "waving the bloody shirt"), and Grant won handily. Grant's presidency would not be as easy as his campaign, however. He had no political experience and was unused to compromise. He frequently fought with his Cabinet, though Secretary of State Hamilton Fish was able to convince him to sign the **Treaty of Washington** (1871), in which Britain compensated the US for aiding the Confederate navy.

## Graft and Corruption Under Grant

### *Crédit Mobilier Scandal, Schuylar Colfax, and Fisk-Gould Scandal*

The Grant administration was so corrupt that the president himself had to apologize. One of the most famous fiascos of the era was the **Crédit Mobilier scandal**: the Union Pacific gave a contract to the Crédit Mobilier of America construction company after the federal government secretly loaned Crédit Mobilier of America money for their bid. Then, Vice President **Schuyler Colfax** was caught accepting a bribe in return for ceasing the investigation. In the **Fisk-Gould scandal**, Jim Fisk and Jay Gould convinced Grant to keep government gold out of the New York Stock Exchange, because they hoped to corner the market. Grant became angry with the men and dumped $4 million worth of gold onto the market. September 24, 1869, is known as **Black Friday** on Wall Street; this was the day that Grant's gold flood caused the price of gold to drop so rapidly that the entire market crashed. Gould was able to survive this catastrophe; Fisk was not.

### *Tammany Hall, Congressional Salary Grab, and Whiskey Ring Scandal*

**William Marcy "Boss" Tweed** was the political boss of New York City. He ran the **Tammany Hall** political machine, a group that fixed elections by recruiting voters with food and jobs. Another instance of corruption under Grant was the **Congressional salary grab**: Congress voted to give themselves a 50% raise, set retroactively by two years. The public was outraged by this avarice, and so, though they kept the pay raise, Congress gave up the back pay. In the **Whiskey ring scandal**, some tax agents who were supposed to be taxing barrels of whiskey were found to have been accepting bribes; this scandal went up as high as Secretary of the Treasury Benjamin Bristow. When historians look at this period and try to figure out why there was so much corruption, they generally decide that it was a carryover from the brutality of the war, combined with the naiveté of the president.

## Opposition to Grant and Corruption Under Grant

**Thomas Nast** was one of the first famous political cartoonists; he made his name satirizing corrupt politicians like Boss Tweed. Grant established the **Civil Service Commission** in 1871, an organization whose mission was to study corruption and make recommendations to the president. Grant paid little attention to this group, however, and it died a quiet death in 1875. During Grant's first term, a group of upper-class Republicans, calling themselves the **Mugwumps**, began to call for a civil service based only on merit. At the same time, the **Liberal Republicans**, another splinter group of the Republican party, spoke out against the graft in civil service, the use of paper money, and the Republican Reconstruction policy. This group supported a lower tariff and better treatment for farmers.

## Industrial Era Scandals and Innovations

The infamous **Credit Mobilier scandal** occurred during Grant's presidency in 1872 and involved the Union Pacific Railroad. A more egregious crime was perpetrated on the stockholders of the Erie Railroad; the owners were trying to avoid being bought out by Vanderbilt, and thus they printed up a huge amount of new stock, making it impossible for Vanderbilt to get a majority interest but also vastly diminishing the value of each share. During this era, the following **innovations** and inventors accelerated industry: sleeper cars (George Pullman), air brakes for trains (George Westinghouse), time zones, double tracking (so that two trains could run on the same line), and the standardization of the distance from one rail to another.

**Review Video: Industrialization**
Visit mometrix.com/academy and enter code: 893924

## Election of 1872 and Final Collapse of Grant

In the election of 1872, **Grant** won a second term (over Liberal Republican Horace Greeley) because of his enduring status as a war hero, and because the worst scandals of his administration had yet to be exposed. Quickly, though, Grant's administration fell apart. Five Cabinet members would be found guilty of **corruption**. Then came the **Panic of 1873**. This was the result of three factors: the withdrawal of European investment (Europeans were funneling their money into the Franco-Prussian War), the stock market crash caused by the Fisk-Gould scandal, and the inflexibility of the banks caused by heavy investment in non-liquid assets. As a result of these factors, **Jay Cooke and Co.**, one of the largest banks in the US, collapsed, taking several other banks with it. Eighty-nine railroads soon went under, and then the iron and steel mills had no business. By 1875, half a million Americans were unemployed, and farmers were beginning to lose their land to foreclosure.

## Ku Klux Klan and Amnesty Act of 1872

In the 1870s, Southern white people, as members of the Conservatives or Redeemers, began to regain control of the local governments; they sought to do away with "Negro rule." The **Ku Klux Klan** was founded in 1867 by former Confederate General Nathan Bedford Forrest and other ex-Confederates. Though founded as a social club, this group quickly got out of hand, causing the passage of the **Ku Klux Klan and Force Acts** (1870-1), unsuccessful attempts to subdue the Klan by allowing for black militias. The **Amnesty Act of 1872** extended the right to vote to many more ex-Confederates. Gradually, the North began to lose interest in the South for the following reasons: they were disgusted by the corrupt governments, they were frustrated by the persistent racism, and they had agreed to remain distant in exchange for a higher tariff.

## Solutions to the Panic of 1873

By 1873, **currency deflation** was a major problem in the US. There were a number of supporters of cheap money, and they encouraged the US government to issue $26 million in greenbacks to stimulate the economy; this plan failed. There was another group of hard-money advocates who suggested using a gold standard, so the government made a compromise called the **Specie Resumption Act of 1875**. This act increased the number of national banks in the South and West, allowed national banks to issue as many notes as they wanted (up to a $300 million limit), and named a "day of redemption," on which all greenbacks could be exchanged for gold coins. The day of redemption never came to pass, however, which seemed to be a victory for the cheap money supporters. Instead, it became evident that the promise of gold exchange caused the public to treat greenbacks as if they were "good as gold." By 1879, the economy was back on track and the Republicans had acquired the reputation as the party in favor of business.

## Subordination of Western Native Americans Until 1874

The Native Americans who roamed the Great Plains were known as fierce hunters, and there were a few bloody encounters between settlers heading west and the natives. In 1851, the US established the **Concentration policy**, which encouraged Native Americans to live close to one another. This strategy was untenable, however, and the period from 1860-90 was marked by frequent conflict. In the **Sioux Wars** of 1865-7, the Sioux were led by **Red Cloud**; they fought and lost to American troops after their sacred hunting ground was mined. For a while, the US tried to group tribes on reservations in Oklahoma and the Black Hills; from 1869-74, Generals Sherman and Sheridan engaged in a **War of Extermination** to kill those who refused to move.

## Subordination of the Western Native Americans from 1875-1887

According to **Grant's Peace Program**, each Native American tribe would be put under the control of different religious groups. In 1875, miners were allowed back into the Black Hills, prompting the **Sioux War** of 1875-6, during which Sitting Bull defeated Custer at the **Battle of Little Big Horn**. Around this time, Chief Joseph attempted to lead his Nez Perce tribe to Canada; this mission failed and the Nez Perce were sent to Oklahoma. The Apache leader Geronimo was defeated in Arizona in 1887. At the **Battle of Wounded Knee**, the US army massacred 300, mostly women and children. Native Americans were doomed by their inferior weapons; by the destruction by white people of their food supply, the buffalo; and by railroads which made it easier for white people to encroach on their hunting grounds.

## Election of 1876 and National Self-Evaluation

The election of 1876, won by **Rutherford B. Hayes** (Republican) over Samuel J. Tilden (Democrat), coincided with the **US centennial**, so people were compelled to consider the history of the country thus far. When Americans of 1876 looked back, they had some reason to be pleased: they had survived a Civil War intact and had witnessed the end of slavery. They also had developed a strong national government. On the other hand, many Americans were disillusioned at this time by the scandals of the Grant administration. There had also been violent and disheartening struggles between black militiamen and the Ku Klux Klan in the South. Finally, many in the country were still reeling from Custer's bloody defeat at the Battle of Little Big Horn.

## Election of 1876 and Compromise of 1877

In 1876, **Rutherford B. Hayes** (Republican) defeated Samuel Tilden (Democrat) after an electoral commission composed mostly of Republicans ruled that certain votes by carpetbag governments should have gone to him. As part of the ensuing **Compromise of 1877**, the South was given federal money for improvements to infrastructure, a Southerner was placed in Hayes' Cabinet, and the Union troops propping up the carpetbag governments were removed. This election established the tradition of the "**Solid South**": it was assumed that every year the majority of Southerners would vote for the Democratic candidate.

## Hayes Presidency

### *Highlights*

Foolishly, **Rutherford B. Hayes** made himself a lame-duck president by announcing soon after taking office that he would not seek a second term. Hayes' wife was nicknamed "Lemonade Lucy," because she would not allow any alcohol in the White House. Hayes tried to restore the power of the presidency after the debacle of Grant, but he was weakened by intense struggles over his Cabinet confirmations. One thing Hayes can be credited with is making a gallant attempt to destroy the **spoils system**. He replaced the Collector of the Customs House after discovering the corruption of that body, and he appointed Carl Schurz Secretary of the Interior on the basis of merit. In turn, Schurz established a merit system in his department, creating an entrance exam for potential employees.

### *Low-Points*

One of the failures of the Hayes administration was its handling of the **Great Rail Strike of 1877**. When over two-thirds of the rail lines were shut down by strikes, Hayes sent in federal troops, and there was considerable bloodshed. This set a bad precedent for how strikes would be handled in the future. Hayes vetoed an attempt by western labor unions to restrict Chinese immigration, saying that this would be a violation of the **Burlingame Treaty**. One of the main issues in the Hayes years was monetary policy. Farmers, who were often in debt, wanted a soft currency not backed by anything; they were willing to settle for a silver standard. In **Hepburn v. Griswold** (1869), the Supreme Court had ruled that there could not be paper money without a gold standard; in the **Legal Tender cases of 1871**, however, the Court reversed itself. The bickering over these conflicting rulings plagued the Hayes administration.

### *HAYES VS. GREENBACKERS AND THE SILVERITES*

After the **Specie Resumption Act of 1875**, Hayes worked to minimize the effects of the oncoming "day of redemption," in which paper money could be exchanged for gold coins. He began a policy of contraction, wherein the government gradually took in paper money and issued gold, and he funded attempts to mine more gold. The **Greenbackers** were those who wanted Hayes to postpone the day of redemption; he did not, and it ultimately proved anticlimactic, as people assumed their paper money was "good as gold" and didn't bother to redeem it. Hayes also had to deal with the **Silverites**. In 1873, the government had enraged silver prospectors by announcing that it would no longer make coins out of silver. In answer to their fury, Hayes pushed through the **Bland-Allison Act**, which established that a minimum of $2 million of silver had to be purchased and coined by the government every month.

### COMPETITION AND DISORDER IN THE INDUSTRIAL ERA

The late 19th century was marked by intense competition between the railroads. Railroads offered secret illegal refunds to big customers, and in areas where they had no competition, they charged exorbitant prices. After the 1870s, various states tried to tame the railroads; one such instance of this kind of regulation was the **Granger Laws**. Farmers often felt that they were charged more than others. In **Munn v. Illinois** (1877), the Supreme Court asserted that the state governments had the right to regulate the railroads. In Wabash, St. Louis, and **Pacific Railroad Co. v. Illinois** (1886), the Supreme Court reversed its former opinion and declared that only the federal government could regulate the railroads. Finally, with the **Interstate Commerce Act of 1887**, the federal government forbade discriminatory practices like refunds and price-fixing; unfortunately, these laws were rarely enforced.

### GREAT STRIKE OF 1877, THE HOMESTEAD STRIKE, AND THE PULLMAN STRIKE

The Great Strike of 1877 occurred in West Virginia when state police and militiamen were sent to break up a railway strike and joined it instead. President Hayes sent in the army, and at least 100 people were killed breaking up the strike. This debacle set a bad precedent for future strikes. In the **Homestead (PA) Strike** of July 1892, a group of soldiers called by Henry Clay Frick (temporarily in charge of one of Carnegie's steel mills) brutally broke up a strike. In 1894, a group of **Pullman railcar employees** began a strike, supported by the American Railway Union of Eugene V. Debs. All rail workers then went on strike out of sympathy for the Pullman workers. The rail owners got an injunction, claiming that the rail workers were interfering with interstate trade and therefore violating the **Sherman Anti-trust Act**. This did not end the strike, and thus President Grover Cleveland had to send in the army under the false premise that the strike was holding up the US mail.

### ELECTION OF 1880

In the election of 1880, the **Republican party** was beset by internal squabbling between the stalwarts and half-breeds over the issue of patronage. This led to a chaotic nominating convention in which a campaign manager, **James A. Garfield**, became the candidate. Garfield won a narrow victory over the Democrat Winfield Scott Hancock, a war hero with no political experience. Garfield was a charismatic figure whose administration began with a successful compromise among

Republicans; unfortunately, he was shot and killed in 1881. Garfield was succeeded by his vice-president, **Chester A. Arthur**. The major event of his presidency was the **Civil Service Act of 1883**, which established a commission to create competitive examinations for potential government employees. Arthur also helped create the modern US navy.

## New South in the 1880s

In the 1880s, the old Southern plantations began to break up, in part because the high taxes imposed by the new governments made them unprofitable. The land was mainly worked by tenant farmers and sharecroppers: **tenant farmers** worked and paid rent on someone else's land, while **sharecroppers** worked the whole plantation and got a share of the crop. Tenant farmers were mostly poor white people, while sharecroppers were mostly freed black people. There was considerable diversification in agriculture around this time, brought on not only by innovation (cotton picker, tractor), but by the **Morrill Land Grant Act**, which gave grants for the creation of agricultural colleges. Clarence Birdseye's development of the refrigerated railroad car spurred farming as well. Also, as the road and rail infrastructure improved in the South, so did Southern industry.

## Gilded Age

### *Characteristics*

The period in American history between Reconstruction and the Progressive Era is commonly known as the **Gilded Age**. During this period, the US seemed to be simultaneously abandoning the ideals of the past and failing to anticipate the future; this was in large part due to the confusion of a horrendous Civil War and massive immigration, industrialization, and urbanization. During this period, many Americans sought refuge in **community organizations** like the Moose Lodge, the Elks Club, and the Masonic Lodge. The politicians of the Gilded Age tended to avoid the major issues of **social injustice and inequality**, instead focusing on minor issues like public v. parochial schools, and the blue laws (laws restricting commercial activity on Sunday).

**Review Video: The Gilded Age: An Overview**
Visit mometrix.com/academy and enter code: 684770

### *Politics*

Although the **Republicans** dominated the executive branch during the Gilded Age, Congress was evenly divided. The Republican party was composed mainly of people from the Northeast and Midwest. Black people typically were Republicans (that is, when they were allowed into the political process). In general, the Republicans supported high tariffs and sound money. One of the main internal disputes in the Republican party was between the **stalwarts**, who supported the spoils system, and the **half-breeds**, who did not. As for the **Democrats**, they were largely based in the South or in the big cities of the North. The Democrats and Republicans butted heads over ethnic, religious, and cultural issues, but they tended to avoid larger economic and social issues. Extremely talented individuals were more likely to go into business than politics during this era. Another trend of the Gilded Age was the domination of the president by Congress.

## American Labor in the Gilded Age

As the US emerged from the Civil War, one of the main economic problems was that most workers were **unskilled**. In general, working conditions were horrendous and wages were low. There was little homogeneity in the labor force, either, making it difficult for workers to switch jobs. **Immigrants** were usually willing to take more dangerous jobs than natives; during the 1880s, more than 5 million immigrants entered the US. In 1882, the **Chinese Exclusion Act** put a 10-year moratorium on Chinese immigration. In 1885, the **Foran Act** prohibited American businessmen from traveling to China to recruit workers. Both of these acts were open violations of the **Burlingame Treaty of 1868**, which had provided for open Chinese immigration.

## Social Critics and Dissenters in the Gilded Age

In his book *Dynamic Sociology*, **Lester Frank Ward** railed against the Social Darwinism espoused by the upper class; he declared that humans were more than mere animals. In *Progress and Poverty*, **Henry George** asserted that poverty was the result of poor legislation rather than any inherent weakness in the poor. **Edward Bellamy** promoted socialism in his novel *Looking Back* (1888); in it, a man of the year 2000 describes how America was turned into a utopian society through the abolition of corporations. Also, at this time, **Thorstein Veblen** exposed the phenomenon of "conspicuous consumption" in his *Theory of the Leisure Class*. All of these critics were disgusted by the hypocrisy of the **robber barons**; these magnates claimed to support laissez-faire government, yet they wanted high tariffs to protect their businesses.

## Laissez-Faire Conservatism and the Gospel of Wealth

The so-called "**Gilded Age**" of American history, which ran roughly from 1880 to 1900, only looked prosperous from a distance. Many at this time believed that wealth justified itself and that God showed his favor in people by making them rich. Many business leaders did not trust politicians because they did not feel that they had had to fight their way to the top. Businessmen believed that the role of the government was to protect property and trade through tariffs. **William Graham Sumner** wrote the essay "What the Social Classes Owe Each Other," in which he declared that corporations shouldn't demand high tariff rates, but the government shouldn't respond to requests to clean up the slums. There was a general sense that the poor were responsible for their plight. Around this time, the popular imagination was inspired by the rags-to-riches fables of **Horatio Alger**.

## Redeemers

The Redeemers sought to prevent black people from voting and to return power to the "natural leaders." In response, the **Populist party** was formed; it was an uneasy alliance of black people and poor white people. Southern Democrats tried to exploit the tension within the Populist party. In order to keep black people from voting, Democrats subjected voters to literacy tests, property tests, criminal background checks, residency requirements, and the so-called **Grandfather Clause**, which stated that individuals could not vote unless their ancestors had voted before January 1, 1867. These restrictions, known collectively as the **Mississippi Plan**, were upheld by the Supreme Court, which ruled in **Williams v. Mississippi** (1898) that they were legal because they never explicitly stated that black people could not vote.

## Black Southerners and Segregation

Most Southern Democrats supported **segregation**, or the separation of the races. Although the **Civil Rights Act of 1875** had outlawed segregated restaurants and hotels, among other things, the Supreme Court ruled in 1883 that this act violated the 14th amendment because only states, and not individuals, could be forbidden from segregation. The **Jim Crow laws** were those rules that segregated black people and white people. Although de facto (by custom) segregation had existed in the North for years, the South began to implement segregation de jure (by law). In **Plessy v. Ferguson** (1896), the Supreme Court ruled that accommodations should be "separate but equal." In **Cummings v. Board of Education** (1898), the Supreme Court allowed public schools to be segregated.

### Booker T. Washington and W.E.B. DuBois

Booker T. Washington was an ex-slave who founded the Tuskegee Institute in 1881; he felt that black people should establish economic independence before worrying about political rights. In his **Atlanta Exposition speech**, he declared that black people needed to humble themselves to white people. Professor **W.E.B. DuBois** attacked Washington's speech as a compromise; DuBois believed black people should take everything they were due. In 1914, both Washington and DuBois met with Marcus Garvey, who believed that black people should return to Africa and establish a separate country (interestingly, most of Garvey's financial support came from the KKK). At around this time, Paul Laurence Dunbar was achieving renown as the "poet laureate of the Negro race," and Charles Waddell Chestnut was admired as a popular black novelist.

### Election of 1884

In 1884, the incumbent Arthur was passed over by his party in favor of Secretary of State James G. Blaine. This proved to be a bad move, as the **Democratic** candidate, **Grover Cleveland**, was able to win the support of conservative Republicans (Mugwumps) and claim a narrow victory. The highlights of the Cleveland administration include the further reform of civil service and the government's successful stand against ex-Union soldiers who were protesting for large pensions. Cleveland reluctantly signed the **Interstate Commerce Act**, and he was correct in predicting that it would not be enforced. Cleveland also spent a great deal of time on tariffs: he attempted to reduce the overall duty with the **Mongrel Tariff** and the **Mills Bill of 1888**, neither of which were very successful.

### Solutions to the "Indian Problem"

The US government constructed several policies in an attempt to solve the so-called "**Indian Problem.**" The **Dawes (Severalty) Act of 1887** asserted that Natives needed to be assimilated into American society; tribes were moved onto "allotments of severalty" (reservations), which they supposedly owned, although they had no control of the land. The **Indian Reorganization (Howard-Wheeler) Act of 1934** encouraged a return to tribal life and offered Natives money for college. In 1953, with the so-called "**termination policy**," Natives became the responsibility of the states rather than the federal government. In 1970, the new strategy was "self-determination without termination": Natives were allowed to move where they choose and were promised money (which they did not receive).

### Election of 1888

In 1888, the Republican **Benjamin Harrison** narrowly upset the incumbent Cleveland, despite having less of the popular vote. Harrison did not accomplish much civil service reform and spent a great deal of time managing insubordination in Congress. Harrison's Republican agenda promoted the **Federal Election Bill**, which was a response to the Mississippi Plan designed to protect the voting rights of freedmen. The **Silver Purchase Bill** was favored by the west but lacked the votes to get through. In the **Compromise of 1890**, the Western Republicans got the silver purchase (Sherman Silver Purchase Act), Southern Democrats got the defeat of the Federal Election Bill, and the Northern Republicans got a higher tariff (McKinley Tariff of 1890). Harrison's administration became known for giving money away for virtually any reason: pensions were excessive, the silver purchase cost federal money, and all of the income tax taken during the Civil War was given back to the people.

### Election of 1892 and the Panic of 1893

**Grover Cleveland** (Dem) defeated Benjamin Harrison (Rep) in the election of 1892 primarily because of his financial conservatism, his promise to change the tariff, and Harrison's weakened state following the epidemic of strikes in 1892. Then came the **Panic of 1893**, caused by labor troubles, over-speculation in the railroads, and an agricultural depression. First, the Philadelphia and Reading Railroads collapsed, then the stock markets collapsed, then the banks folded, draining the gold reserves, then the other railroads folded, and finally the factories were forced to close. Cleveland believed that the cause of this Panic was the **Sherman Silver Purchase Act**, so he repealed it. This plan did absolutely nothing financially, and it split the Democratic party politically.

## Panic of 1893 and Domestic Affairs Under Cleveland

After the Panic of 1893, a group known as the **Silverite school** declared that the economic problems could be solved if the US would begin coining silver again. Cleveland, however, ignored this advice and elected to buy gold with the profits from the sale of government bonds. This strategy was somewhat successful. It was during the **Panic of 1893** that the suggestion to battle economic depression by employing people on public works was first made. One of Cleveland's major policy moves in his second term was the **Wilson-Gorman Tariff of 1894**. This lowered the tariff rate and established trade with Latin America. It also established a small income tax on wealthy individuals, though this income tax would be repealed in the **Supreme Court case Pollock v. Farmer's Loan and Trust** (1895). Cleveland's last term was diminished by ineffective enforcement of the **Sherman Anti-trust Act** and the **Interstate Commerce Act**.

## J.P. Morgan and Banker Control

The **Panic of 1893** was brought on by the collapse of the **Philadelphia and Reading Railroads**; soon after, 192 railroads failed. In a panic, railroad magnates turned to bankers, especially the "Railroad Doctor," **J.P. Morgan**. Morgan insisted that all of the business' records be opened to him. His usual strategy was to encourage old investors to reinvest; to sell more, "watered-down" stock; and to place either himself or one of his associates on the Board of Directors. In this way, Morgan was able to create a set of "interlocking directories," conglomerations of businesses in which he had an interest. He created many large companies this way, among them General Electric, Western Union, and Equitable.

## Andrew Carnegie and Steel

The potential for making money in **steel** was made possible by the development of the **Bessemer process**, whereby iron ore was converted into wrought iron and then had its impurities removed with cold air. **Andrew Carnegie**, an immigrant from Scotland who rose to the top of the Pennsylvania Railroad, was one of the first to make his fortune in steel. He was not especially knowledgeable about steel, but he was the first manager to make a point of **vertical integration**; that is, control of every step of the production process. Carnegie bought out most of his competitors, until he was eventually bought out by J.P. Morgan. Carnegie and his fellows believed in a sort of "gospel of wealth," the idea that they had risen to the top through a process like natural selection. They also believed in using their money for the community.

> **Review Video: Andrew Carnegie and the Steel Industry**
> Visit mometrix.com/academy and enter code: 696753

## John D. Rockefeller and the Trust

John D. Rockefeller came from a working-class background but gradually rose to become the owner of the wildly profitable **Standard Oil company**. Rockefeller was known for spying on his competitors and intimidating his employees. In 1870, Standard allied itself with 40 other companies; when this alliance began, the group controlled 10% of the market, but by 1881 they controlled almost 95%. In 1882, Standard Oil created a **trust**: alliance members gave their stock to Standard in exchange for trust certificates. The federal government began to get suspicious of these powerful trusts, and in 1890 the **Sherman Anti-trust Act** was passed. This act forbade trusts, but it was worded so vaguely that it was ineffective. In the case of **US v. E.C. Knight Co.** (1895), the Supreme Court ruled that the Knight sugar refinery was not a monopoly because it didn't hurt interstate trade; businesses saw this ruling as a call to monopolize.

## Republican Ascendancy in the Election of 1896

The Republicans had been successful in the Congressional elections of 1894, and they nominated **William McKinley** for president in 1896. McKinley was in favor of high tariffs and the gold standard. He was opposed by William Jennings Bryan of the Democrats. McKinley had a wealth of political experience and money, and the Democrats were blamed by many for the economic depression under Cleveland; McKinley won fairly easily. This election marked a 36-year period of domination by the **Republicans**. It also spelled the end of the Populist party. Around this time, gold was found in the Yukon, lending credence to the Republican belief in the gold standard.

## Imperialism

### *During the Period of Withdrawal (Civil War to 1880s)*

In the period after the Civil War, the US for the most part withdrew from **foreign affairs**. The Secretaries of State in this period, however, were very aggressive: **Seward** interfered in Korean politics, tried to assert influence in the Caribbean, and famously purchased Alaska from Russia in 1867 for $7.2 million. **Hamilton Fish** tried and failed to annex Santo Domingo. Aside from these instances, though, the US kept its distance. For the most part, this was because it was preoccupied with its own problems. There was also a common belief that invading and colonizing other countries would be a violation of the US **Declaration of Independence**. Many were remembering Washington's farewell address, in which he advised the US to avoid military entanglements, and others were wary of violating the **Monroe Doctrine**.

### *During the New Manifest Destiny (1880s to 1920s)*

In the 1880s, the US began to take a stronger interest in **foreign affairs**. This was in part due to humanitarian concern; the US felt it could improve the standard of living around the world. There was also, of course, an economic motive; manufacturers wanted to find a new source of raw materials, as well as a new market for their products. Missionaries began to travel abroad in this period, trying to convert foreigners to Christianity. There were also military reasons for the increased activity abroad; the US decided it would be a good idea to acquire naval bases in the Pacific, and a group known as the **Jingoists** openly looked for a military conflict. Theodore Roosevelt and Henry Cabot Lodge were both Jingoists.

### *Bering Sea, Pan-American Union, and Samoan Islands Conflict*

The "**Seal Battle**" was fought in the Bering Sea between British Canada and the US mainly over boundary lines. In 1893, the two sides met and established mutual boundaries between Alaska and Canada. In 1889, the first meeting of the **Pan-American Union** was held in Washington, DC. In 1878, the US had established a naval base at Pago Pago. Both the British and Germans demanded access to the base. In 1889, the US allowed both the British and Germans to jointly occupy the base. In 1899, the **Samoan islands** were divided up among the US and the European powers.

### *Conflict with Italy, Baltimore Incident, Boundary Disputes in South America, and Hawaii*

Between the years 1889 and 1891, the US came into conflict with **Italy** after members of the **Sicilian Black Hand**, a terrorist group, were lynched without just cause in New Orleans. The US also sparred with Chile after 2 sailors from the ***USS Baltimore*** died during a bar fight in Valparaiso, Chile. At around this time, a boundary dispute erupted between **British Guiana** and **Venezuela** after gold was discovered in the vaguely defined border region. Britain was ready to send troops into South America, but the US dissuaded them from doing so, citing the Monroe Doctrine. Meanwhile, all throughout the 19th century, the US had been closing in on a conquest of **Hawaii**. After New England missionaries stumbled upon the islands, the US had gotten the natives to sign trade treaties with various US companies. In the 1890s, the US army, led by pineapple magnate Sanford Dole, ousted the native leadership. Hawaii was annexed by the US in 1898.

**Review Video: An Overview of American Imperialism**
Visit mometrix.com/academy and enter code: 629170

## Spanish-American War

### *Causes*

The **Spanish-American War** centered around **Cuba**. There had already been several revolts against the Spanish leadership on that island, and the **Wilson-Gorman Tariff** had damaged the Cuban economy. In 1896, the Spanish sent General Valeriano Weyler to establish a reconcentration camp, where the dissenting Cubans could be weeded out. Many in the United States pushed the government to intervene in Cuba; businessmen were worried about their crops, Christians and humanitarians were worried about the Cuban people, and imperialists saw a good chance to seize the island. The two final causes of the war were the **DeLome letter**, in which the Spanish minister to the US insulted President McKinley, and the explosion of the ***USS Maine*** in Havana Harbor. Although the Spanish still claim to not have caused this explosion, the US nevertheless declared war on April 25, 1898.

### *Overview*

The Spanish-American War only lasted between six and eight weeks before the US claimed victory. The first phase of it was fought in the Philippines and the second in Cuba. In Cuba, the United States scored a crucial victory when a rag-tag group of soldiers known as the **Roughriders** (Theodore Roosevelt among them) took Kettle Hill and secured Santiago. Although the **Teller Amendment of 1898** had promised independence to Cuba after the war, the **Platt Amendment**, which was inserted into the Cuban Constitution in 1901, made Cuba a protectorate of the US. The US control of **Guantanamo Bay** dates back to this amendment. In 1934, Cuba received its independence. The Spanish-American War formally ended with the signing of the **Treaty of Paris** in 1898. The US received Guam, the Philippines, Puerto Rico, Cuba, and Wake Island. The US also paid the Spanish $20 million because Manila had supposedly surrendered after the end of the war, making it an invalid wartime concession.

## Debate over the Philippines and the Filipino War

In the years 1898 and 1899, the question of what to do about the **Philippines** was hotly debated in the US. **Imperialists** (including Henry Cabot Lodge and Theodore Roosevelt), wanted to make the group of islands into a state, argued against **Anti-imperialists** (e.g., Andrew Carnegie, Mark Twain) who felt that the US would be drawn into Asian conflicts. Some politicians, like William Jennings Bryan, voted for the Treaty of Paris and the acquisition of the Philippines because they felt it would be a disaster that would discourage further imperialism. In 1899, the Filipino leader **Aguinaldo** led the people against US forces. This uprising was only crushed after much cruelty. Later, the **Tydings-McDuffie Act of 1934** promised independence to the Philippines within 10 years but they did not receive it until 1946. Some relevant Supreme Court rulings from this period were in the **Insular Cases of 1901**: the Court asserted that citizens of US territories do not have the same rights as citizens of the continental US.

# American History 1899 to the Present

## John Hay's Defense of China

From 1898 to 1905, **John Hay** was the Secretary of State. One of his great achievements was establishing the **Open Door Policy** with respect to China. China had just been defeated by Japan and was in the process of being carved up by the European powers into various spheres of economic influence. Hay asserted that each nation should allow equal access for all nations and should respect the rights of the Chinese. Somewhat surprisingly, Europe agreed to this policy of goodwill. The Open Door Policy did not, however, keep China from being exploited by foreign traders. In the **Boxer Rebellion of 1900**, the Chinese rose up against foreigners and were promptly routed by an international coalition (including the US).

## Election of 1900 and Theodore Roosevelt

In the election of 1900, **McKinley** and Theodore Roosevelt of the Republicans defeated William Jennings Bryan of the Democrats. McKinley was then assassinated on September 6, 1901, and **Roosevelt** took over. Roosevelt is known as a follower of the African proverb, "Speak softly and carry a big stick." He was known for having very little respect for the system of checks and balances. If the Constitution were too rigid on an issue for his tastes, he ignored it; if Congress acted up, he would subdue them with a mixture of compromise and coercion. Roosevelt displayed his blunt skill in diplomacy in the **Alaska Panhandle dispute of 1903** (in which he decided which islands the US would get, and which would belong to the British) and in the **Morocco Dispute of 1905**, in which he (along with Britain and France) dissuaded Germany from trying to take the North African country.

## Panama Canal

### *Beginnings Under Roosevelt*

The Spanish-American War had demonstrated that the US needed a **Latin American canal** in order to become a major naval power. At that time, however, their hands were tied by the **Clayton-Bulwer Treaty of 1850**, which had stated that neither the US nor Britain would build a canal in Latin America without the other. Fortunately for the US, the British were distracted by the Boer War in South Africa and thus were willing to sign the **Hay-Pauncefote Treaty** in 1901, allowing the US to go it alone. Many in the US, including Roosevelt, wanted to build the canal in Nicaragua because it has a number of lakes that could be connected, and because it is mostly flat. Others lobbied for Panama, pointing out that a French contractor had already started work on a canal there and that Panama was narrower than Nicaragua.

### *Organization Required to Build*

In 1902, the United States struck a deal with a Panamanian builder for the control of the canal project. The US then needed to acquire the land. Panama at this time was owned by Colombia; the Colombians rejected the first offer made by the US, leading Roosevelt to call them "blackmailers." Then, in 1903, a rebellion broke out in Panama; Roosevelt recognized the new, independent country after less than a day of fighting. Fifteen days later, the US purchased the **Panama Canal Zone** from the new foreign minister for $10 million initially and $250,000 per year. Many observers were embarrassed by the deal the United States had won from a fledgling country. Nevertheless, Roosevelt then hired engineer John Stephens to finish the job.

### *Building and Opening*

Once Roosevelt finally secured the building supplies and the land to construct the Panama Canal, the brutal and dangerous work began. In order to prevent malaria, the US paved streets, drained swamps, and built houses so that the workers would not have to sleep in tents. Nevertheless, the workdays were long and the pay was low. In the end, the canal cost about $400 million; it was finished in 1913 but did not open until the next year. Roosevelt's visit to Panama made him the first president to leave the US during his term. In 1920, a guilty Democratic Congress gave Colombia $25 million. At present, about 12,000 ships go through the canal every year, and it takes about 8 hours to get from one end to the other.

## Roosevelt and the 2nd Venezuelan Crisis

In 1902, many Latin American countries were deep in debt to Europe and were not making any moves to repay their debts. Enraged, European countries began to use military force. At first, Roosevelt supported this policy, but he gradually changed his mind, in part because the American public was opposed to it. When Germany, therefore, sent ships to Santo Domingo in 1904, Roosevelt announced the **Roosevelt Corollary** to the Monroe Doctrine. This document stated that nations may not use force to collect debts. Roosevelt asserted that the US would peaceably arbitrate these disputes before Europe could get violent; he felt these interventions would help Latin America and prevent European recolonization. The US developed a reputation as "the policeman of the Caribbean."

## Roosevelt Republicans and Roosevelt as a "Trustbuster"

For Roosevelt Republicans, the principles of good **domestic policy** could be summed up as the "3 Cs": control of the corporations, consumer protection, and the conservation of natural resources. Roosevelt had made his name as a member of the **Roughriders** in the Spanish-American War. Interestingly, his presidency was a result of his unpopularity in his own party: his fellow Republicans had nominated him as vice president because this was felt to be a weak position. They were of course quite displeased when McKinley was assassinated and Roosevelt became president. Roosevelt quickly became famous for his attacks on the trusts. He went after the **Northern Securities Company**, run by, among others, J. P. Morgan and John D. Rockefeller. Morgan attempted to bribe Attorney General Philip Knox to halt the investigation; Knox promptly reported this to Roosevelt. In all, 44 **anti-trust cases** were heard during Roosevelt's presidency.

## Roosevelt's Square Deal

Roosevelt's Square Deal was a domestic agenda designed to help the working class and diminish the power of the corporations. The **Elkins Act** made railroad rebates illegal, making it difficult for preferential treatment to be given to corporations. Roosevelt formed the **Department of Commerce and Labor** to help workers. One telling episode was the **Anthracite Coal Strike** in 1902. When the owner of the mines asked Roosevelt for an injunction forcing the employees back to work, Roosevelt instead sent troops in to mine the coal for the government! The owner and the labor leader then met at the White House to settle their differences. This was the first time both sides in a strike had accepted an executive commission, and the first time the president had threatened to seize property. It was also the first time a president had sided with a labor union.

## Election of 1904

In the election of 1904, Roosevelt used the **Square Deal** as his platform and was able to defeat the Democrat Judge Alton B. Parker. As part of the Square Deal, Roosevelt mandated an **open shop policy**; workers would be free to join a union without being obliged to do so. A case in which Roosevelt's government did not benefit workers was the **Danbury Hatters' Strike**. During this dispute, the workers organized a general boycott of Danbury Hats. The management argued that this boycott violated the **Sherman Anti-trust Act** and the **Interstate Commerce Act**, and the Supreme Court agreed. Many workers blamed Roosevelt for this decision.

## Roosevelt's Reforms

The **Hepburn Act of 1906** gave the ICC the authority to set shipping prices in the event that a shipper complained about the rates. This act also allowed the government to regulate pipelines and express and sleeping car companies. The **Pure Food and Drug Act of 1906** established the Food and Drug Administration to regulate what had become a very corrupt industry. The **Meat Inspection Act of 1906** was inspired by Upton Sinclair's novel *The Jungle*, which exposed the corruption of the meatpacking industry. It established tougher regulation of meat handlers. Not all of Roosevelt's legislation passed, however. He was unable to pass laws against child labor, establish a national worker's compensation, or restrict the power of the **National Association of Manufacturers** to gain injunctions against strikers.

## Roosevelt's New Programs and the Old Guard Republicans

Many Old Guard Republicans disagreed with Theodore Roosevelt on the issue of resource conservation. The **Newlands Reclamation Act of 1902** tried to reclaim the wilderness through the construction of dams. Roosevelt believed that the United States only had about a quarter of its original trees; this act set aside land in the Grand Canyon, Yosemite, and Yellowstone for the preservation of forests. Roosevelt also had to endure the **Panic of 1907**, which was caused by too much supply, a decrease in demand, and a short money supply resulting from a lack of gold. The **Aldrich-Vreeland Act of 1908** authorized national banks to issue emergency currency. Over time, it seemed that Roosevelt had become more radical. The **Employers Liability Act of 1906**, for instance, had provided for workman's compensation but was struck down by the courts. Roosevelt promptly went after the courts.

## Second Hague Disarmament Conference, Treaty of Portsmouth, Japanese Laborers, and Great White Fleet

At the Second Hague Disarmament Conference in 1907, a number of nations gathered to reaffirm the **Hague Conference rules** of humane warfare and agreed upon how the collection of debts should be pursued. After the **Russo-Japanese War**, Roosevelt rather reluctantly agreed to mediate between the two countries. The result was the **Treaty of Portsmouth**, in which the Japanese lost some land (though not as much as the Russians felt was appropriate). For this, Roosevelt received the 1906 **Nobel Peace Prize**. After the Russo-Japanese War, many **Japanese workers** came to the US; Roosevelt had to intervene and prevent them from being discriminated against. Finally, Roosevelt promoted the **US Navy** by painting a number of ships white and parading them past the Asian coast.

**Review Video: The Treaty of Portsmouth**
Visit mometrix.com/academy and enter code: 566070

## Progressive Movement

### *Demographic Trends and Working Class*

The **Progressive Movement** was marked by advances in rights for workers, women, and minorities. As the 20th century began, it seemed as if the rich were getting richer and the poor were becoming more numerous. Per capita income and population had both increased dramatically, but wealth seemed to be concentrated in a smaller and smaller group. Between one-third and one-half of all factory workers lived in poverty and management showed no concern for these workers in the form of unemployment or worker's compensation. Many of the wealthy magnates felt the poor were that way because of their sinfulness and thus had no desire to provide aid. At the same time, many in the middle class feared that the lower class would revolt, although they didn't want to cause trouble themselves.

### Labor Unions, Immigrants, and Black People

By 1914 the **American Federation of Labor** had 2 million members, although most Americans still did not trust labor unions. Meanwhile, immigrants had withstood several challenges to their legitimacy. The **Immigration Restriction League** had tried many times to require immigrants to pass a literacy test. For their part, immigrants were annoyed that they had to go to school, they hated Prohibition, and they hated the settlement houses into which they were often forced by the government. Black people were one group that would not receive much help during the Progressive era. In 1905, W. E. B. DuBois had spearheaded the Niagara Movement, which led to the formation of the **National Association for the Advancement of Colored People**. In 1911 the **National Urban League** was formed to help black people move into the cities.

### Effects on Women and Farmers

During the early part of the 20th century, women aggressively pursued more rights. **Sarah Platt Decker** led the **General Federation of Women's Clubs**, a group that worked hard to improve working conditions for women and children. The **International Ladies' Garment Workers Union** was also popular; it received a great deal of publicity after 146 women died in a fire at the Triangle Shirt factory. **Jane Addams** supported Prohibition, as did the Women's Christian Temperance Union and the Anti-Saloon League. **Carrie A. Nation** became famous for attacking saloons with an ax. For their part, farmers were doing much better in the early years of the 20th century than in years past; those who were still struggling joined with the Progressives.

### Social Critics and State Reforms

**Eugene V. Debs** was a prominent Socialist leader during the Progressive era. The **Industrial Workers of the World**, established in 1905 by "Big Bill" Haywood and known as the "Wobblies," was a radical and militant labor union that appealed to unskilled workers. There were some interesting state and local experiments in this period. In Galveston, Texas, the city switched to a commission system in which the heads of various departments were elected. In Staunton, Virginia, the office of the mayor was done away with in favor of a managing council. **Robert LaFollette's** many reforms in Wisconsin led Roosevelt to refer to this state as the "laboratory of democracy." LaFollette tied the university system, the railroads, and the banks to the state government. Governor Woodrow Wilson of New Jersey planned to use corporate taxes to pay for public education.

### National Reforms

The **16th amendment** (1913) allowed for an income tax. The **17th amendment** (1913) provided for the direct election of US senators. The **18th amendment** (1919) prohibited alcohol. The **19th amendment** (1920) gave women the right to vote. In the case of **Muller v. Oregon** (1908), the Supreme Court upheld Oregon's 10-hour workday for women. In **Hammer v. Dagenhart** (1918), the Supreme Court declared the Keating-Owen Act of 1916 was unconstitutional. This act had prohibited interstate shipping of goods made in factories that employed children. The Court declared that the regulation of factories was the concern of the states. In response to this decision, many states passed acts banning child labor. The first **minimum wage** (25¢) was established in Massachusetts in 1912. New York established the first lasting workman's compensation rules in 1910. In 1896, Utah had become the first state to limit the workday, to ten hours.

### Summary

It is important to note that Progressivism is not synonymous with Socialism; **Progressives** wanted to change the system, while **Socialists** wanted to destroy it altogether. Progressives believed that the government should regulate all business. Moreover, the Progressives wanted to take government out of the hands of the rich and put it into the hands of the common people. Often,

Progressives had difficulty getting organized. This problem had been the death knell of the Populists; the Progressives were able to succeed in spite of their turmoil because they had great leaders: Roosevelt, Taft, and Wilson. The Progressive philosophy was started by a small minority of liberal intellectuals, including William James and Henry Adams. Among the authors who wrote on Progressive themes were Jacob Riis (*How the Other Half Lives*), Frank Norris (*The Octopus*, on railroad corruption), and Upton Sinclair (*The Jungle*, on corruption in the meatpacking industry).

## Theodore Roosevelt's Legacy and the Election of 1908

Theodore Roosevelt, like Andrew Jackson, was truly a public servant. Most of his domestic policies really seemed aimed at improving the lot of the common American. During his administration, Roosevelt greatly enlarged the powers of the president. He created the national parks system and gave the Progressive Movement some respectability. In the 1908 election, Roosevelt chose **William Howard Taft** to become his successor. Roosevelt felt confident that Taft would carry on the mission of the Progressives. Taft ran against William Jennings Bryan of the Democrats, a veteran leader who favored a lower tariff and limited injunctions against strikers. Taft won the election, primarily because of his association with Roosevelt.

## Taft Presidency

### *Foreign Policy of Taft (1909-13)*

Roosevelt was succeeded in the White House by **William Howard Taft**, who became known for "**dollar diplomacy**"; the United States would loan money to Latin American countries so that these countries could pay off their European debts. The US would also dabble a bit in Latin American politics, trying to influence the governments for the benefit of American business. The Taft administration also wanted to encourage trade with China and therefore helped prop up some American banking interests there. Taft is also known for his association with the creation of the **World Court**. The US, Britain, and France tried to establish an international judiciary. This idea enraged former president Roosevelt; he preferred settling differences on the battlefield.

### *Tariffs and the Payne-Aldrich Act*

**Taft** was a very cautious president. His administration saw the deepening of the gradual split between Progressive and Old Guard Republicans. Though Roosevelt had promoted him as a Progressive, Taft slowly began to act more like a member of the **Old Guard**. These tensions came to a head over the tariff in 1909. The Old Guard wanted to keep the tariff as it was, while Progressives fought for reductions. After the House and Senate came up with conflicting tariff bills, Taft was able to engineer a compromise; the **Payne-Aldrich Act of 1909** brought the tariff down to 40.8%. This act also contained a corporate tax and the promise of an income tax in the future.

### *Split Between Taft and Roosevelt*

In the Congressional elections of 1910, the radical Progressives (known as the **insurgents**) were able, with the help of the Democrats, to diminish the power of the Old Guard Republicans in the House. Meanwhile, President Taft drifted closer and closer to the side of the Old Guard. In 1909, Secretary of the Interior **Richard Bollinger** leased national land to corporations, incurring the wrath of forester Gifford Pinchot, who asked for a Senate investigation. Bollinger was forced to resign to take the heat off of Taft. In the Congressional election of 1910, former President Roosevelt announced a mixture of Progressive and Liberal ideas called the **New Nationalism program** and was labeled a Marxist. Then, finally, Taft destroyed a merger between US Steel and Tennessee Coal and Iron that Roosevelt had supported, infuriating the former president.

## 1912 Election and the Legacy of Taft

At the Republican convention before the election of 1912, the incumbent **Taft** was nominated even though **Theodore Roosevelt** had won most of the primaries. Enraged, Roosevelt left the Republicans and formed the **Progressive (Bull-Moose) party**. Roosevelt ran on his platform of **New Nationalism**: voting rights for women and a ban on child labor were among the initiatives. As an interesting side note, while campaigning in Wisconsin, Roosevelt was shot in the torso during a speech but managed to finish the speech in spite of the injury. Ultimately, the election came down to a contest between Roosevelt and **Woodrow Wilson** of the Democrats. These two candidates had similar views on a number of issues, but while Roosevelt was willing to allow some trusts, Wilson wanted to eliminate trusts across the board. Wilson ended up winning a rather comfortable victory. As the Taft presidency came to a close, most observers saw his greatest accomplishments as the "rule of reason," in which the judiciary was allowed to pick which trusts to bust; the **Mann-Elkins Act**, which brought the telephone and telegraph industries under the control of the federal government; and the creation of the **Department of Labor**.

## Wilson Presidency

### *Tariff Reform and the Federal Reserve Act*

Woodrow Wilson appointed **William Jennings Bryant** as his Secretary of State; Bryant became known for his policy of "cooling off," wherein volatile situations would be ignored until all parties had a chance to reconsider their positions. One of Wilson's first major acts as president was to push through the **Underwood-Simmons Tariff of 1913**. This reduces the duty rate to 27% and drastically reduced the tariff on a thousand other items. It also included a slightly greater income tax. Another important economic move was the **Federal Reserve Act of 1913**. This set up a national banking system to be overseen by a Federal Reserve Board. The Federal Reserve system would become the first effective national banking system since the Second Bank of the United States and would be one of the great legacies of Wilson's term. It gave the government a ready means to adjust the amount of currency in circulation.

### *Effects on Trusts*

When Wilson entered office, he declared that there was no such thing as a good trust. With the **Federal Trade Commission Act of 1914**, a bipartisan committee of 5 was created to investigate trusts and issue reports to the government and to the public. The creation of the FTC slowed the growth of monopolies. Peeved by the ineffectiveness of the Sherman Anti-trust Act, Wilson supported the passage of the **Clayton Anti-trust Act of 1914**. This prohibited businesses from selling at reduced prices to favored customers if this price discrimination helped create a monopoly. It also prevented so-called "tying contracts," which forbade a purchaser from buying or selling the products of a competitor. The act also outlawed large interlocking directories; formally allowed the existence of labor unions and farm organizations, as well as strikes and boycotts; and declared that no injunctions could be issued unless property was at stake.

### *Accomplishments of Wilson's New Freedom Agenda*

The **Smith-Lever Act of 1914** brought public education into rural areas. The **Smith-Hughes Act of 1917** allocated money for vocational training and home economics courses. The **Federal Farm Loan Act of 1916** divided the US into 12 agricultural districts and established federal farm loan banks with low interest rates. The **Adamson Act of 1916** asserted that railway workers should be paid for a 10-hour day, though they should only be required to work 8 hours. During Wilson's presidency, **Lewis Brandeis** became the first Jewish member of the Supreme Court. In general, then, Wilson believed in regulating business and improving social welfare. He did not, however, see anything wrong with segregation.

### *Wilson's Moral Diplomacy*

Along with his Secretary of State William Jennings Bryant, Woodrow Wilson promoted the view that nations should treat one another ethically. For instance, the **Panama Canal Tolls Act of 1912** had made it so that the US did not have to pay tolls to use the canal, unlike every other nation; Wilson did away with this measure. Wilson's actions in the **Dominican Republic** were more dubious. The Dominican Republic had been in deep debt early in the 20th century, and the Roosevelt administration had been glad to help in exchange for keeping some troops in the country. When in 1916 the Dominican Republic asked the US to leave, Wilson refused and sent in the Marines. It was only in 1940 that the Dominican Republic was no longer considered a US protectorate. A similar scenario occurred in **Haiti**: the US offered to help the tiny nation, but was unwilling to leave when asked (mainly because of economic interest).

## US and Mexican Revolution

Mexicans traditionally resented the US for its seizure of Texas and the Southwest. When the US-friendly leader **Porfirio Diaz** was overthrown in 1910 and eventually replaced by the murderous dictator **Victoriano Huerto**, the US sent weapons to his opponents. Then, in April 1914, two American soldiers of the *USS Tampico* were jailed in Mexico, and the US did not receive an apology upon their release. This angered the US, and they, in turn, seized a German ship that was believed to be unloading war materials to Mexico. The only thing that kept the US out of a more serious conflict was the **ABC Mediation**: Argentina, Brazil, and Chile met and convinced Huerto to retire. Still, **Pancho Villa**, a challenger for control of Mexico, continued to antagonize the US; he killed several Americans and was unsuccessfully pursued by American forces.

## World War I

### *America's Role in the Build-Up to War*

There had been relative peace in Europe since the end of the Napoleonic Wars in 1815. Many even felt that the age of great wars was over. In 1910, the US had become involved in the **Pan-American Union**, which was organized to settle differences with diplomacy rather than violence. At the **First Hague Conference** in 1899, 26 nations agreed on the principles of mediation, the humane rules of war, and the creation of a permanent court of arbitration. At the **Second Hague Conference** in 1907, 44 nations reaffirmed the old agreements and declared that the payment of debts could not be forced through war. Unfortunately, there would be no Third Hague Conference; it was canceled due to World War I.

### *Causes*

The rise in **nationalism** at the beginning of the 20th century helped contribute to the possibility of war. There was also some conflict between the **imperialist** (France, Britain, and the US) and the **non-imperialist** (Germany, Italy) nations. Many large nations were seeking economic expansion outside of their own borders, and the competition for foreign markets was intense. There was also a complex system of entangling alliances; many countries were involved in several different alliances at the same time. The spark for World War I, though, was the assassination of **Archduke Franz Ferdinand**, heir to the throne of Austria-Hungary, in April of 1914 by a Serbian nationalist. When Emperor Franz Joseph declared war on Serbia, it set off a chain reaction that involved virtually every nation in Europe.

### *US Attempts at Neutrality*

For a while, the US tried to remain **impartial** in World War I, not least because it was making a great deal of money producing supplies for both sides. Among the general public, there was general support for Britain and France, but many German and Irish immigrants supported the Central powers. There were a small group of American citizens who flew missions for the French, known as the Lafayette Escadrille. Gradually, the US government became angry with both sides, even as it tried to maintain trade with both sides. The British blockade of neutral Scandinavia annoyed the US, as did the German's flouting of the rules of war with their aggressive U-boats. In 1915, the British ship ***Lusitania*** was sunk off the coast of Ireland, killing 128 Americans. This convinced many Americans that neutrality could not be maintained.

### *Increasing American Involvement*

During the early years of WWI, the tide of **nationalism** was rising in the US. Many people felt it would be impossible for America to remain neutral; even Theodore Roosevelt decried conscientious objectors. Nevertheless, many **pacifists** objected to any involvement. William Jennings Bryant resigned as Secretary of State after the sinking of the *Lusitania*, advising the US to stay off of British ships, to stop selling weapons to both sides, and to not side so unthinkingly with the British. At around this time, Roosevelt began recruiting and training men as part of the **Plattsburg Experiment**. Finally, Wilson increased the number of troops in both the Army and the Navy with the **National Defense Act of 1916**. Wilson also set into motion a campaign to build more ships.

### *Election of 1916 and Entrance into WWI*

In the election of 1916, **Wilson** narrowly defeated the Republican Charles Evans Hughes. Wilson ran on a **peace platform**. Soon after, however, diplomatic relations were broken off with the Central powers and submarine warfare began. The American entrance to WWI was accelerated by the "**Zimmermann Note**," in which the German minister to Mexico encouraged that country to attack the United States. In 1917, merchant vessels were ordered by Wilson to arm themselves. Among the reasons the US sided with the Allies was the fact that American business was more deeply connected with these countries than with the Central powers. Also, the US had traditionally had stronger ties with Britain and France.

### *Wilson's War Agenda*

On April 2, 1917, Wilson addressed the nation on the subject of World War I. He declared that the conduct of the German U-boats was "a war against humanity itself," and that, if managed successfully, WWI would be "a war to make the world safe for democracy." Four days later, a **declaration of war** was passed. The **Selective Service Act of 1917** registered and drafted millions of American men for military service; about 4.7 million Americans served in the war. The American war effort was mainly paid for with borrowed money, though an increased income tax and the sale of war bonds contributed. Wilson also mobilized American industry; the **War Industries Board**, headed by Bernard Baruch, strove to cut waste and create new industries to aid the war effort. The **National War Labor Board**, headed by ex-President Taft, tried to streamline the labor force to aid the war effort.

### *Contributions of the American Public and Public Opinion of the War*

The **18th amendment** to the Constitution, otherwise known as the **Volstead Act**, outlawed alcohol in 1920. This amendment was purported to conserve food, though it was really an attempt to influence public morality. Through the **Food Administration**, Wilson encouraged people to plant "victory gardens," and to skip meat one day a week. The war was also supported through the **Espionage and Sedition Acts of 1917-8**, which made it illegal to say negative things about the war or to interfere with the sale of war bonds. In **Schenck v. US** (1919), the arrest of the Socialist leader Charles Schenck for criticizing the war was upheld by the Supreme Court, which asserted that First Amendment rights were only exercisable when they did not present a clear and present danger to the nation. In **Abrams v. US** (1919), a Russian immigrant critical of the US actions in Russia was also declared to be a clear and present danger.

### *Perception of Americans Soldiers*

The situation for the Allies was desperate after Russia left the war under the **Brest-Litovsk Treaty of 1917**. The US began to convoy British and French ships in an attempt to prevent U-boat attacks. The American soldiers in Europe were referred to as Doughboys, Yanks, and Devil Dogs. Some of the American heroes in the war were **Alvin York** ("Sergeant York"), who reportedly killed 20 and captured 132; **J.J. Pershing**, who led the American Expeditionary Force; and **Eddie Rickenbacker**, a pilot credited with 22 kills. Americans were praised for their efforts at Cantigny, at Reims, and in the Argonne Forest campaign, where there were over 128,000 American casualties.

### *Wilson's Fourteen Points Program*

Wilson issued his Fourteen Points program supposedly to try to create a quick and lasting peace. Also, however, Wilson hoped to draw the Russians back into the war, to inspire the war-weary Allies, and to demoralize the enemy nations by appealing to the dissenting contingents. Some of the changes called for in the **Fourteen Points** were open diplomacy, freedom of the seas, no tariffs, reduced land artilleries, right of self-determination for all people, temporary international control of colonies (not imperialism), and the creation of the **League of Nations**. Wilson's proposal encouraged the Slavic peoples in Germany and Austria-Hungary to resist the war. Its success in defusing the German war effort allowed Wilson to insist that he would only negotiate with a ruler of the people's choice; **Kaiser Wilhelm** was forced to abdicate the throne.

### *Armistice of WWI and the Treaty of Versailles*

On November 11, 1918, the Germans agreed to an **armistice** provided that Wilson's Fourteen Points be used as a treaty. Overall, between 9 and 10 million people died in the war, including 320,000 Americans. In the **Treaty of Versailles** (1919), the **League of Nations** was created to handle international disputes. A number of new countries, such as Poland and Czechoslovakia, were created by this treaty; also, Germany was disarmed and forced to pay war reparations. Later, the Treaty of Versailles would come to be seen as an uneasy mixture of vengeance and conciliation. It also relied too much on the good faith of the signers. Wilson recognized many problems with the treaty, but he felt the League of Nations would be able to correct them in the future.

## US and the League of Nations

The League of Nations had five permanent members: Japan, Britain, Italy, France, and the US. Germany and Russia were not included. The League would have a **General Assembly** and a **Court of International Justice**. It would try to use economic sanctions and, if necessary, force to guarantee the territorial integrity and political independence of every nation. The problems the League developed in practice were many: it was almost impossible to set into motion, because a unanimous vote was required for action; it created a number of artificial and unsuccessful countries (Sudetenland, for example); it had no power to regulate economics; it excluded two major nations (Russia and Germany); and it had no power to force a nation to disarm.

**Review Video: WWI Overview**
Visit mometrix.com/academy and enter code: 659767

## US Response to the Treaty of Versailles and the League of Nations

The US Senate rejected both the Treaty of Versailles and the League of Nations. Republicans, including Henry Cabot Lodge, created the "**Round Robin Manifesto**" guaranteeing that the Treaty would not be approved; some felt that the Republicans were hurt that none of their members had been invited to the table in Versailles. Other politicians were simply angry that the Kaiser had not been killed. Wilson attempted to take the matter of the treaty directly to the American people, but he suffered a stroke in 1919 and both the Treaty and the League were rejected by Congress. Lodge issued the **Lodge Reservations**, a rebuttal to Wilson's Fourteen Points, in which he declared that it was an infringement on Congress' power for Wilson to assert that the US military would be used to protect other nations. In the national climate of isolationism and disillusionment that followed the war, it was perhaps inevitable that the US would never sign the Treaty or join the League.

## 1920s

### *Election of 1920 and the Background to the 1920s*

The election of 1920 was known as the "solemn referendum." In it, Republican **Warren G. Harding** (who had voted against the League of Nations) defeated Democrat James Cox (who had Franklin Roosevelt as his running mate). Harding's election was in part due to his opposition to the League, but also it was due to his being a radical departure from Wilson. As the 1920s began, Americans felt disillusioned; few people felt that WWI would be the end of war, and massive immigration had left the US scrambling for an identity. There was also hostility lingering from the war: anti-radical, anti-immigration, anti-black, and anti-urban groups had broad followings. The general negativity at the beginning of the decade was not helped by the post-war **recession** and a massive outbreak of **influenza** that killed half a million people.

### *Immigration and Labor Issues at the Beginning of the 1920s*

The radical **International Workers of the World** was defunct by 1920, but many people still feared the influx of new ideas (including communism) and immigrants to the US. Indeed, immigrants became the scapegoat for many of the nation's problems. With the **Immigration Restriction Act of 1921**, only a certain quota of immigrants would be allowed into the country. The **National Origins Act of 1924** restricted immigration even further and stipulated that no Japanese would be allowed into the US. Basically, Americans only wanted Nordics to be able to enter the country. Anti-communist sentiment flared up for the first time during this period; **A. Mitchell Palmer**, the attorney general under Wilson, encouraged citizens to "rouse the Reds."

### *Race Relations in the Early 1920s*

In July 1919, there were violent **race riots** because of competition for jobs; in Chicago, a black swimmer crossed into the wrong area of Lake Michigan, sparking another riot. At around this time, the **KKK** increased in popularity in part because of D.W. Griffith's movie "Birth of a Nation," which depicted the Old South as a paradise led by the Klan. The KKK was led by Hiram Evans and had between 4 and 5 million members; it was anti-black, anti-immigration, anti-Jewish, anti-Catholic, and anti-alcohol. Membership in the Klan declined slightly in the wake of some lynchings and as the economy improved. Nevertheless, many black people sought refuge in the big cities, as part of the **Great Black Migration**. Also, at this time, the **Harlem Renaissance** was reinvigorating black culture; this movement included Langston Hughes, Countee Cullen, Duke Ellington, Paul Robeson, and Louis Armstrong. Many black people subscribed to the beliefs of Marcus Garvey, who thought black people should return to Africa.

### *Provincialism v. Modernity*

At the beginning of the 1920s, the American population was evenly divided between city-dwellers and country-dwellers. While the cities were booming in the post-war period, **farmers** found themselves in economic trouble because of their surpluses. At around this time, many writers, including Ernest Hemingway, F. Scott Fitzgerald, and the members of the **Ashcan School,** sharply criticized the growing materialism of the **urbanites**. In 1920, the "noble experiment" of **Prohibition** began; it was constantly undermined by corrupt government and organized crime, and the government lost the money it had made on the taxation of alcohol. Another incident that brought the differences between Americans into sharp relief was the **Scopes Monkey Trial** in Dayton, Tennessee (1925). In this trial, Clarence Darrow successfully defended a science teacher who had taught the students Darwin's theory of natural selection.

**Review Video: 1920's**
Visit mometrix.com/academy and enter code: 124996

## Harding Presidency

When Warren G. Harding came into office, he promised a "return to normalcy." He almost immediately passed the **Esch-Cummins Act of 1920**, which allowed for virtual trusts in the railroad industry. Harding raised tariffs and was known for having a strong Cabinet, which included **Herbert Hoover** as Secretary of Commerce. Harding's administration was also known for a large number of scandals. It was discovered at one point that Attorney General Harry Daugherty was selling pardons, parole, and liquor; his successor, Jesse Smith, was later found to be doing exactly the same thing. In the **Forbes Scandal**, the head of the Veterans Bureau was found to have embezzled $250 million from the organization. In the **Teapot Dome Scandal**, the Secretary of the Interior was discovered to have sold government oil reserves to private interests. Near the end of his term, Harding had a stroke and was succeeded by **Calvin Coolidge**.

## Coolidge Presidency and the Election of 1924

Calvin Coolidge won the election of 1924 by distancing himself from the scandals of the Harding administration. He is famous for saying, "The business of America is business," and his administration embodied that credo. He allowed the return of **trusts** (now known as "mergers"), and he made major efforts to protect American business abroad. When struggling farmers looked to the government for help, Coolidge responded by vetoing the **McNary-Haugan Bill**, which would have established a minimum price for agricultural products. The **Clayton Anti-Trust Act** was totally ignored during the Coolidge presidency.

## Election of 1928 and Hoover's Agricultural Program

The election of 1928 pitted **Herbert Hoover** of the Republicans against **Alfred E. Smith** of the Democrats. Hoover, who had served as Secretary of Commerce under Harding, was associated with rural voters, Prohibition, and Protestantism and earned a solid victory over Smith after a dirty campaign. Hoover immediately put into action his "self-help" program for agriculture. With the **Agricultural Marketing Act,** he established cooperatives. He also established the **Federal Farm Board** to loan money to farmers and the Grain and Cotton Stabilization Corporation to buy surpluses. Hoover passed the **Hawley-Smoot Tariff of 1930**, which allowed the president to adjust the tariff at his own discretion; Hoover set it at the highest peacetime rate in American history.

## Causes of the Great Depression

The Great Depression was the result of a number of converging factors. For one thing, there was an agricultural depression in the 1920s brought on by tremendous post-war surpluses. The automobile and housing industries both experienced diminished demand in the 20s. One major problem was that wealth was so unevenly distributed: one-third of the nation's wealth was controlled by 5% of the population. There was not much in the way of international trade, in part because of Hoover's high tariff. Overproduction on assembly lines led to factory surpluses and unemployment. Finally, there was persistent unsound speculation in the stock markets. By 1929, many stocks were considered to be overvalued and thus no one was buying them. This caused the catastrophic market crashes of **Black Thursday** and **Black Tuesday** (October 24 and 29, 1929), in which 40% of the market value (about $30 billion) was lost.

## Hoover and the Great Depression

Hoover's first strategy for combating the Great Depression was to balance the budget, reduce federal spending, keep the US on the gold standard, and just wait it out. Later, he developed some **work-relief programs**, employing people on public work projects. The **Hoover Dam** was one of those projects. Hoover also created the **Reconstruction Finance Group**, which loaned money directly to state and local governments as well as to railroads and banks. Hoover's aid projects were unprecedented; still, he resisted giving direct aid to the people in the form of welfare. World War I veterans descended on Washington in 1932 when they were told that their pensions would not be paid until 1945. These so-called "**Bonus Marchers**" eventually had to be dispersed with force, leading many citizens to believe that the country was descending into anarchy. The **20th amendment**, known as the anti-Hoover amendment, actually brought the date of the next inauguration forward.

**Review Video:** Causes of the Great Depression
Visit mometrix.com/academy and enter code: 635912

## Franklin Delano Roosevelt and the New Deal

Franklin D. Roosevelt was elected president in the election of 1932. He was determined to preserve the US government and tried to calm the general public with his folksy "**Fireside Chats**." As the governor of New York, Roosevelt had been able to experiment with social welfare programs. He was a pragmatist and a follower of the **Keynesian school of economics** which insisted that the government had to spend money in order to get out of the Depression. Unlike Hoover, then, Roosevelt supported massive government spending and little volunteerism; he wanted the government to regulate agriculture and industry and also for it to take an interest in the daily economic decisions of the people.

In the early days of his term, FDR promoted the **3 Rs**: relief, recovery, and reform. He announced a bank holiday for five days to stop the drain on the cash flow. The **Emergency Banking Act** authorized the **Reconstruction Finance Group** to buy bank stocks in order to finance repair. The **Glass-Steagall Act** made it illegal for banks to loan money to people for the purpose of playing the market and established the **Federal Deposit Insurance Corporation** to protect banks. The **Economy Act** cut $400 million from veterans' payments and $100 million from government salaries. Roosevelt had the gold standard and prohibition repealed. The **Federal Emergency Relief Administration** was established to provide $3 billion in direct relief to people.

The **Civil Works Administration**, headed by Harry Hopkins, was established to give people work. The **Civilian Conservation Corps** was a civilian army that built things such as the Blue Ridge Parkway. Other organizations created to **employ** people were the Public Works Administration, the Works Progress Administration, the Tennessee Valley Authority (responsible for the construction of 21 dams), the National Youth Administration (gave work to high school students), and the Rural Electrification Administration. The **National Industrial Recovery Act** tried to encourage fair competition and create scarcity to drive prices up. It established a minimum wage, a maximum number of weekly hours, and the right of labor to organize. In **Schechter Poultry v. US** (1935), the Supreme Court would rule that the NIRA should have been made up of laws instead of codes, because there were too many loopholes.

As part of his **New Deal program** to help the US recover from the Great Depression, FDR established the **First Agricultural Adjustment Administration**. This agency provided farmers with loans to help them with mortgage payments and paid them not to plant or sell agricultural products. The formation of the **AAA** was economically successful but was one of the least popular measures in the New Deal; it would later be declared unconstitutional in Butler v. US (1936). The **Federal Securities Act** stated that the securities dealers must disclose the prices of stocks and bonds. The **Wagner Act of 1935** made it illegal for employers to have blacklists of unionized workers. The **Federal Housing Administration** was established to provide lower interest rates for people willing to repair or purchase a house. The **US Housing Authority** was created to loan money to state and local governments for the construction of low-cost housing.

### *Resistance to FDR's New Deal*

**Father Coughlin** was a priest who became famous for his radio broadcasts; he blamed the banks and an "international Jewish conspiracy" for the Depression. **Dr. Francis E. Townsend** was a famous advocate for senior citizens who advocated a national sales tax. **Alf Landon** ran against FDR in the 1936 presidential election and was defeated soundly because of his ties to big business. In the **"Court Packing" controversy** of 1937, FDR tried to overcome Supreme Court resistance to the New Deal by increasing the number of justices on the Court from 9 to 15. This attempt was unsuccessful, but Roosevelt was able to fill Court vacancies with New Deal supporters. A final bit of resistance to the New Deal occurred during the so-called "**Roosevelt Recession**" of 1937-8, in which the economy seemed to be making much less progress than before. Many historians attribute this recession to the fact that New Deal programs were getting much less use in this era.

## Life of Black Americans and the Great Depression

In the **Scottsboro (AL) case of 1932**, 9 young black men were accused of raping 2 white women. Although the evidence was scant, all 9 of the men were convicted. In **Powell v. Alabama**, the Supreme Court would rule that the men had not been given a fair trial because they had not had adequate representation. At around this time, the white **Harold Ickes** was the head of the NAACP. He worked hard to get New Deal jobs for black people, Thurgood Marshall among them. **Eleanor Roosevelt** also was an advocate for black people in this period. She came into open conflict with the Daughters of the American Revolution after this group denied Marian Anderson, a black opera singer, the right to sing at Constitution Hall. In general, the New Deal helped many black people obtain leadership positions that otherwise would have been closed to them. The Roosevelt administration was the first to show any real concern for black people, so most black people became life-long Democrats.

## Latin American Foreign Policy from 1920 to 1945

The US had tremendous financial investments in **Latin America** and most of the government's policy there was aimed at securing these investments. In 1921, the US paid $21 million to **Colombia**, in part for stealing the land for the Panama Canal and in part to keep them from seizing US oil investments. At this time, the US also had bad relations with **Mexico** until the election of President Calles, a pro-American politician. During the Hoover administration, the US tried to promote "good neighborism" with respect to Mexico and the rest of Latin America. In 1934, the **Platt Amendment** gave Cuba full independence. When Batista came to power, however, the US backed him completely and refused to acknowledge any other elected leaders.

## America's Introduction to WWII

After the First World War, the US became obsessed with isolating itself from foreign conflicts. The **Nye Committee** studied the war and determined that it had been fought for financial reasons and could have been avoided. Isolationist parties achieved some popularity during this period, including the **America First Committee**, led by Charles Lindbergh, and **SOS** (Stop Organized Slaughter). The **Neutrality Laws** of 1935-7 declared that the US could not sell weapons to another country in a time of war and that US citizens could not travel on the ships of a nation at war. In 1937, FDR delivered the **Quarantine Speech**, in which he asserted that the Nazi "disease" must be contained. Finally, after conflict in Europe had escalated considerably, FDR declared that the US needed to help Britain and be an "arsenal of democracy in the world." The **Neutrality Act of 1940** made it legal for the US to sell weapons on a cash and carry basis. In August of 1941, FDR and Churchill drew up the **Atlantic Charter**, which vowed to destroy Nazism, protect the right of self-determination, and create a World Peace Organization.

### Buildup to the Attack on Pearl Harbor

A number of events had created a stormy relationship between the US and Japan long before the invasion of Pearl Harbor. The US influence over the **Treaty of Portsmouth**, which ended the Russo-Japanese War, created a great deal of tension between the two countries. The Japanese were also antagonized by Theodore Roosevelt's parade of the **Great White Fleet** and by the **National Origins Act of 1924** and the **Segregation Laws**, which kept Japanese from entering and assimilating into the US. America also had a cordial relationship at this time with Japan's longtime rival, China. As the Japanese became more belligerent, the US froze all Japanese assets in America and denied Japan the purchase of any more oil or scrap metal. The Japanese then launched surprise attacks both on the American naval base at **Pearl Harbor** and on the **Philippines**, where they hoped to secure some oil.

### US Involvement in WWII Concerning Europe and Africa

After the Japanese attack on Pearl Harbor in 1941, the US declared **war** on Japan, after which Germany declared war on the US. Before going after Japan, however, the US first attacked Germany; this was done because the US underestimated Japan industrially and militarily, and because the US feared Britain was on the verge of defeat. **Operation Overlord**, the Allied invasion of the European continent at Normandy, was led in part by General **Dwight D. Eisenhower**. The American generals Omar Bradley and George Patton took part in the **Allied Operation Torch**, aimed at taking back North Africa. At the **Battle of the Bulge**, in Belgium, the Germans tried to break the Allied lines, but were unsuccessful, in part because of the heroism of American soldiers.

### US Involvement in WWII Concerning Asia and the Pacific

The US strategy for controlling the Pacific was known as "island hopping." In the **Coral Sea Battle of 1942**, Americans stopped the Japanese from taking Australia and New Guinea. In the same year, the **Doolittle raids** of Japanese naval bases boosted American morale. In the **Battle of Midway** (1942), the US sunk four Japanese aircraft carriers. In the **Battle of Leyte Gulf**, General Douglas MacArthur took back the Philippines and also took control of Iwo Jima and Okinawa. During this period, a team of American scientists led by Robert Oppenheimer was developing the **atomic bomb** in Los Alamos, New Mexico. Japan was warned several times by President Truman that the bomb would be used if they did not surrender. Surely enough, Americans dropped atomic bombs on **Hiroshima** on August 6, 1945, and on **Nagasaki** three days later. Japanese leaders surrendered aboard the USS Missouri on August 15, 1945.

### Election of 1940 and American Home Front During WWII

In 1940, **FDR** easily defeated the Republican Wendell Willkie. After his election, Roosevelt pledged that every resource would be devoted to winning the war. FDR created a number of war-time bureaucracies, including the **War Production Board** (which was devoted to manufacturing goods for war), the **War Manpower Commission** (which organized the draft and created jobs for women), and the **Office of Price Administration**, which set prices and rations. In total, the US war effort cost between $330 and $360 billion. Most of this cost was covered through taxation and the sale of government bonds. The US frequently denied civil liberties to Japanese Americans during this period, forcing many to live in internment camps. In **Korematsu v. US** (1944), the Supreme

Court ruled that the internment camps were legal, but in **ex parte Endo** (1944), the Court adjusted its decision to state that the US could only intern those whose disloyalty could be proven.

### Yalta Conference

The Yalta Conference was held on an island in the Crimean Sea in February of 1945. It was attended by FDR, Churchill, and Stalin. At the Conference, FDR tried to make sure that Germany would not be split into smaller nations (this would happen later). Stalin "liberated" the countries along the border of Nazi Germany, and in exchange, FDR allowed the Red Army to remain in those countries. This Conference established boundaries and a provisional government for Poland (this provisional government was led by the Soviets, and would last until 1989). One of the more important moves of this Conference was that the US and Britain allowed a Communist government under **Mao Zedong** to remain in Mongolia; this group of Communists would eventually take over China in 1949.

### Truman and the Fair Deal

When Truman came into office after the death of Franklin Roosevelt in 1945, he was already fighting an uphill battle. Many people felt that the Democrats had controlled the executive branch for too long, and many expected **Truman** to have the personal charisma of FDR. Truman gamely attempted to continue the reforms of the New Deal, which he renamed the **Fair Deal**. Nevertheless, he was frequently thwarted by the Republican Congress. Truman surprisingly won a narrow victory over Dewey in the election of 1948, and continued to pursue reforms in education, health care, and civil rights. He gradually became worn down by his conflicts with Congress, however, and he declined to run in 1952.

### Korean War

The Korean War took place during the Truman presidency. Korea had been divided after WWII into a **northern half** (under Soviet control) and a **southern half** (under American control). When foreign troops finally withdrew from the peninsula, North Korea attacked South Korea in an attempt to unify. The United Nations Security Council declared that North Korea was an aggressor, and sent troops led by the American General **Douglas MacArthur** to the region. MacArthur had some early victories, but progress slowed when China began to send men and supplies to the North Koreans. Gradually, combat gave way to armistice talks, yet those these too seemed to drag on endlessly.

### Election of 1952, Eisenhower, and the Suez Canal

General **Dwight Eisenhower**, a Republican, defeated the Democrat Adlai Stevenson in the election of 1952. One of the first crises of the Eisenhower administration concerned the **Suez Canal** in Egypt. The conflict began after Israel attacked Egypt in response to attacks on the new Jewish nation that were launched at Egyptian bases; at the same time, England and France withdrew plans to build a dam on the Suez Canal because of Egypt's recognition of Communist China. Angered by these events, Egyptian President **Nasser** seized the assets of the European company that administered traffic on the canal. The United States was eventually able to defuse the situation; this marked the introduction of the so-called **Eisenhower Doctrine**, in which American troops and money would be used to undermine Communism in various regions around the world.

### Anti-Communism in the United States

As the US was becoming more embroiled in the Cold War, Americans became increasingly paranoid about the spread of **Communism**. There were numerous investigations aimed at weeding Communist spies out of the government, and two people, Julius and Ethel Rosenberg, were executed for spying. The leader of much of this was Senator **Joseph McCarthy**, who was famous for promoting and prolonging the "**Red Scare**" as the often-termed witch-hunt for communists in the government was known (Soviet communications released after the fall of the Soviet Union confirmed the vast majority of his accusations). The tide of anti-communism extended into a general disapproval of organized labor. The **Taft-Hartley Act** restricted the ability of labor unions markedly. In order to survive, the nation's two largest labor unions combined, forming the **AFL-CIO**.

### Civil Rights Under Eisenhower

For a long time, the problems of black people had been considered a Southern issue; however, massive black migration into the Northern cities made civil rights a national question. In **Brown v. Board of Education** (1954), the Supreme Court ruled that segregation in public schools is unconstitutional. After some southern states defied this decision, Eisenhower was forced to send in federal troops. At the same time, black people were staging nonviolent protests across the south. **Rosa Parks** famously refused to give up her bus seat in Montgomery, Alabama, and four black men staged a sit-in at a whites-only lunch counter in Greensboro, North Carolina. With the **Civil Rights Acts** of 1957 and 1960, black people were given the right to vote, but these acts were not enforced.

### US Foreign Policy Under Eisenhower

The Secretary of State under Eisenhower was **John Foster Dulles**, who wanted to pursue an aggressive foreign policy to "roll back Communism." This was also the period in which the national defense budget skyrocketed, as both the US and USSR believed that peace could be maintained by threatening the other side with total annihilation. It was in this climate that the US first became involved in **Vietnam**. The French had been kicked out of this Southeast Asian nation for good in 1954, and the country had been divided into a northern and southern half in the **Geneva Truce** of the same year. The US then tried to bolster the standing of the non-communist leader **Ngo Dinh Diem** in the south, as he batted the communist **Viet Cong**. Increasingly, Eisenhower was funneling money to the anti-communist forces in South Vietnam, believing that if this country became communist, others would follow (the "Domino effect").

### Election of 1960, Kennedy and the Space Program, and Assassination of JFK

In the election of 1960, the Democrat **John F. Kennedy** defeated Richard Nixon; this was the first election in which television was a major factor. One of the most important issues of the Kennedy presidency would be the **space race** with the Soviet Union. It was under Kennedy that the **National Aeronautics and Space Administration** was established. Alan Shepard became the first American in space in 1961, and in 1969, Neil Armstrong would become the first human to walk on the moon. Kennedy, unfortunately, would not witness this event: he was shot and killed by **Lee Harvey Oswald** in Dallas in November of 1963. Though some still claim that Oswald was a part of a broader conspiracy, an investigation led by Chief Justice Earl Warren declared that he had acted alone.

### Civil Rights During the Kennedy Years

The black struggle for **civil rights** intensified during the Kennedy administration. After integration at Southern universities was mandated, National Guardsmen were deployed to keep the peace. The situation was especially tense in Alabama, where Governor George Wallace declared that segregation would stand in his state forever. In July of 1963, **Martin Luther King, Jr.** led the famous **March on Washington**, during which he made his "I Have a Dream" speech. King would receive the **Nobel Peace Prize** in 1964. The **23rd and 24th amendments** to the Constitution were aimed at redressing the issue of black suffrage; they gave electoral votes to Washington, DC, and eliminated the poll tax.

### LBJ and Election of 1964

**Lyndon Baines Johnson** took over as president after the assassination of Kennedy. He was able to use the "ghost" of the assassinated president to pass the **Civil Rights Act of 1964**. Johnson also declared a "war on poverty," a system of programs aimed at helping the poor. In the election of 1964, the escalating conflict in Vietnam was much in the public's mind, and the Republican candidate, Barry Goldwater, was viewed as a war-monger. The election of Johnson, however, did not keep the US out of Vietnam. After being elected, Johnson promoted legislation under the banner of the "Great Society." He created Medicare and Medicaid with the **Social Security Act of 1965** and established the agency of **Housing and Urban Development**.

## Civil Rights Movement During the Johnson Years

The summer of 1964 saw more violence in the South as three civil rights workers were murdered while trying to register voters. After the passage of the **Voting Rights Act of 1965**, Johnson would have to deploy Federal Marshals to escort black people to the polls. Frustrated by the slow advance to equality, many black people became more militant. During the summer of 1967, there were riots in 150 cities, most of which were sparked by economic concerns, as black people felt they were being mistreated in the marketplace. Advocates of **Black Power** joined groups like the Black Panthers and the Mau Mau, and even formerly moderate groups like the SNCC would begin to endorse violence. Many white Americans who sympathized with the black struggle were alienated by this militancy. There were more riots in 1968 after the assassination of Martin Luther King, Jr. in Memphis. The **Civil Rights Act of 1968** gave full rights to black people but contained restrictions aimed at reducing racial violence.

## Foreign Policy Under Johnson

After an American ship came under fire from **North Vietnam** in the Gulf of Tonkin, Johnson received a blank check for American involvement in the region. **General Westmoreland** oversaw troops during this period of escalation. Soon, 184,000 American soldiers were in Vietnam, and the government was spending a million dollars every day. Coupled with inflation, this expense bled Johnson's domestic program dry. The **peace movement** in the US took off during this period. Many people protested what they saw as inequities in the draft system (for instance, black people seemed to be unfairly overrepresented). The US problems in Vietnam were exposed to the world during the **Tet Offensive** of January 1968; during this period, the Viet Cong damaged American forces in virtually every city in the region.

## Election of 1968 and Domestic Policy of Nixon

In the election of 1968, the Republican **Richard M. Nixon**, who had narrowly lost to Kennedy in 1960, defeated the Democrat Hubert Humphrey. The **Democratic National Convention** had endured violent protests over the Vietnam War. Though much of Nixon's administration would be concerned with the war (and later with the Watergate investigation), he did institute a somewhat successful policy of sharing revenue with states. The economy was languishing in a state of stagflation (high inflation and high unemployment) during this period and thus Nixon tried to jolt it with a ninety-day wage and price freeze. This move, known as the **New Economic Policy** (or Nixonomics) was a total failure.

## Nixon and Vietnam

Nixon had won the election on a platform of "Peace with Honor," and upon entering office, he began slowly withdrawing troops from Vietnam. The **Nixon Doctrine** asserted that the US would honor its commitment to South Vietnam with material rather than men. Nixon did, however, order an invasion of purportedly neutral **Cambodia**, where the Viet Cong were stockpiling weapons. It was also during Nixon's presidency that four students at Kent State University were killed by the National Guard during a protest. In the election of 1972, Nixon crushed George McGovern after Foreign Advisor Henry Kissinger claimed that peace was "at hand." After the election, Kissinger and Le Duc Tho would negotiate the **Paris Peace Accords of 1973**.

### Watergate Scandal

On June 17, 1972, a break-in was thwarted at the **Democratic National Committee office** at the Watergate Hotel in Washington, DC. It was eventually discovered that the burglars had ties to the Nixon administration. This began the unraveling of an enormous conspiracy of corruption in the Nixon administration. Many of Nixon's advisers would be forced to resign, though Nixon still refused to cooperate with the investigation. Eventually, though, evidence would mount against him, and Nixon would be forced to release tapes of his Oval Office conversations. Nixon **resigned** on August 8, 1974, although he never admitted any guilt. The **Watergate scandal** left a permanent stain on the presidency.

### Gerald Ford Interlude

Gerald Ford, a congressman from Michigan, had been appointed vice president under Nixon after the resignation of Spiro Agnew, and became president after Nixon resigned. His was a mostly uneventful term, as the nation recovered from the shocks of Vietnam and Watergate. Ford talked a great deal about battling inflation but never did very much to back up his rhetoric. It was during the Ford administration that **South Vietnam** fell once and for all to the North Vietnamese. Ford's most famous act may have been his full **pardon** of Nixon. Though Ford at the time declared that "our long national nightmare is over," this unpopular move may have cost him the election in 1976.

### Election of 1976 and the Carter Administration

The Democratic governor of Georgia, **Jimmy Carter**, defeated the incumbent Gerald Ford in the election of 1976. Carter was popular with black voters and was generally believed to be outside the cesspool of Washington politics. Carter immediately made an $18 billion tax cut, and inflation soared. Carter also made the controversial move of pardoning all those who evaded the draft during the Vietnam War. "As for foreign policy, Carter became known for his humanitarian efforts, working for peace between Israel and Egypt at Camp David and in 2002 earned the Nobel Peace Prize 'for his decades of untiring effort to find peaceful solutions to international conflicts'" (www.nobelprize.org). Carter signed a bill to give the **Panama Canal** back to the Panamanians, and endured a severe oil shortage. This, along with the failed rescue of fifty American hostages in Iran, led to Carter's defeat in 1980.

### Election of 1980 and Foreign Policy Under Reagan

In the election of 1980, known as the **Conservative Revolution**, **Ronald Reagan** easily defeated Jimmy Carter. Reagan presided over the last few years of the Cold War. In 1983, Reagan authorized the invasion of Grenada, where there was an airstrip that was supposedly being used by the Cubans and the Soviet Union. Later in 1983, a Marine barrack in Lebanon was blown up by terrorists, killing hundreds of American soldiers. Reagan introduced the **"Star Wars" program**, a strategic defense initiative in which incoming missiles would be destroyed from outer space by laser-armed satellites. Reagan promoted the "**Peace through strength**" method of foreign policy, whereby the economic might of the United States would furnish such an intimidating military that the Soviet Union would be unable to compete financially and thus fail. This eventually played a major role in the **fall of the Soviet Union** in 1989. Reagan nevertheless improved relations with the Soviet Union diplomatically, even signing a treaty with Soviet Premier **Mikhail Gorbachev** to ban a certain class of nuclear weapon.

### Domestic Affairs Under Reagan

Upon entering office, Reagan implemented **tax cuts** in the hopes of stimulating the economy. While this had a very positive effect on the economy by the end of his first term, the American trade deficit continued to grow wider. Reagan's presidency was tarnished by the **Iran-Contra affair**, in which it was determined that the US had sold weapons to a hostile nation. In 1984, due to an impressive economic recovery and unprecedented growth, Reagan defeated Walter Mondale (whose running mate was Geraldine Ferraro, the first female vice-presidential candidate) in a landslide, winning 49 states electorally. In the case **Wallace v. Jaffree** (1985), the Supreme Court ruled that schools could provide for a moment of silence, but could not endorse any particular religion. In **US v. Eichman** (1990), the Court ruled that burning the American flag qualified as expressive conduct, and was therefore permitted under the First Amendment.

## Overview of George H. W. Bush's Foreign and Domestic Policies

In the election of 1988, the Republican Vice President **George H.W. Bush** defeated Michael Dukakis easily. Under Bush, the **federal deficit** continued to rise, and the US role in the Iran-Contra affair continued to cast a shadow over the executive branch. One of the major crises during the Bush administration was the wreck of the **Exxon Valdez**, which created the largest oil spill ever along the Alaskan coast. Meanwhile, Bush led the US military into the **Persian Gulf War** in 1990-1 after Iraq invaded neighboring Kuwait. American troops routed the Iraqis. It was also during Bush's administration that the **Berlin Wall** fell and the Communist regime in the Soviet Union finally crumbled.

## Election of 1992 and Domestic Policy Under Clinton

The Democratic governor of Arkansas, **Bill Clinton**, defeated the incumbent George H. W. Bush and H. Ross Perot (Independent) in the election of 1992. Clinton tried to reduce the federal deficit. He also pushed for gays to be allowed into the military. Clinton appointed Janet Reno as the first female Attorney General and also reversed most of the restrictions on abortions that had been established by the Reagan and Bush administrations. Clinton's presidency would be plagued by scandals throughout; he and his wife were accused of making illegal land deals in the **Whitewater scandal**, and Clinton would later be **impeached** for lying under oath and obstructing justice in regard to an extramarital affair. A Democrat majority in the Senate elected not to remove him from office.

## Election of 1996 and Foreign Policy Under Clinton

In the election of 1996, the incumbent **Bill Clinton** narrowly defeated Kansas Senator Bob Dole. During Clinton's two terms, the United States trade deficit would continue. In the aftermath of the collapse of the Soviet regime, the US gave substantial aid to Russia and many of the new republics. The United States would also supply troops for a **NATO peacekeeping effort** during the Civil War in the former Yugoslavia between the years 1992 and 2000. American troops also participated in peacekeeping missions in Somalia, Bosnia, and Haiti. Finally, Clinton ordered air strikes against Iraq after it was determined that Iraqi leader **Saddam Hussein** had been part of a conspiracy to assassinate President Bush.

## Election of 2000 and George W. Bush

In the election of 2000, **George W. Bush**, the son of ex-President Bush, defeated Vice President Al Gore, despite losing to Gore in the popular vote. Bush immediately instituted a major tax cut; critics claimed that this tax cut only benefited the very rich. On September 11, 2001, the US suffered the worst **terrorist attack** in its history, as four planes were hijacked and two of them destroyed the **World Trade Center** towers in New York. The attacks were planned and funded by **al-Qaeda**; an Islamic fundamentalist group led by Osama bin Laden. The United States almost immediately launched **Operation Enduring Freedom**, an attack on the Taliban government of Afghanistan that had harbored bin Laden.

### BARACK OBAMA

In 2008, Barack Obama, a senator from Illinois, became the first African American US president. His administration focused on improving the lot of a country suffering from a major recession. His major initiatives included:

- Economic bailout packages
- Improvements in women's rights
- Moves to broaden LGBT rights
- Health care reform legislation
- Reinforcement of the war in Afghanistan

### DONALD TRUMP

In 2016, Donald Trump, previously a real estate developer and television personality, was elected 45th president after a tumultuous election in which he won the electoral college but lost the popular vote. Marked by tension between the administration and domestic media, Trump's initiatives included:

- Appointing three Supreme Court Justices: Neil Gorsuch, Brett Kavanaugh, and Amy Coney Barrett
- Passing a major tax reform bill
- Enacting travel and emigration restrictions on eight nations: Iran, Libya, Syria, Yemen, Somalia, Chad, North Korea, and Venezuela
- Recognizing Jerusalem, rather than Tel Aviv, as the capital of Israel
- Responding to the novel coronavirus (SARS-CoV-2) outbreak

Almost completely along party lines, Donald Trump was impeached by the House on charges of abuse of power and obstruction of Congress; he was acquitted by the Senate.

## Chapter Quiz

Ready to see how well you retained what you just read? Scan the QR code to go directly to the chapter quiz interface for this study guide. If you're using a computer, simply visit the online resources page at **mometrix.com/resources719/texeshist7-12** and click the Chapter Quizzes link.

# Texas History

## History of Texas

The history of Texas (as part of the United States) began in 1845, but settlement of the region dates back to the end of the **Upper Paleolithic Period**, around 10,000 BC. Its history has been shaped by being part of **six independent countries**: Spain, France, Mexico, the Republic of Texas, the Confederacy, and the United States. Starting in the 1820s, American and European immigrants began arriving in the area; joined by Hispanic Tejanos they revolted against a very culturally distant Mexico in 1836 in search of state freedom and defeated an invasion army led by General Antonio López de Santa Anna. After nearly a decade as an independent country, the Republic of Texas joined the **Union** (the United States) in 1845. The name Texas derives from táysha, a word in the **Caddoan** language of the Hasinai, which means "friends" or "allies."

## People Indigenous to Texas

Texas lies within the regions of three North American civilizations which had reached their developmental peak prior to the arrival of European explorers: the **Pueblo** from the upper Rio Grande region, the **Mound Builder** of the Mississippi Valley region, and the civilizations of the **pre-Colombian** cultures of Mexico and Central America. Native American tribes that lived inside the boundaries of present-day Texas include the Alabama, Apache, Atakapan, Bidai, Caddo, Coahuiltecan, Comanche, Cherokee, Choctaw, Coushatta, Hasinai, Jumano, Karankawa, Kickapoo, Kiowa, Tonkawa, and Wichita. No one culture was dominant in the present-day Texas region and many different peoples inhabited the area.

## First Established Europeans in Texas

The first Europeans established in the main part of Texas were the **French**. However, the French colonial presence was short-lived. After exploring the interior of what is now the United States, French nobleman **La Salle** returned with a large expedition designed to establish a French colony on the Gulf of Mexico, at the mouth of the Mississippi River. They left France in 1684 with four ships and 300 colonists. The expedition, however, was plagued by pirates, hostile Native Americans, and poor navigation. They set up **Fort Saint Louis** of Texas, near Victoria, Texas. La Salle led a group eastward on foot on three occasions to try to find the shortest route from Texas to the Mississippi. During the last such search his remaining 36 followers mutinied, and he was murdered by four of them near the site of modern Navasota, Texas. The colony lasted only until 1688, when Karankawa-speaking Native Americans massacred the twenty remaining adults and took five children as captives. Tonti sent out search missions in 1689 when he learned of the expedition's fate, but failed to reach a fort with survivors. Despite the failure of their colony in Texas, the French continued to claim Texas, even after the Spanish had arrived and colonized it. The failure of the French colony became known throughout the world. This French period of Texan history is memorialized in the Texas state seal and as the first (or second) of the traditional "six flags over Texas."

## Texas Towards End of 18th Century

Towards the end of the 18th century Texas remained a sparsely settled territory, heavily dependent on the military and continually exposed to the depredations of Native Americans who resisted Spanish sovereignty in the region. Crown efforts during much of the 18th century to bolster the small population and thus improve the province's viability proved in general unsuccessful. The population remained a mixture of hispanized Native Americans centered on the missions, Spanish and Mexican soldiers with their families, Spanish colonial officials and their families, and various communities of French, British, Italian, German, and American settlers who had been assimilated into the Spanish system. Then in the early years of the 19th century Spain once again faced concerted efforts by rivals, now including the United States, to wrest from it important parts of its North American empire. Relations with the United States had come dangerously close to war over navigation rights on the Mississippi River and the expansion of Anglo-American frontier settlements into the Spanish Floridas. Napoleon's coerced acquisition of Louisiana in 1800 and his subsequent sale of the vast territory to the United States in 1803 left Spanish North America divided and vulnerable.

## Early 19th Century Texas

The early 19th century position of Spanish Texas did not look promising. Foreign encroachments, Native American warfare, and insurrectionary activity all contributed to demographic and economic **collapse**. In the end, desperate Spanish authorities authorized Anglo-American **colonization** in an effort to bolster the province and so produced a new set of problems for the Mexican authorities who soon replaced them. In the years following the Louisiana Purchase and the acquisition of New Orleans by the US, American settlers had begun to move westward into Mexican claimed territory. Some settlers were active filibusters, who sought the long-term annexation of the area by the US In 1812-1813; the **Gutiérrez-Magee Expedition** attempted to separate Texas from the Spanish Empire. In response the Spanish government in Mexico ordered a virtual genocide of the entire Tejano-American population and any of their collaborators amongst the Tejano-Spanish population. The result was the utter devastation of Texas which left it with a population size it had at the beginning of the 18th century. Spanish Texas was a failing colonial policy.

## Oldest and Largest Colonial Texas Community

Spanish Texas had solidified upon three primary centers. The oldest and largest of colonial Texas communities was **San Antonio de Béxar**. In its eighty-year history the settlement had evolved from a presidio-mission complex to the first chartered municipality and finally to the provincial capital. Its population of approximately 2,000 was composed chiefly of Mexican settlers from Coahuila, Nuevo León, and other frontier provinces mixed with a small number of Canary Islanders. After the United States acquired Louisiana, reinforcement of the Spanish military presence in Texas resulted in the transfer of the Second Flying Company of San Carlos de Parras (the Álamo de Parras company) to San Antonio, where it was headquartered in 1803 at San Antonio de Valero Mission, which had been closed. Other units from Nuevo Santander and Nuevo León swelled the population to over 3,000 by 1810.

## Texas in the 1820s and 1830s

In the 1820s, the population in Texas was very sparse and the Mexican government had difficulty in attracting Mexicans to the area. Thus, in order to populate and develop the area Mexico sought **settlers** from Europe and especially the neighboring United States. When Mexico reached an agreement with **Stephen F. Austin**, it allowed several hundred families from the United States, known as **Texians**, to move into the region. Thousands of additional settlers soon flooded into Texas. When Mexico abolished slavery nationwide, some immigrants from the US refused to comply with the law. This was coupled with complaints about the tightening political and economic control over the territory by the central government in Mexico City, which expected its citizens to be members in good standing of the Catholic Church, whereas the settlers from the United States were Protestant. In 1835, Mexican President **Antonio López de Santa Anna** abolished the Constitution of 1824 and sought to centralize national power in Mexico City. This caused much political unrest throughout Mexico, an example of which was the rebellion and resulting massacre in Zacatecas. As a result, the new government's efforts to tighten political and economic control over the territory of Texas would only rouse emotions in the Texian settlers and local Tejanos, leading to the **Texas Revolution**.

## Mexican Texas

Mexican Texas is the name given by Texas historians to the brief period between 1821—1835, when Texas was part of Mexico, as a part of the **State of Coahuila y Tejas**. The period begins with Mexico's victory over Spain in its war of independence in 1821 and ends with Texas's **Declaration of Independence** from Mexico in 1836, forming the **Republic of Texas**. The Rio Grande and South Texas areas have a long and turbulent history of independence movements by the local Mexican population on account of unitary and perceived dictatorial and unconstitutional practices by the central Mexican government. North Texas and East Texas, meanwhile, remained largely in the hands of Native American tribes, some of whom were hostile to Spanish and then Mexican rule.

## Battles of the Texas Revolution

Four days after the first declaration of independence, the two-week long **Battle of the Alamo** ended as Mexican General **Antonio López de Santa Anna's** forces defeated the nearly 200 Texans defending the small mission (which would eventually become the center of the city of San Antonio). "Remember the Alamo!" became the battle cry of the Texas Revolution. The **Battle of San Jacinto** was fought on April 21, 1836 (interestingly, the anniversary for the founding of the city of Rome) near the present-day city of Houston. General Santa Anna's entire force of 1,600 men was killed or captured by Texas General **Sam Houston's** army of 800 Texans; only nine Texans died. This decisive battle resulted in Texas's independence from Mexico. Sam Houston, a native of Virginia, was **President** of the Republic of Texas for two separate terms, 1836–1838 and 1841–1844. He also was **Governor** of the state of Texas from 1859 to 1861.

## Third Center of Colonial Spanish Power in Texas

The third center of Spanish power and the one with the most limited amount of Spanish royal control was far to the northeast, near the Louisiana border. **North-Eastern Texas** had traditionally been a community of English, French, and Spanish settlers who had established the Presidio de Las Adacs as the first capital of Texas. However, North-East Texas was even further removed from Mexico City than San Antonio de Bexar. Consequently, the area was downgraded in colonial status and by Imperial edict the settlement was ordered abandoned. The viceroy eventually did permit the resettlement of East Texas, but would not consent to dwellings within 100 leagues of Natchitoches (Nacogdoches), Louisiana. Nevertheless, the refugees in San Antonio viewed any concession as encouraging. In August 1774 they founded the settlement of **Bucareli** on the Trinity River at a site in what is now Madison County. The town had attracted 347 inhabitants by 1777, but it was plagued by floods and Comanche raids. Without authorization, the population moved again in 1779 to **Nacogdoches**. The new town began to be garrisoned in 1795 by a detachment from Bexar as a means of further solidifying the interests of San Antonio over the province. By the beginning of the 19th century, the settlement was attracting increasing numbers of immigrants, legal and otherwise, from the Anglo-American frontier.

## Legacies of Spanish Texas

The Spanish occupation of Texas lasted for just 105 years. However, the **legacies of Spanish Texas** are lasting and significant. Perhaps most obvious, yet superficial in importance, is the use of **Spanish names** for hundreds of towns, cities, counties, and geographic features in Texas. San Antonio, the first formal municipality in Texas, is one of the ten largest cities in the United States. Forty-two of the 254 counties in Texas bear either Hispanic names, or an Anglicized derivation such as Galveston or a misspelling such as Uvalde. The names of physiographical features such as Llano Estacado, Guadalupe Mountains, and Padre Island serve as reminders of Spanish explorers and conquistadors who crossed portions of Texas well before the English settled the Atlantic Coast of North America. Spaniards introduced numerous European crops, irrigation at San Antonio and other mission sites, livestock, and livestock-handling techniques. **Farming**, initially practiced by some Native American groups in Texas, was likewise expanded and improved by Spanish missionaries and settlers. The restored **missions** at San Antonio and Goliad stand as enduring monuments to the Franciscans who brought the mantle of Christianity to Native Americans in Texas. With the exception of those in California, the finest examples of Spanish mission architecture in the United States are found in Texas.

### BEGINNING OF REPUBLIC OF TEXAS

The first declaration of independence for modern Texas, by both Anglo-Texan settlers and local Tejanos, was signed in Goliad on December 20, 1835. The **Texas Declaration of Independence** was enacted at Washington-on-the-Brazos on March 2, 1836, effectively creating the **Republic of Texas**.

## Chapter Quiz

Ready to see how well you retained what you just read? Scan the QR code to go directly to the chapter quiz interface for this study guide. If you're using a computer, simply visit the online resources page at **mometrix.com/resources719/texeshist7-12** and click the Chapter Quizzes link.

# Foundations, Skills, Research, and Instruction

## Social Studies Skills

### COLLECTING INFORMATION AND ORGANIZING AND REPORTING RESULTS

The first step of compiling data for useful implementation requires narrowing down on a **topic**. The student should first read background information to identify areas that are interesting or need further study and that the student does not have a strong opinion about. The research question should be identified, and the student should refer to general sources that can point to more specific information. When he or she begins to take notes, his or her information must be **organized** with a clear system to identify the source. Any information from outside sources must be acknowledged with **footnotes** or a **bibliography**. To gain more specific information about his or her topic, the student can then research bibliographies from general sources to narrow down on information pertinent to the topic at hand. He or she should draft a thesis statement that summarizes the main point of the research. This should lead to a working **outline** that incorporates all the ideas needed to support the main point in a logical order. A rough draft should incorporate the results of the research in the outlined order, with all citations clearly inserted. The paper should then be edited for clarity, style, flow, and content.

#### *FORMULATING RESEARCH QUESTIONS OR HYPOTHESES*

Formulating research questions or hypotheses is the process of finding questions to answer that have not yet been asked. The first step in the process is reading **background information**. Knowing about a general topic and reading about how other people have addressed it helps identify areas that are well understood. Areas that are not as well understood may either be lightly addressed in the available literature or distinctly identified as a topic that is not well understood and deserves further study. Research questions or hypotheses may address such an unknown aspect, or they may focus on drawing parallels between similar, well-researched topics that have not been connected before. Students usually need practice in developing research questions that are of the appropriate scope so that they will find enough information to answer the question, yet not so much that they become overwhelmed. Hypotheses tend to be more specific than research questions.

#### *IDENTIFYING MAIN IDEAS IN A DOCUMENT*

Main ideas in a paragraph are often found in the **topic sentence**, which is usually the first or second sentence in the paragraph. Every following sentence in the paragraph should relate to that initial information. Sometimes, the first or second sentence doesn't obviously set up the main idea. When that happens, each sentence in the paragraph should be read carefully to find the **common theme** between them all. This common theme is the main idea of the paragraph. Main ideas in an entire document can be found by analyzing the structure of the document. Frequently, the document begins with an introductory paragraph or abstract that will summarize the main ideas. Each paragraph often discusses one of the main ideas and contributes to the overall goal of the document. Some documents are divided up into chapters or sections, each of which discusses a main idea. The way that main ideas are described in a document (either in sentences, paragraphs, or chapters) depends on the length of the document.

### *Using Electronic Resources and Periodicals for Reference*

Electronic resources are often the quickest, most convenient way to get background information on a topic. One of the particular strengths of **electronic resources** is that they can also provide primary-source multimedia video, audio, or other visual information on a topic that would not be accessible in print. Information available on the internet is not often carefully screened for accuracy or for bias, so choosing the **source** of electronic information is often very important. Electronic encyclopedias can provide excellent overview information, but publicly edited resources like Wikipedia are open to error, rapid change, incompleteness, or bias. Students should be made aware of the different types and reliabilities of electronic resources, and they should be taught how to distinguish between them. Electronic resources can often be too detailed and overwhelm students with irrelevant information. **Periodicals** provide current information on social science events, but they too must be screened for bias. Some amount of identifiable bias can actually be an important source of information, because it indicates prevailing culture and standards. Periodicals generally have tighter editorial standards than electronic resources, so completeness and overt errors are not usually as problematic. Periodicals can also provide primary-source information with interviews and photographs.

### *Using Encyclopedias, Bibliographies, or Almanacs for Social Science Research*

Encyclopedias are ideal for getting background information on a topic. They provide an overview of the topic and link it to other concepts that can provide additional keywords, information, or subjects. They can help students narrow their topic by showing the subtopics within the overall topic and by relating it to other topics. **Encyclopedias** may sometimes prove to be more useful than the internet because they provide a clearly organized, concise overview of material. **Bibliographies** are bound collections of references to periodicals and books, organized by topic. Students can begin researching more efficiently after they identify a topic, look it up in a bibliography, and look up the references listed there. This provides a branching network of information a student can follow. A pitfall of bibliographies is that when in textbooks or other journal articles, the references in them are chosen to support the author's point of view and so may be limited in scope. **Almanacs** are volumes of facts published annually. They provide numerical information on just about every topic, and are organized by subject or geographic region. They are often helpful for supporting arguments made using other resources and do not provide any interpretation of their own.

### *Primary and Secondary Resources*

Primary resources provide information about an event from the perspective of people who were present at the event. They might be letters, autobiographies, interviews, speeches, artworks, or anything created by people with first-hand experience. **Primary resources** are valuable because they provide not only facts about the event but also information about the surrounding circumstances; for example, a letter might provide commentary about how a political speech was received. The internet is a source of primary information, but care must be taken to evaluate the perspective of the website providing that information. Websites hosted by individuals or special-interest organizations are more likely to be biased than those hosted by public organizations, governments, educational institutions, or news associations. **Secondary resources** provide information about an event but were not written at the time the event occurred. They draw information from primary sources. Because secondary sources were written later, they have the added advantage of historical perspective, multiple points of view, or resultant outcomes. Newsmagazines that write about an event even a week after it occurred count as secondary sources. Secondary sources tend to analyze events more effectively or thoroughly than primary sources.

**Review Video: Primary and Secondary Sources**
Visit mometrix.com/academy and enter code: 383328

### *Organizing Information Chronologically and Analyzing the Sequence of Events*

To organize information chronologically, each piece of information must be associated with a time or a date. Events are ordered according to the time or date at which they happened. In social sciences, chronological organization is the most straightforward way to arrange information, because it relies on a uniform, fixed scale—the passage of time. Information can also be organized based on any of the "who, what, when, where, why?" principles.

**Analyzing the sequence of chronological events** involves not only examining the event itself but the preceding and following events. This can put the event in question into perspective, showing how a certain thing might have happened based on preceding history. One large disadvantage of chronological organization is that it may not highlight important events clearly relative to less important events. Determining the relative importance of events depends more strongly on interpreting their relationships to neighboring events.

### *Recognizing Cause-and-Effect and Comparing Similarities and Differences*

Cause-and-effect relationships are simply linkages between an event that happened (the **effect**) because of some other event (the **cause**). Effects are always chronologically ordered after causes. Effects can be found by asking why something happened or looking for information following words like *so, consequently, since, because, therefore, this led to, as a result,* and *thus*. Causes can also be found by asking what happened. **Comparing similarities and differences** involves mentally setting two concepts next to each other and then listing the ways they are the same and the ways they are different. The level of comparison varies by student level; for example, younger students may compare the physical characteristics of two animals while older students compare the themes of a book. Similarity/difference comparisons can be made by listing written descriptions in a point-by-point approach, or they can be done in several graphic ways. Venn diagrams are commonly used to organize information, showing non-overlapping clouds filled with information about the different characteristics of A and B, and the overlapping area shows ways in which A and B are the same. Idea maps using arrows and bubbles can also be developed to show these differences.

### *Distinguishing Between Fact and Opinion*

Students easily recognize that **facts** are true statements that everyone agrees on, such as an object's name or a statement about a historical event. Students also recognize that **opinions** vary about matters of taste, such as preferences in food or music, that rely on people's interpretation of facts. Simple examples are easy to spot. **Fact-based passages** include certainty-grounded words like *is, did*, or *saw*. On the other hand, **passages containing opinions** often include words that indicate possibility rather than certainty, such as *would, should*, or *believe*. First-person verbs also indicate opinions, showing that one person is talking about his or her experience. Less clear are examples found in higher-level texts. For example, primary-source accounts of a Civil War battle might include facts ("*x* battle was fought today") and also opinions ("Union soldiers are not as brave as Confederate soldiers") that are not clearly written as such ("I believe Union soldiers..."). At the same time that students learn to interpret sources critically (Was the battle account written by a Southerner?), they should practice sifting fact from these types of opinion. Other examples where fact and opinion blend together are self-authored Internet websites.

**Review Video: Distinguishing Fact and Opinion**
Visit mometrix.com/academy and enter code: 870899

### *Determining the Adequacy, Relevance, and Consistency of Information*

Before information is sought, a list of **guiding questions** should be developed to help determine whether information found is adequate, relevant, and consistent. These questions should be based on the **research goals**, which should be laid out in an outline or concept map. For example, a student writing a report on Navajo social structure might begin with questions concerning the general lifestyle and location of Navajos and follow with questions about how Navajo society was organized. While researching his questions, he or she will come up with pieces of information. This information can be compared to his or her research questions to determine whether it is **relevant** to his or her report. Information from several sources should be compared to determine whether the information is **consistent**. Information that is **adequate** helps answer specific questions that are part of the research goals. Inadequate information for this particular student might be a statement such as "Navajos had a strong societal structure," because the student is probably seeking more specific information.

### *Drawing Conclusions and Making Generalizations About a Topic*

Students reading about a topic will encounter different facts and opinions that contribute to their overall impression of the material. The student can critically examine the material by thinking about what facts have been included, how they have been presented, what they show, what they relate to outside the written material, and what the author's conclusion is. Students may agree or disagree with the author's conclusion, based on the student's interpretation of the facts the author presented. When working on a research project, a student's research questions will help him or her gather details that will enable him or her to **draw a conclusion** about the research material.

**Generalizations** are blanket statements that apply to a wide number of examples. They are similar to conclusions but do not have to summarize the information as completely as conclusions. Generalizations in reading material may be flagged by words such as *all*, *most*, *none*, *many*, *several*, *sometimes*, *often*, *never*, *overall*, or *in general*. Generalizations are often followed by supporting information consisting of a list of facts. Generalizations can refer to facts or the author's opinions, and they provide a valuable summary of the text overall.

## Evaluating and Interpreting Maps

The **map legend** is an area that provides interpretation information such as the key, the scale, and how to interpret the map. The **key** is the area that defines symbols, abbreviations, and color schemes used on the map. Any feature identified on the map should be defined in the key. The **scale** is a feature of the map legend that tells how distance on the map relates to distance on the ground. It can either be presented mathematically in a ratio or visually with a line segment. For example, it could say that one inch on the map equals one foot on the ground, or it could show a line segment and tell how much distance on the map the line symbolizes. **Latitude** and **longitude** are often shown on maps to relate their area to the world. Latitude shows how far a location is north or south from Earth's equator, and longitude shows how far a location is east or west from Earth's prime meridian. Latitude runs from 90°N (North Pole) to 0° (equator) to 90°S (South Pole), and longitude runs 180°E (International Date Line) to 0° (prime meridian) to 180°W (International Date Line).

**Review Video: Elements of a Map**
Visit mometrix.com/academy and enter code: 437727

### *Popular Map Projections*

- **Globe**: Earth's features are shown on a sphere. No distortion of distances, directions, or areas occurs.
- **Mercator**: Earth's features are projected onto a cylinder wrapped around a globe. This generates a rectangular map that is not distorted at the equator but is greatly distorted near the poles. Lines of latitude and longitude form a square grid.
- **Robinson**: Earth's features are projected onto an oval-looking map. Areas near the poles are truer to size than in the Mercator. Some distortion affects every point.
- **Orthographic**: Earth's features are shown on a circle, which is tangent to the globe at any point chosen by the mapmaker. This generates a circular, 3D-appearing map similar to how Earth is seen from space.
- **Conic maps**: This family of maps is drawn by projecting the globe's features onto a cone set onto the globe. Some distortion affects most points.
- **Polar maps**: The land around the poles has been projected onto a circle. This provides much less distortion of Antarctica and the land around the North Pole than other map types.

### *Cartographic Distortion and Its Influence on Map Projections*

Cartographic distortion is the distortion caused by projecting a three-dimensional structure, in this case, Earth's surface, onto the two-dimensional surface of a map. Numerous map projections have been developed to minimize distortion, but the only way to eliminate distortion completely is to render Earth in three dimensions. Most map projections have minimal distortion in some location, usually the center, and the distortion becomes greater close to the edges of the map. Some map projections try to compromise and distribute the distortion more evenly across the map. Different categories of maps preserve, or do not distort, different features. Maps that preserve directions accurately are **azimuthal**, and maps that preserve shapes properly are **conformal**. Area-preserving maps are called **equal-area maps**, and maps that preserve distance are called **distance-preserving**. Maps that preserve the shortest routes are **gnomonic projections**.

**Review Video: Map Projections**
Visit mometrix.com/academy and enter code: 327303

### *Comparing Maps of the Same Place from Different Time Periods*

Maps of the same place from different time periods can often be initially aligned by **geographic features**. Political and land-use boundaries are most likely to change between time periods, whereas locations of waterways and geologic features such as mountains are relatively constant. Once geographic features have been used to align maps, they can be compared side-by-side to examine the changing locations of human settlement, smaller waterways, etc. This kind of map interpretation, at the smallest scale, provides information about how small groups of humans **interact with their environment**. For example, such analysis might show that major cities began around ports and then moved inland as modes of transportation, like railroads and cars, became more common. Lands that were initially used for agriculture might become incorporated into a nearby city as the population grows. This kind of map analysis can also show the evolution of the **socio-economics** of an area, providing information about the relative importance of economic activities (manufacturing, agriculture, or trade) and even the commuting behavior of workers.

### *Natural, Political, and Cultural Features on Maps*

Map legends will provide information about the types of natural, political, or cultural features on a map. Some maps show only one of these three features. **Natural features** such as waterways, wetlands, beaches, deserts, mountains, highlands, and plains can be compared between regions by type, number, distribution, or any other physical characteristic. **Political features** such as state and county divisions or roads and railroads can be compared numerically, but examining their geographic distribution may be more informative. This provides information on settlement density and population. In addition, road and railroad density may show regions of intense urbanization, agricultural regions, or industrial centers. **Cultural features** may include roads and railroads, but might also include historic areas, museums, archaeological digs, early settlements, and even campgrounds. Comparing and contrasting the number, distribution, and types of these features may provide information on the history of an area, the duration of settlement of an area, or the current use of the area (for example, many museums are found in current-day cultural centers).

### *Comparing Maps with Datasets or Texts*

Maps can provide a great deal of information about an area by showing specific locations where certain types of settlement, land use, or population growth occurred. **Datasets** and **texts** can provide more specific information about events that might only otherwise be hypothesized from maps. This specific information may provide dates of significant events (for example, the date of a fire that gutted a downtown region, forcing suburban development) or important numerical data (e.g., population growth by year). Written datasets and texts enable map interpretation to become concrete and allow observed trends to be linked with specific causes ("Real estate prices rose in 2004, causing middle-class citizens to move northwest of the city"). Without specific information from additional sources, inferences drawn from maps cannot be put in **context** and interpreted in more than a vague way.

## Evaluating and Interpreting Other Graphic Formats

The type of information being conveyed guides the choice of **format**. Textual information and numeric information must be displayed with different techniques. Text-only information may be most easily summarized in a diagram or a timeline. If the text includes numeric information, it may be converted into a chart that shows the size of groups, connects ideas in a table or graphic, or shows information in a hybridized format. Numeric information is often most helpfully presented in tables or graphs. When information will be referred to and looked up again and again, tables are often most helpful for the reader. When the trends in the numeric information are more important than the numbers themselves, graphs are often the best choice. Information that is linked to the land and has a spatial component is best conveyed using maps.

### *Interpreting Charts and Tables*

Charts used in social science are a visual representation of data. They combine graphic and textual elements to convey information in a concise format. Often, **charts** divide the space up in blocks, which are filled with text and/or pictures to convey a point. Charts are often organized in tabular form, where blocks below a heading all have information in common. Charts also divide information into conceptual, non-numeric groups (for example, "favorite color"), which are then plotted against a numerical axis (e.g., "number of students"). Charts should be labeled in such a way that a reader can locate a point on the chart and then consult the surrounding axes or table headings to understand how it compares to other points. **Tables** are a type of chart that divides textual information into rows and columns. Each row and column represent a characteristic of the information. For example, a table might be used to convey demographic information. The first column would provide "year," and the second would provide "population." Reading across the rows, one could see that in the year 1966, the population of Middletown was 53,847. Tracking the columns would show how frequently the population was counted.

### *Interpret Graphs and Diagrams*

Graphs are similar to charts, except that they graphically show numeric information on both axes. For example, a **graph** might show population through the years, with years on the *x* axis and population on the *y* axis. One advantage of graphs is that the population during the time in between censuses can be estimated by locating that point on the graph. Each axis should be labeled to allow the information to be interpreted correctly, and the graph should have an informative title.

**Diagrams** are usually drawings that show the progression of events. The drawings can be fairly schematic, as in a flow chart, or they can be quite detailed, as in a depiction of scenes from a battle. Diagrams usually have arrows connecting the events or boxes shown. Each event or box should be labeled to show what it represents. Diagrams are interpreted by following the progression along the arrows through all events.

### *Using Timelines in Social Science*

Timelines are used to show the relationships between people, places, and events. They are ordered chronologically and usually are shown left-to-right or top-to-bottom. Each event on the **timeline** is associated with a date, which determines its location on the timeline. On electronic resources, timelines often contain hyperlinks associated with each event. Clicking on the event's hyperlink will open a page with more information about the event. **Cause-and-effect relationships** can be observed on timelines, which often show a key event and then resulting events following in close succession. These can be helpful for showing the order of events in time or the relationships between similar events. They help make the passage of time a concrete concept and show that large periods pass between some events, while other events cluster very closely.

### *Using Political Cartoons in Social Science Studies*

Political cartoons are drawings that memorably convey an opinion. These opinions may be supportive or critical and may summarize a series of events or pose a fictional situation that summarizes an attitude. **Political cartoons** are, therefore, secondary sources of information that provide social and cultural context about events. Political cartoons may have captions that help describe the action or put it in context. They may also have dialogue, labels, or other recognizable cultural symbols. For example, Uncle Sam frequently appears in political cartoons to represent the United States government. Political cartoons frequently employ caricatures to call attention to a situation or a person. The nature of the caricature helps show the cartoonist's attitude toward the issue being portrayed. Every element of the cartoon is included to support the artist's point and should be considered in the cartoon's interpretation. When interpreting political cartoons, students should examine what issue is being discussed, what elements the artist chose to support his or her point, and what the message is. Considering who might agree or disagree with the cartoon is also helpful in determining the message of the cartoon.

## Analyzing Artifacts

Artifacts, or everyday objects used by previous cultures, are useful for understanding life in those cultures. Students should first discover, or be provided with, a **description** of the item. This description should depict what time period the **artifact** was used in and what culture used it. From that description and/or from examination of the artifact, students should be able to discuss what the artifact is, what it is made of, its potential uses, and the people who likely used it. They should then be able to draw **conclusions** from all these pieces of evidence about life in that culture. For example, analysis of coins from an early American archaeological site might show that settlers brought coins with them, or that some classes of residents were wealthy, or that trade occurred with many different nations. The interpretation will vary depending on the circumstances surrounding the artifact. Students should consider these circumstances when drawing conclusions.

# Historiography

## Introduction to Historiography

Historiography is the study of the methods and approaches that historians use to create histories. It involves examining how historical evidence is chosen, interpreted, evaluated, analyzed, and used in the writing of history. Historiography is not concerned with the events that make up history but rather the manner in which that history was recorded. The sources, techniques, and theoretical frameworks used to record the history of a certain subject constitute that subject's historiography.

## Common Terminology Used When Studying History

When studying history, it is important to have a clear understanding of various terms that can be used interchangeably. The term **time** refers to the continuous passing of events in the past, present, and future. Time is a scientific measure that conventionally uses minutes, hours, days, and years as its **standard measures**. Time passes with or without significant events taking place. **History** is distinct from time as it is the record of **significant events** throughout the past. The term **chronology** refers to the arrangement of events in their correct order. As history contains uncertainty, the chronology of particular events is up for debate. Terms used to describe the ebb and flow of history are change and continuity. **Continuity** refers to periods of time that are relatively stable in history with no major changes, whereas times of **change** refer to rich periods in history with significant events that alter the common practices of that time, often leading into a new era. When describing what has changed for a civilization over time, it is common to focus on political, economic, social, and technological aspects. For instance, the United States government was established in 1776 and continues today. This demonstrates a change at the beginning of the timeline related the United States, but since then, there has been political continuity as it has existed for roughly 250 years. Other aspects of life in this period may have experienced other changes, such as the innovation of electricity, steam engines, and automobiles. When a portion of time has relatively stable conditions such that it can be summed up by a common characterization, it is called a **period of time**; this process of summing up time into periods is called **periodization**.

## Civilization, City-States, and Empires

Since history is the study of recorded events throughout time, it is naturally tied to organized society with a developed language to record the events. The development necessary to record history generally coincides with early civilization. A **civilization** is a human society that has established complex means of surviving as a group. These **functions** are developing a food supply, a social structure, a shared language, a culture, and technology. The first known complex civilization is Mesopotamia, which was more easily developed due to its fertile farmlands, access to water through an available river. Mesopotamia is a good example of a **city-state**, which is essentially an independently sovereign city that does not depend on another government. Mesopotamia, as an early civilization, was the central hub and government in its region. The model of city-states still exists today, though they are often comparatively less significant in size and economy compared to other nation-states. Examples of modern city-states include Monaco, Vatican City, and Singapore. As the early civilizations continued to develop, they would eventually grow into **empires**, which are larger sovereign states with multiple territories, though they are usually governed centrally by a monarch or emperor.

## Interpreting Timelines

Timelines are a useful tool for visualizing the chronology of events as well as a great method to map out periods and view changes or continuity throughout history. Timelines can focus on either small or large ranges and can be multifaceted so that one period or type of event can be compared with another. A key element of a timeline is having a consistent interval mapped out. For instance, if we wanted to construct a timeline to map the events that happened for a single day, we would likely use hours to plot out the continuum. One might start the timeline at 12am and end the timeline at 12am the next night to show the picture of the entire day. Each event or period, such as sleeping, waking up, eating, going to work, and special occurrences can be marked on the timeline to plot out the day. If someone wanted to compare multiple days, these timelines could be lined up and compared and contrasted to find what is common to all days and what is unique. These same concepts can be applied to historical timelines as well. Instead of mapping just one day, one might consider mapping the events leading up to and throughout a particular war. The significance of events should change with the focus of the timeline. Seeing events plotted on a steady continuum of time can be very helpful in understanding the pacing of events throughout history.

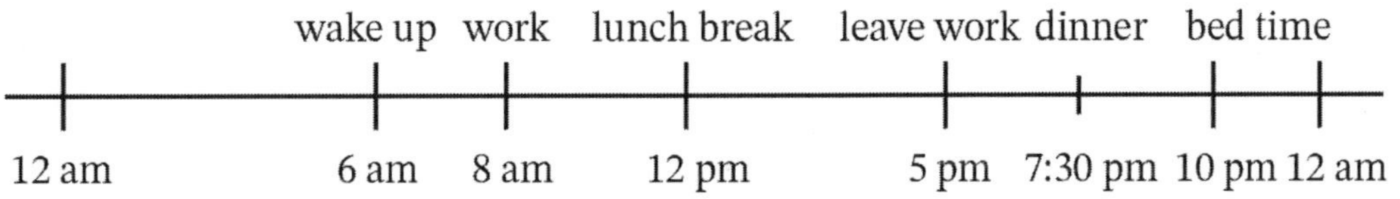


## Relationships Between Historical Events and Their Implications

As one aspect of society changes, it frequently proves to have significant effects on other parts of society. One of the easiest ways to see this effect is the innovation of new technologies. An example of a highly impactful technology is the printing press. Prior to this invention, all written documents had to be written by hand, which was time-consuming and costly. Books were very expensive and rare, which put the burden of education on mainly religious authorities and very wealthy classes of people. This new innovation allowed for more written works to be spread, which caused a need for literacy and education, ultimately evoking huge cultural and political changes. Technology tends to be a much quicker influencer of change in civilization, as it is sudden and can have dramatic impacts on how things are done. Cultural, political, and economic effects tend to move more gradually but likewise have strong effects that can change civilization forever.

## Primary and Secondary Sources of Historical Information

When studying history, it is important to consider the reliability, validity, and availability of sources of information. **Primary sources** are first-hand accounts of an event, such as a transcript of a speech, a recording, statistics, or a work of art. **Secondary sources** are indirect records, such as text books, newspapers, and other forms of reviews of the primary sources. Secondary sources of information can still be valid and useful, but are more open to **interpretation** and **bias**. Information from recent history, such as the election of a president in the 2010s is very reliable, as there are many sources of information that are in consensus about the objective event. Furthermore, many people still alive are primary sources since they were alive and witnessed the election. This is not true of less modern history, such as the election of Abraham Lincoln in 1860. There are still plentiful records of the information, but all witnesses to the election have passed away at this point. This event took place in an era where newspapers and legitimate documentation was widespread and available. The clarity and objectivity of sources are indisputable because they are so abundant. If, however, we only had political cartoons and election campaign brochures to go by, the reliability and accuracy of the information may be up for debate because the source materials are only secondary sources of information and are likely to contain biases. Generally, the further back in history one researches, the fewer sources are available due to lack of documentation, technological limitations, and language barriers. With fewer sources, and possibly conflicting information, historians must put together the most reasonable explanation of what took place during the period in question, given the amount of information available to them.

## Types of Sources of Information Used in Historical Research

- **Almanacs**—books that are published each year to express current information for consideration in the coming year. These often act as time capsules for that particular year and can give historians insight into economic and technological details of the time.
- **Encyclopedias**—resources that cover a variety of topics broadly for the purpose of giving the reader an overview. Wikipedia is an internet-based version of an encyclopedia that is useful for finding leads or obtaining general information about a topic.
- **Bibliographies**—a list of resources used in composing a scholarly work. These are usually primary and secondary sources that can be used to check an author's sources or to give leads on similar research. Similar concepts include works-cited pages and literature reviews.
- **Periodical Guides**—a series of publications over time, usually in the form of magazines or journals. These usually broach a more specific category of information, such as on research methods, psychology, or medical procedures, and are intended to help members of a particular field stay up-to-date with current research in their field.
- **Biographical Dictionaries**—a resource that contains a list of important names to know about the given subject and a description of how they contributed to the field. For instance, if one were interested in the Revolutionary War, a biographical dictionary would include information on each of the founding fathers and other significant individuals of the time.
- **Maps**—representations of land and territories that can display a variety of factors, including geographical features, political features, economics, demographics, and many more aspects. Digital maps can generally be manipulated to show multiple features at once.

## Uses and Limitations of Various Historical Source Materials

Historical source materials are a type of primary source material that offer historians the opportunity to study people, places, and events that occurred in the past. Unfortunately, there are limitations to what these materials can tell us. A limitation of **historical source materials** is that they may be biased by those who created them. For example, those who create historical documents such as letters may leave out details or exaggerate parts in order to make their points more convincing. Another limitation might be that some historical sources only provide evidence for certain points of view, as they were recorded by those with specific interests and perspectives.

- An **oral history** provides an account of an event that happened in the past, which is told by the person who was there when it happened. Oral histories are important because they allow us to learn about things that may not be written in books or recorded in documents.
- **Newspapers** are important source materials for scholars because they provide a detailed account of the past, which cannot be found in books or other sources. Newspapers are not always reliable as they may not be based on fact, while others might omit certain information or give undue weight towards one side of an issue at the expense of another.
- **Diaries** and personal **journals** can provide valuable information for historians because they are detailed histories of people's lives. However, the reliability of these accounts is always in question because they were created by just one person and aren't always written with the intention of sharing.
- **Artifacts** can be defined as objects created by humans, which can give hints at the peoples' material culture and intangible culture. Material culture includes things like buildings or furniture while intangible culture includes things like music or dance. The benefits of artifacts are that they can offer insights into how people lived in the past. They can also be used to shed light on the thoughts, feelings, fears, tensions, customs, rituals, and other social practices at that time.

- **Tax lists** and **census data** are useful sources of insight into how people lived during a certain time. They provide us with reliable information about the income, demographics, and beliefs of the people living in a particular time.
- **Personal correspondence** has been an important form of historical information for historians. It gives an insight into the lives and interactions of ordinary people. The main benefits of using personal correspondence as a source for history is that it provides an authentic portrayal of the author's thoughts and feelings during a time period or in response to significant events.

### Historical Interpretation and Biases

History is a discipline that relies on the interpretation of **facts** to create **narratives**. Due to the types and availability of sources, history tends to leave itself open to **subjectivity**. Often, this means that **biases** are introduced at either the source of information, the interpretation of the information, or at the explanation of the information. For instance, if the only **sources of information** about an event are newspapers, the author of these historical sources may have been biased, causing the **interpretation** of the actual events to be skewed from the start. Similarly, the person interpreting the source may have their own biases that they introduce or even **teach** to others in the process of communicating the historical narrative. Commonly described biases in modern interpretation of history generally revolve around sociopolitical issues such as Eurocentrism, popular political parties, economic biases, and cultural favoritism.

### Historical Revisionism

Historical revisionism is the act of reinterpreting a historical account through established historical methodologies. This is often done when new information is discovered or old information is reinterpreted in such a way that it warrants reconsidering the previously accepted history of an event or period. Historical revisionism is an essential and necessary process in creating accurate histories. Revisionism can, sometimes, be used incorrectly and in a way that leads to a less accurate interpretation of historical events. An example of this would be when the historical record is denied or deliberately distorted. This can involve using falsified records, purposefully misrepresenting the meaning of a piece of historical evidence, manipulating statistics, or unjustly denying the validity of historical evidence. A common example of this is Holocaust denial, which is an antisemitic theory that the Holocaust was either fabricated or greatly exaggerated.

## Social Science Classroom Management

### Overview of Classroom Management

- **Organization**—the state or manner of being organized
- **Discipline**—training expected to produce a specific character or pattern of behavior, especially training that produces moral or mental improvement
- **Procedures**—a set of established forms or methods for conducting the affairs of an organized body
- **Learner responsibility**—the student must have responsibility for their actions or non-actions
- **Interventions**—interference so as to modify a process or situation

**Review Video: Classroom Management - Rhythms of Teaching**
Visit mometrix.com/academy and enter code: 809399

## Instructional Approaches to Classroom Management and Student Motivation

- Model-based classroom management
- Concise and efficient instructions
- Developmentally and age-appropriate instruction
- Large (whole) group instruction
- Small group instruction

Be able to create and maintain an atmosphere that encourages questions, conjectures, problem-solving, and experimentation.

## Reteaching, Enrichment, and Extensions

- **Reteaching**—The act of teaching over again
- **Enrichment**—above and beyond the given
- **Extensions**—small add-ons that help in teaching

## Curriculum Components

- **Scope and sequence**—effective instruction focusing on the essential skills and concepts commonly found on standardized tests.
- **Curricular materials**—equipment and materials needed to teach a subject.
- **Learner objectives**—types and levels of objectives of what will be taught.

## Prior Knowledge

Prior knowledge is a combination of one's existing attitudes, experiences, and knowledge. Attitudes can range from beliefs about ourselves as learners or being aware of our own strengths and weaknesses. It can also be our level of motivation and responsibility for our own learning. The experiences from our daily activities, especially ones with our friends and families, give us a background from which we derive most of our understanding. Individual events in our lives provide us experiences we can draw from, both bad and good, and influence how we deal with future situations. This knowledge is drawn from a wide variety of things, from knowledge of specific content areas and the concepts within, to the goals that we have for ourselves academically.

## Using Computers to Better Manage the Classroom

Computers have revolutionized virtually every area of society, and teaching is no exception. Various forms of digitalization can significantly increase the efficiency of a teacher's ability to manage the classroom. Teachers can use the computer to do traditional paperwork and help free them from a number of tasks that are classified as noninstructional. A computer will not make a classroom a success by itself, and a teacher must know, like a business manager, what programs will do and how they are used. Teachers can use computers to:

- Keep student progress records, tests, and cumulative and average scores.
- Prepare individualized notes and observations for each student.
- Keep thorough records of attendance.
- Keep an inventory of supplies that include what quantities are available and where they are located.
- Generate tests and worksheets, as well as often grade them instantly. Students may also be able to take the test on the computer.
- Produce posters and calendars and generally provide more options for time organization.
- Appreciably increase communication between the teacher, parents, and their children.

## TEACHER PLANNING AND PREPARATION

Despite the status of the teacher's knowledge on instructional matters, he or she selects certain curricular content, makes decisions about groupings, and allocates specific time periods for activities. These are the crux of teacher preparation and planning. Teachers must turn curricular goals and related content into a plan that works; the planning may be informal, or it may be formal and explicit. This includes textbook and material selection, content strategies, learning assessments for particular pupils, scheduling lessons, and detailing instruction for particular days. A skillful teacher plans his or her school day before they ever enter into the classroom. Teachers have perceptions of the students' needs in different subject areas, but very little is accomplished if the teacher is hindered in their plans.

## QUESTIONING STRATEGY IN RECIPROCAL TEACHING

One of the surest signs of proficiency in a subject is the ability to teach the concepts that have been learned to others. Reciprocal teaching provides students with the opportunity to absorb the information that has been read or taught and begin summarizing, questioning, clarifying, and ultimately predicting the content that they read, as though they might have to teach it to someone else. Students first identify the kind of information significant enough for the substance of a question when those questions are first generated as they read through a text. They then ask this information in the form of a question and test themselves to find out if they might answer their own questions. The generation of questions is a flexible strategy insofar as students can be taught and encouraged to ask questions on a number of different levels. When students know before reading that they need to think of questions about the text, they then read while aware of the important ideas in that text. This helps increase comprehension, process the meaning, and make inferences and connections to prior information before forming a question.

## ORAL QUESTIONING IN CLASS

One easy way for teachers to conduct a formative assessment in class is to briefly quiz students on the material covered. Whether it is to be done for a grade or not, it is generally useful to give a brief overview of the previous day's lesson at the beginning of class. Oftentimes, this can be best accomplished by allowing students to articulate the material and to critique one another's understanding. Some probing questions from the teacher can ensure that the recent material is understood in the context of the material that has already been learned. It is not always necessary to formally grade students on their participation or performance in an informal question-and-answer session; the main thing is to develop an idea of the students' progress.

## FORMS OF ASSESSMENTS AND USING STUDENTS' WORK TO GUIDE INSTRUCTION

- Identify what students are doing correctly.
- Identify the concepts that your class is developing.
- Point out your students' misconceptions and errors.
- Identify appropriate measures of scoring aptitude.
- Figure out appropriate methods of remediation and acceleration.
- Know the appropriate uses of rubrics.

**Review Video: Assessment Reliability and Validity**
Visit mometrix.com/academy and enter code: 424680

## HURDLES STUDENTS FACE STUDYING AT HOME

The personal difficulties students have and priorities that compete with classwork have drastically changed as the world has become digitally saturated. The presence and ubiquitous nature of social media influences culture and mindsets in ways that society still does not fully comprehend. Students may have difficulties with homework because parents come home tired after a hectic day and are unable to properly monitor the students' assignments, or the parents are less familiar with the more modernized methods of teaching and assignments and become frustrated or apathetic—choosing to simply remain in ignorance rather than confront the unfamiliar territory. Oftentimes, the parents do not actually realize that their child is having a problem until they see that their child's grades are suffering. Students may also be involved in various extracurricular activities that vie for their time or suffer specific personal difficulties such as an unstable home life, a lack of adult role models, or drug problems.

## Strategies to Have Students Complete Homework Assignments

Teachers should make known their expectations early in the school year before the first piece of homework is ever assigned. Ensuring that the students clearly understand the rules of the classroom, the types of assignments they are likely to encounter, the methods and means for turning the assignments in, and how those assignments will be graded, can prevent much of students' confusions and frustrations. A written explanation of expectations helps to increase the chances of students successfully completing homework. In elementary school, as well as to a certain extent in junior high and high school, homework can teach students the fundamentals of working independently, as well as encourage self-discipline through time management and meeting deadlines.

Students should know:

- Homework is important and has meaning.
- Doing assignments or not doing them has consequences such as lower grades if the assignments are not done.
- Students need to be held to a high standard. Research has shown that students make better gains academically when teachers set high expectations and tell the students of their expectations. Students also should know how much and when homework will be assigned.

## Creating Assignments with Purpose in Completing Homework and Study Skills

Assignments that are given to students to complete outside of class should be given with a purpose rather than to provide busywork. If a student believes that the homework given is meaningful or beneficial to them, they will be more likely to consider it as something worth doing. While students may appreciate understanding an assignment's purpose, the purpose might not become clear until students are midway through the assignment or have completed it. The teacher should not just tell a student to read something or answer questions without knowing why they are doing it. Students should be shown the bigger picture of how their assignments fit in the realm of what they are studying, even though the student may not entirely appreciate the project's significance until it is finished or partially finished.

The following are some of the main purposes of homework:

- To review and practice what the students have learned for implementation in the future
- To prepare for exams
- To improve overall study skills by learning to use resources such as the library, reference material, encyclopedias, or the internet
- To explore subjects more deeply than time allows while in class

## Helping Students Better Understand and Study with Focusing Assignments

Assignments that are focused are less difficult for students to complete and understand. Assignments that try to reinforce an overabundant number of ideas are not likely to help a student learn. This is especially the case for students who have not yet developed abstract thinking to the point where they can successfully integrate many of the concepts. Assignments need not be a large, overwhelming dissertation about what it is the teacher expects. The assignment should stick to one issue or concept, and it should ask for maybe four or five examples. A teacher can easily determine if the students are comprehending what is being taught and if not, help can be given in studying for the objective. Focus and the appropriate background information are also important in class discussions of assigned readings because some children can become overwhelmed if asked to read too much at once.

## Helping Students Think Through While Studying with Challenging Assignments

Homework can give a student the ability to apply concepts that are beyond the controlled environment of a classroom. It can also help students collect and connect information from a variety of sources, subjects, and places. The best assignments challenge students to expand or break away from how they normally think. Such an assignment might combine two unassociated ideas. Assignments can range from listing what one finds in a desk drawer to writing paragraphs about family members. In those assignments, students can break the punctuation or capitalization rules in order to better learn the rules. Integrating topics also helps the thinking process, such as putting together an art, writing, and science class.

## Helping Students Study and Complete Their Work by Varying Assignments

If all assignments are alike, students are very likely to get bored. Mixing approaches and styles is one of the fastest ways to elicit change. All students will not be interested in a given assignment, but mixing it up creates better chances that some of the homework will be enjoyed by the students. Short-term assignments can help students practice and review material already covered in class. Long-term projects allow students to vary the pace of their work, get into subjects of interest to them, and to manage time and deadlines. Variety may also help keep teachers engaged and excited about the schoolyear and convince them to try experimenting with their approaches and styles.

## Enhancing Studying by Tying Assignments to the Present

Students may often feel that they cannot relate to assignments about events from long ago. It is hard to teach most types of history unless they are related somehow to the present, so assignments should draw comparisons between what is happening today and events years or centuries ago. For instance, students might approach an assignment on a Civil War battle by contrasting it with more modern battles. They might see the battle through the eyes of a television war correspondent who interviews the principal leaders and ask what they might do differently if they were to "do over" the battle. Students learn the specifics of such battles through these interviews and can appreciate the significance of the events that took place. This is a way of piquing interest in studying.

## Helping Students Study a Subject by Matching Skills, Interests, and Needs

The chances are greater that a student will complete his or her homework assignments if they:

- Are not too hard or too easy.
- Match children's preferred learning styles.
- Let students work on material that they really like. Assignments cannot be customized for every student. But teachers can give assignments to a heterogeneous class that varies in content, format and style. This will better the chance that all students will have some elements of the assignments that are of interest.

Teachers can give the students choices. The student may be expected to master all the same material, but it can be done in different ways. This helps the student feel they control parts of their learning, which encourages studying and helps them to enjoy an assignment that they otherwise might not.

### Test-Taking Tips Benefiting Intermediate Students

When it is time to take a test, the student should:

- Think positively about doing the best that he or she can do.
- Take some deep breaths and relax. Breathe slowly. Clear the mind of worries and anxious thoughts.
- Push his or her feet down on the floor to the count of five. Push them harder and hold. Relax and then repeat.
- Visualize by closing his or her eyes and picturing his or herself in a happy and peaceful place.
- Bring all materials needed for the test.
- Listen carefully to the directions and ask if they are not understood.
- Reread the directions carefully
- Look over the entire test to see what must be done before beginning.
- Determine how much time there is to spend on each question, allowing more time for essay questions.
- Skip difficult questions and go back later to answer those skipped.

### Carefully Reading Entire Test Items and All Answers for Elementary Students

Students should carefully consider each possible option or alternative before selecting an answer on an assignment or exam. It is common for a student to stop reading after determining that one of the answer choices is an acceptable answer rather than ensuring that they have made the best choice. Students should be encouraged to very carefully go over each question and pay particular attention to key terms. This information may be translated by the student into different forms, such as changing the question into their own words or substituting common words. They can use their knowledge to anticipate what an answer might be and to select an answer that appears similar to the one they predicted. These skills may be practiced in regular classroom activities.

### Importance of Checking Work When Taking Tests in Elementary Classes

It is worthwhile to instill into students the idea of checking their work after completion. Confirming that they have correctly answered each question to the best of their ability is an excellent use of any extra time a student may have after finishing an assignment or test. When they check their work, they need to ensure that the answers are correctly marked on the answer sheet and that the answers match the number of questions on the answer sheet. Students should have time to check and reconsider their work if time has been efficiently managed, and they should be encouraged to change answers when they think a better answer is appropriate. Students need reinforcement that their work should be checked daily. Teachers can do this by refusing to accept work until it is confirmed the work has been checked.

### Helping Achieve Positive Learning Outcomes from High Teacher Expectations

Most, if not all, teachers have high hopes for their students. However, some teachers may be better than others at consciously communicating those expectations. Others might unconsciously expect less of students who show little interest in learning or who have significant barriers to hurdle. But by holding all students to high standards, most teachers believe they can help students achieve their full potential. Studies do show that students tend to internalize beliefs teachers have about their ability. When students are not expected to make a lot of progress, they may tend to take on a defeatist outlook. Some students may think their teachers believe they are not capable of handling demanding assignments. Teachers must see themselves as responsible for finding ways to raise performance despite whatever circumstances the students face.

### Home, Cultural, and Parental Involvement

Many of the differences in academic achievement in children can be explained by the quantity and quality of reading materials in the home, the number of pages read for homework, the number of days absent from school, the number of hours in which TV is watched and social media is consumed, and the presence of two parents in the home. There are other environmental factors that impact academic acheivement. For instance, the activities in which children engage outside of school, such as reading storybooks, visiting libraries, or playing word games. Another factor is the potential difference between the home and school cultures. Culture is used in this sense as a broad term to include the behavior and attitudes of parents. If there is a wide gap between the home culture and school culture, children may perceive tasks like reading as unrewarding or devaluing their identity.

### Effect of Peer Influence on Learning

Peer influence on children's behavior, as well as on learning, is well recognized in psychological literature. Peer influence can operate both positively and negatively. Teachers will try normally to exploit the positive influence on peers and promote many of the learning experiences the children may have by organizing them into small groups in which they can become involved in learning. The negative aspects of peer influence are obvious when parents of children expect them to show interest in school work and spend time on homework, but many of the children's peers do not have the same goals for themselves. There may be times where it might become necessary to have a child discontinue his or her association with those peers who are negative influences.

### Literacy Problems Within the School System

There are various statistics that indicate that the overall literacy rates of students within the US school system are well below desired values. According to the Literacy Project in 2019, almost 65% of fourth graders did not read at a proficient level, and roughly 90% of children who were below average readers at the end of first grade remained that way by the end of fourth grade. There also appears to be at least some correlation between literacy and income, as over 80% of the fourth graders who were reading below the proficient level were from low-income families. While many solutions have been proffered, no major solution has been discovered to significantly reduce or eliminate this issue. To further complicate matters, recent studies have also shown that over 85% of juvenile offenders have difficulty reading. Debates over policy and methodology continue as no one-size-fits-all strategy has been determined to be effective at reducing overall illiteracy rates within the school system.

### Ensuring Literacy for Students of Lower Socioeconomic Classes

There are disagreements among scholars as to the nature of the correlation between a child's socioeconomic level and comprehension level in school. Some see a direct correlation, while others say the correlation is more in degrees. Most data shows that children who are from low-income families are significantly more likely to fall behind in reading. This typically compounds as those with poor literacy skills through school tend to maintain them into adulthood often resulting in lower paying jobs, which then continues the cycle of poverty. There are many debated reasons as to why certain children may not be excelling in school, but in order to progress effectively, one needs to have a good foundation, and that foundation is being able to read and to communicate.

### Improving School Literacy Levels

If a school performs poorly on assessments, they are sometimes required to adjust their entire curriculum. When such changes take place, there are many aims that are incorporated, much more than just a single program or a single type of instruction. These aims may include helping students' lifelong skills, improving the quality of teaching, and making sure all teachers recognize the role that language plays in learning. Another possible aim might be to include a set time for students to read, such as a literacy hour. The focus might include having staff mark all children's books for spelling and grammar as well as content, that all departments provide a glossary of subject-specific words for pupils, and that all departments would use a writing frame to provide writing structure for children in each subject.

### Impact of Family Background on Education

The exact nature of the impact parental education and socioeconomic status has on student achievement is unknown, although it does have an impact. Studies have found that parental education and family socioeconomic status alone are not necessarily predictors of how students will achieve academically. Studies have found that parental education accounts for about a quarter of the variance in student test scores, while socioeconomic status accounts for slightly more than a quarter. Other research indicates that dysfunctional home environments, low expectations from parents, parenting that is ineffective, differences in language, and high mobility levels may account for the low achievement levels among those students that come from lower socioeconomic levels. Other impacts that family culture has on a student's performance might include cultural dispositions that end up isolating a student from his or her peer group. One of the most reliable ways of addressing family or socioeconomic background is by increasing the student's awareness of their future, whether that be in education or a particular career path. Having the student start thinking about his or her future will help to set and achieve short-term goals that will naturally lead to their long-term goals.

### Negative Peer Influences of Learning

Students, teenagers specifically, look to each other to learn, and this sometimes brings about problems. Teenagers are growing and learning, and through this development, the students look to each other to acquire what their peers deem to be acceptable. In many instances, this may lead to inaccurate understandings. Teenagers purposely acquire knowledge sometimes that is unmistakably wrong and continue to use it in everyday situations. Some students are so influenced by their culture that, even though they are capable of speaking properly, they will not do so for fear they will not fit in with their peers. These students—who readily acknowledge that they have been taught formal language—choose to continue using slang because their culture has shaped them to do so.

### The Hispanic Culture in Reading Lessons for Elementary Students

One of the greatest ways to expand cultural intelligence and remove barriers of ignorance is to simply expose children to various cultures and highlight what makes them unique. The Hispanic population is the fastest growing ethnic population in the United States. In order to better incorporate Hispanic culture into lesson plans, teachers will likely need to intentionally implement new strategies to properly engage and inform students. Assigning students the task of researching and presenting famous Hispanic Americans in history, presenting videos with Hispanic speakers and Spanish vocabulary, or reading about major historical events in the formation of Hispanic nations are all excellent ways to celebrate and better understand Hispanic culture. It is imperative to make sure that classrooms have ample amounts of resources for children to properly explore and engage with various cultures and their traditions. Showing how culture influences society, from foods eaten to the names of cities, children are better able to comprehend and understand one another and the larger world around them.

## IEP

Special education teachers help to develop an Individualized Education Program (IEP) for each special education student. The IEP sets personalized goals for each student and is tailored to the student's individual needs and ability. When appropriate, the program includes a transition plan outlining specific steps to prepare students with disabilities for middle school or high school, or, in the case of older students, a job or post-secondary study. Teachers review the IEP with the student's parents, school administrators, and the student's general education teacher. Teachers work closely with parents to inform them of their child's progress and suggest techniques to promote learning at home.

### Observations Assessing Prediction Skills

Teachers observing students will at some point hear the language of prediction. Students might say, "I think..." or "I wonder if..." By observing, the teachers can view certain reading behaviors that students show. When observing students making predictions about fiction text, the teacher should look out for these reading behaviors:

- Do students look at the text cover and make predictions that are based on the title or illustration?
- Do students stop prediction-making while they are reading?
- When reading the text, do students make predictions based on clues from the illustration or text?

These behaviors should be observed for nonfiction text reading:

- Do students use headings or subheadings in order to make predictions?
- Do students use charts, graphs, illustrations, or maps to make predictions?
- Do students predict what is likely to be learned based on clues from the illustration or text?

### Effectively Using Paraprofessional Skills and Time

Especially with special education, teachers do not have enough time to meet all of the needs of every individual student in each classroom, and paraprofessionals are often sent into classrooms to help students with special needs. Regardless of the use, the roles and routines in which the paraprofessional is used need to be carefully and clearly laid out. Say the paraprofessional is in the classroom for reading a half-hour each day. It is important to consider the routines that could be put into place for that time period. One might discuss the benefits of the paraprofessional helping with readers who struggle. Also, one might plot the progress of students that are being helped by the paraprofessional. Ensuring that the paraprofessional is helpful to both the teacher and students and is not being pushed beyond the limitations of their expertise effectively manages the paraprofessional's skills and time.

### Establishing a Successful Learning Center

Effective classrooms have a combination of direct instruction, cooperative learning, independent practice, and learning center activities. Learning centers help play an important part in classroom management and should be established one at a time. Possible centers include a writing center, an alphabet center, a science center, a writing center, or various other centers, but these can always be changed to meet the students' needs. Clear rules and routines for using each center should be understood, and a chart should be posted at each center that indicates how many children should be in the center or what materials and equipment may be used. The center will likely need to be closely supervised at first, as teachers begin determining when children are able to work both independently or cooperatively.

### Curriculum Standards

Standards focus on developing coherency across grade levels, teaching for understanding, and relevancy of subject matter, helping courses to build upon each other in age-appropriate ways. This farsighted statement sets an excellent vision for what students should be learning. The standards are broken into ten areas within two broader categories. Process Standards, the first category, defines how students should "do" the content and how they should be able to use their knowledge. The second category, the Content Standards, deals with the content that students should learn.

### Controversy Over Teacher Expectations on Learning Outcomes

The original Pygmalion study gave teachers false information about the learning potential of certain students in grades 1-6 in a San Francisco elementary school. Teachers were told that one of their students had been tested and found to be on the edge of a period of rapid intellectual growth, but in actuality, the student had actually been selected at random and the tests were measuring how the expectations of the teacher towards a student can impact their success. At the end of the experimental period, some of the targeted students exhibited superior scores on IQ tests compared to those of similar abilities. The results led researchers to claim that inflated expectations of teachers for target students actually caused accelerated intellectual growth. A number of studies have since taken place, and some found technical defects serious enough to cast doubt on the original findings. Whether one accepts or doubts the Pygmalion study, educators and the public are very interested in the power of expectations affecting the outcomes of students.

### Effects of Higher Teacher Expectations Supplemented with Other Measures

High expectations may not be the magic trick needed to close achievement gaps, but raising expectations can make a difference when the effort is accompanied by a relevant and rigorous curriculum, adequate materials,current textbooks, effective teaching strategies, good classroom management, tutoring programs, uncrowded classrooms, and involved parents. It is likely the case that in life, as well as in teaching, there is a need for balance. Teachers should believe and expect that students can learn given time and hard work, and students must be convinced that the reward of an education is worth the effort. When students and teachers mutually understand and believe that success is obtainable and that it can only be obtained through consistent and intentional work, both students and teachers are significantly more likely to achieve their goals.

## Chapter Quiz

Ready to see how well you retained what you just read? Scan the QR code to go directly to the chapter quiz interface for this study guide. If you're using a computer, simply visit the online resources page at **mometrix.com/resources719/texeshist7-12** and click the Chapter Quizzes link.

# TExES Practice Test

Want to take this practice test in an online interactive format?
Check out the online resources page, which includes interactive practice questions and much more: **mometrix.com/resources719/texeshist7-12**

**1. Where was the first great human civilization located?**

a. Egypt
b. Greece
c. Mesopotamia
d. Samaria

**2. Which of the following was NOT an ancient Egyptian ruler?**

a. Anubis
b. Hatshepsut
c. Ramses II
d. Tutankhamen

**3. How did the Crusader army that went on the First Crusade differ from the Crusader armies that Pope Urban II envisioned?**

a. There was no difference. The people of Europe were accustomed to obeying clerical direction and eagerly joined the cause. They created an army that was primarily made up of faithful Christians from all social classes led by a select group of knights who were responsible for leading and training their armies.
b. There was no difference. The people of Europe obeyed clerical direction and stayed home to pray for the success of an army composed entirely of knights and other professional military personnel.
c. Pope Urban II had envisioned an army of skilled knights and professional soldiers; instead, men and women from all classes joined together to retake the Holy Land.
d. Pope Urban II had envisioned an army composed of faithful Christians from all social classes led by a group of select knights; instead, the army was primarily made up of knights and other professional military personnel.

**4. Which western European monastic order developed an early form of banking that helped make pilgrimages to the Holy Land safer for the pilgrims?**

a. The Knights Templar
b. The Knights Hospitaller
c. The Knights of Malta
d. The Barbary Corsairs

**5. Which early feminist work was written by Mary Wollstonecraft?**

a. A Vindication of the Rights of Woman
b. The Declaration of Sentiments
c. Frankenstein
d. The Awakening

**6. What is the historical significance of the Dome on the Rock's site to Jews?**

a. It is the traditional site of Jesus Christ's crucifixion and resurrection
b. It is located on Temple Mount, where the Second Temple previously stood and the traditional site of Solomon's Temple
c. It is the traditional site of Mohammed's ascent into heaven
d. It is the site of the founding of the Islamic religion.

**7. How did the Nile shape the Ancient Egyptian Empire?**

a. It provided a nonnavigable boundary for the Egyptian Empire.
b. It eroded land, creating natural harbors for Egyptian fishermen.
c. It routinely flooded, eroding the limited desert farmland.
d. It routinely flooded, leaving behind fertile silt that helped make large scale agriculture possible.

**8. In which country does a large part of the native, traditionally nomadic people currently live in large tents known as yurts or gers?**

a. Indonesia
b. Mongolia
c. Thailand
d. India

**9. Which of the following was NOT a tax levied on the American colonies by the British government in the 1760s and '70s?**

a. The Sugar Act of 1764
b. The Stamp Act of 1765
c. The Lead Act of 1772
d. The Tea Act of 1773

**10. To whom was the Declaration of Independence addressed and why?**

a. To the British Parliament because the colonists were opposed to being ruled by a king who had only inherited his throne and only considered the popularly elected Parliament to hold any authority over them
b. To the King of England because the colonists were upset that Parliament was passing laws for them even though they did not have the right to elect members of Parliament to represent their interests
c. To the governors of the rebelling colonies so that they would know that they had 30 days to either announce their support of the Revolution or to return to England
d. To the colonial people as a whole because the Declaration of Independence was intended to outline the wrongs that had been inflicted on them by the British military and inspire them to rise up in protest

**11. How did the ruling in *Marbury v. Madison* alter the Supreme Court's power in the federal government?**

a. It lessened it. The Supreme Court was concerned about the possibility of judges overturning laws enacted by voters through referendums and took away that power.
b. It increased it. The decision in *Marbury v. Madison* gave the Supreme Court its now traditional right to overturn legislation.
c. It increased it. The decision in *Marbury v. Madison* strengthened the Supreme Court's Constitutional right to overturn legislation.
d. There was no change. *Marbury v. Madison* was a case involving a president who was unwilling to obey laws enacted by his predecessor; there was nothing about the case or decision that would have more than a cursory connection to federal powers of government

**12. Which President of the United States changed the date of Thanksgiving from the last Thursday of November to the fourth Thursday of November?**

a. George Washington
b. Andrew Jackson
c. Abraham Lincoln
d. Franklin D. Roosevelt

**13. Which of the following is an example of historiography?**

a. An explanation of past treatments of an historical event.
b. A geographer using physical geography to explain historical events.
c. A historical treatise on a single aspect of a larger historical event.
d. Historiography is not a valid historical term

**14. Which of the following questions would most likely be asked by a historian concerned with the philosophy of history?**

a. What issues shaped the writing of Plato's Republic?
b. Should history be measured by changes in individual lives or by larger political trends?
c. Why were the religions of Shinto and Buddhism able to merge in Japan?
d. Should historians study modern primitive cultures as a means of learning about past civilizations?

**15. You are researching the Battle of the Bulge's Malmedy Massacre. Four potential sources offer conflicting accounts of one aspect of the event. Based on the principles of historical research, which source would be considered a primary source?**

a. Wikipedia
b. A newspaper article written by an analyst who synthesized the accounts of several surviving soldiers over the weeks following the massacre.
c. The account of a wounded survivor written immediately following the massacre.
d. One of your teaching colleague's lecture notes.

**16. Which of the following is considered to be the largest cause of death among Native Americans following the arrival of European colonists in North America?**

a. Wounds from wars with the European settlers
b. Wounds from wars with the other Native American tribes
c. European diseases
d. Exposure during the wintry, forced marches on which the European settlers forced them

**17. What is the historical significance of the Dome on the Rock's site to Muslims?**

a. It is the traditional site of Jesus Christ's crucifixion and resurrection
b. It is located on Temple Mount, where the Second Temple previously stood and the traditional site of Solomon's Temple
c. It is the traditional site of Mohammed's ascent into heaven
d. It is the site of the founding of the Islamic religion.

**18. What method did Johannes Gutenberg use to create printing plates for his printing press?**

a. Woodcuts – he had a team of apprentices carve each page out of wood plates.
b. Metal etchings – the letters were etched into specially treated metal plates which were then placed in special acid baths to create printing plates.
c. Moveable clay type - Gutenberg carved moveable type out of clay and would press the letters into hot wax tablets to create printing plates.
d. Moveable type – Gutenberg cast metal type through the use of molds in order to achieve the individual letters which were then loaded into composing sticks, which were then used to form printing plates.

**19. Which group(s) of people were originally responsible for selecting the members of the US Senate?**

a. State legislatures
b. State governors
c. State electors
d. State residents, subject to voting eligibility

**20. The Erie Canal is 363 miles long and connects which body of water to Lake Erie?**

a. The Mississippi River
b. The Hudson River
c. The Susquehanna River
d. The Lehigh River

**21. The telephone was a solution to which of the following problems with the telegraph?**

a. Telegraph lines were thick and difficult to maintain.
b. Telegraph messages could only be received by people who had specialized equipment.
c. Telegraphs could only relay one message at a time.
d. Telegraphs frequently broke down if subject to extended use.

**22. Why did each Incan ruler have to earn his own fortune?**

a. A tradition that all the wealth an Incan king accumulated during his reign would be used to house and care for the king's mummified remains.
b. A tradition that all of a deceased king's wealth would be added to the main Incan temple's treasury.
c. A tradition that all of a deceased king's wealth would be used to create a large public work in the king's memory.
d. A belief that the new king needed to prove his worth through conquest and adding to the royal treasury.

**23. How would this picture be most appropriately used?**

*Credit:* National Archives and Records Administration.
http://teachpol.tcnj.edu/amer_pol_hist/thumbnail297.html

a. As an example of a Suffragist picket sign.
b. As an example of American response to Versailles Treaty.
c. As an example of early American use of Biblical allusions.
d. As an example of an early American response to the German Nazi movement.

**24. What was the ancient Agora of Athens?**

a. It was the main temple to Athena, where scholars would go to give lectures and pray for wisdom.
b. It was the Athenian ruling body.
c. It was the city of Athens's main source of drinking water and a place where Athenian women traditionally gathered.
d. It was the name of the primary marketplace and also an important gathering center for Athenians.

**25. Who was Genghis Khan?**

a. The founder of the Mongol Empire
b. The leader of the Hunnic Empire in the 5th Century who led his people to attack into Western Europe.
c. The leader of the 19th Century Taiping Rebellion
d. None of the above

**26. Which of the following is NOT necessarily an example of an educator introducing his own bias into the educational process?**

a. A teacher only using materials and sources that he knows are reputable and declining to use unverified material in his lessons
b. A textbook author choosing to only use sources that place his favorite US president in a good light and his least favorite US president in a bad light
c. A teacher only using primary sources that he agrees with and ridiculing a student who provides a verifiable primary source that offers a conflicting opinion
d. An administrator only selecting textbooks that were written before a certain date to be included in classroom instruction

**27. Which of the following words can be defined as "a list of events organized in order of their occurrence?"**

a. Anachronism
b. Anno Domini
c. Chroma
d. Chronology

**28. Who was Lewis and Clark's guide?**

a. Pocahontas
b. Sacagawea
c. Squanto
d. Wauwatosa

**29. What was the standard government economic principle in the late nineteenth and early twentieth centuries?**

a. Laissez faire
b. Social Darwinism
c. Keynesian Economics
d. Monetarism

**30. What was the purpose of Lyndon Johnson's Great Society?**

a. To eliminate poverty and racial injustice in America
b. To erase the last vestiges of the Great Depression from the American economic landscape
c. To encourage economic prosperity through trickledown economics
d. To increase educational standards in the United States

**31. What were Woodrow Wilson's Fourteen Points?**

a. A list of reasons why women should not be given the right to vote.
b. A list of conditions to which France and Great Britain had to agree before the United States would enter World War I.
c. His plan for creating lasting peace in Europe after World War I
d. His plan for stimulating the economy and turning the United States into a major economic power.

**32. Which of the following American cities was not founded by people fleeing religious persecution?**

a. Plymouth, Massachusetts
b. Jamestown, Virginia
c. Boston, Massachusetts
d. Providence, Rhode Island

**33. Which of the following is not a skill that a student should have learned by the beginning of eighth grade?**

a. Identifying important events in the European exploration and colonization of North America.
b. Evaluating the relationships between past and present conflicts.
c. Identifying the reasons that the US entered World War I.
d. Creating a timeline.

**34. Which of the following is an example of providing a connection between history and economics?**

a. Using maps showing post-World War II migration patterns.
b. Using charts and maps to illustrate the growth of US cities.
c. Discussing the effects of weather on world history.
d. Discussing the role of food shortages and inflation in the Russian Revolution.

**35. Which economic crisis led to the creation of the SEC?**

a. The Panic of 1907
b. The Post World War I Recession
c. The Great Depression
d. The Recession of 1953

**36. What was the purpose of the Mayflower Compact?**

a. To create and enact a series of laws for the Pilgrims.
b. To create a temporary government for the Pilgrims.
c. To memorialize the Pilgrims' promises to raise their children according to their religious ideals.
d. To memorialize the laws under which the Pilgrims had previously been living

**37. What was Manifest Destiny?**

a. The idea that the United States was intended by God to expand to fill North America.
b. The idea that England was intended by God to expand its empire to fill the world.
c. The idea that England was intended by God to colonize the non-European world.
d. The idea that the United States was intended by God to spread democracy throughout the world.

**38. What was the purpose of the Marshall Plan?**

a. To rebuild Europe after World War I and strengthen the United States' Western allies.
b. To rebuild Europe after World War II and prevent the spread of Communism in post-war Europe.
c. To create jobs for US servicemen following World War II.
d. To build hospitals for wounded war veterans following World War I.

**39. Most of the earliest civilizations flourished in or near what sort of geographic feature?**

a. Mountains
b. Valleys
c. Oceans
d. Rivers

**40. Which of the following is a true statement concerning the Magna Carta?**

a. Its main purpose was to prevent the Church from increasing its holdings.
b. It created a system of majority rule in England.
c. It was meant to protect the rights and property of the few powerful families that topped the feudal system.
d. It was concerned with the rights of all Britons and frequently mentions the common people.

**41. Which statement is an accurate reflection of Mayan urban life?**

a. The Mayas were a sophisticated urbanized culture, whose people predominately lived in large cities.
b. The Mayas lived in urban communities, supported by a small number of highly productive farms.
c. Mayan cities were primarily used as religious centers.
d. Mayan cities were primarily used as government centers.

**42. What were Martin Luther's 95 theses?**

a. His charter for the Lutheran Church
b. Criticisms of practices in the Catholic Church
c. A document explaining his differences with other Protestant churches
d. Reasons why the Bible should be translated into popular languages.

**43. Which US Founding Father is credited with founding the Federalist Party?**

a. John Adams
b. Thomas Jefferson
c. Alexander Hamilton
d. George Washington

**44. Who were the Shoguns?**

a. Chinese military leaders
b. Japanese military leaders
c. Chinese religious leaders
d. Japanese religious leaders

**45. Which of the following is a true statement concerning the Iroquois Confederacy?**

a. It was a Confederacy of French fur trappers and settlers and members of the Iroquois tribes during the French and Indian War.
b. It was a group of seven Native American tribes who joined together to protect themselves against European incursions into their territories.
c. Its members were also known as the Five Civilized Tribes.
d. It made decisions through a democratic process.

**46. Which of the following was one of reasons that James Oglethorpe wished to found the colony of Georgia?**

a. To create an escape-proof penal colony in North America.
b. To create a refuge for England's "worthy poor."
c. To increase the Virginia Company's profitability
d. To build a new port city to aid in the existing colonists' plans for westward expansion.

**47. Which of the following is not a true statement concerning the beginnings of slavery in the Virginia colony?**

a. Slavery was established quickly as a means of securing a cheap source of labor.
b. Initially slaves could become free through converting to Christianity.
c. The number of slaves in Virginia increased as tobacco planters required a steady supply of labor.
d. Early Virginian slaves included both Africans and Native Americans.

**48. Why were the "Five Civilized Tribes" given that name?**

a. They had advanced military systems.
b. In recognition of the assistance they gave early European settlers.
c. They had advanced social and government systems.
d. They had formed a complex Confederacy dedicated to preserving peace amongst themselves.

**49. Who famously crossed the Rubicon in 49 BC?**

a. Julius Caesar
b. Cleopatra
c. Mark Antony
d. Marcus Brutus

**50. What was the basis of Edward Jenner's original smallpox vaccine?**

a. Liquid from chickenpox sores
b. Liquid from cowpox sores
c. Liquid from smallpox sores
d. Liquid from acne sores

**51. Which Japanese city was the first to be attacked with an atomic bomb?**

a. Hiroshima
b. Nagasaki
c. Nagoya
d. Tokyo

**52. Which of the following peoples did not practice a form of feudalism?**

a. The Norsemen (Vikings)
b. The Germans
c. The Persians
d. The Byzantines

*Refer to the following for questions 53–55:*

The United States' Constitution is the longest-lived written constitution in world history and has served as the model for the constitutions of other nations. Several factors contribute to its survival into the twenty-first century, the most important being the Constitution's simplicity and the built-in permission to amend it as necessary.

Simplicity gives the Constitution flexibility. In it, basic rules do not change but within these rules, laws and practices can and are modified to meet the needs of the people and the state. If the Constitution had specific rules and laws concerning dynamic forces such as the economy, it would have quickly become outmoded or obsolete as the United States came to face challenges and situations that the original framers could not have predicted. The Constitution's framers realized that they could not anticipate the future and so created a document that provided a basic framework of government that could be amended without being cast aside as new situations and needs arose. This ability to amend the Constitution aided the pro-Constitution Federalists in the fight to ratify it as they gained support with the promise of the Bill of Rights which soothed early concerns regarding the rights of man.

**53. Assuming that the above passage was from a student's essay, which of the following questions would it best answer?**

a. How is the US Constitution a simple document?
b. Why was the United States' Constitution used as a model for other countries' constitutions?
c. Which attributes have contributed to the US Constitution's longevity?
d. What was the Federalist Party's earliest public action?

**54. Which of the following is the best explanation of how the information in the above passage could be used in a class focused on a subject other than History?**

a. To describe the formation of the US Constitution in a government class.
b. To explain the basis of US law in a government class.
c. To explain why the US Constitution can be amended in a current events class
d. To describe attributes of the US Constitution in a government class.

**55. How could the information in the above passage be used to form a connection between history and modern government?**

a. To explain how Enlightenment ideas shaped American legal theory.
b. To explain why the Constitution's framers chose to create a basic framework for government rather than create a strict, unchangeable model.
c. To explain how the American two-party political system began.
d. To explain why it was necessary to have a written Constitution.

**56. Which of the following was a contemporary argument against The Bill of Rights?**

a. The concern that it didn't apply to the states.
b. The belief that a bill of rights would infringe upon states' rights.
c. The concern that specifically stating one right would create an argument against an unstated right.
d. The belief that the Bill of Rights would be too great a check on government's ability to function.

**57. What were the Federalist Papers meant to accomplish?**

a. To encourage people to join the Federalist Party
b. To explain the necessity of the federalist system
c. To assist in the ratification of the Constitution
d. To expose a series of scandals relating to the Federalist Party

**58. What was Franklin D. Roosevelt's "court packing" plan?**

a. A plan to influence court outcomes by packing the observation gallery with his own supporters.
b. A plan to prevent cases from coming to trial by filing a large number of other cases in order to create judicial gridlock.
c. A plan to keep Roosevelt surrounded by his own supporters to give him a greater impression of popularity.
d. A plan to appoint a second justice for every federal justice over the age of seventy.

**59. How did the invention of the cotton gin change the cotton industry in the United States?**

a. It decreased the amount of labor needed to grow cotton, thereby decreasing the demand for slaves.
b. It had no overall effect on the cotton industry.
c. It made Southern cotton plantations dependent on Northern textile factories who could use the gins to efficiently clean cotton.
d. It turned cotton into a viable cash crop resulting in cotton becoming a major Southern export.

**60. What was the purpose of the Sherman Anti-Trust Act?**

a. To prevent unions from striking
b. To prevent restraints on free trade
c. To encourage international trade
d. To prevent corporate tax evasion

**61. How were the Mexican-American War and the US annexation of Texas connected?**

a. Mexico had informed the United States that annexing Texas was the same as a declaration of war.
b. The Mexican War began as Texas's war of independence.
c. Mexico wanted Texas to remain independent as a buffer between itself and the US and declared war in hopes of halting the annexation.
d. There was no relation. Mexico did not care what Texas did.

**62. What did the landmark Supreme Court case, *Brown v. The Board of Education of Topeka* decide?**

a. That school busing was inherently Constitutional.
b. That the doctrine of separate but equal was Unconstitutional.
c. That racially separate educational facilities deprive people of equal protection under the laws.
d. That Plessy v. Ferguson was appropriately decided.

**63. Which of the following did not occur during or because of the French Revolution?**

a. The Reign of Terror
b. Economic crisis
c. The ending of feudal practices and slavery in France
d. The calling together of the Estates General

**64. Before 1854, which of the following countries had regular trading relations with Japan?**

a. The Netherlands
b. Great Britain
c. France
d. Italy

**65. Which of the following was a power granted to the US Congress under the Articles of Confederation?**

a. The power to collect taxes
b. The power to enter into treaties with foreign governments
c. The power to enforce laws
d. The power to regulate interstate commerce

**66. According to Plato's *Republic*, which sort of person would make the best head of state?**

a. A philosopher
b. A great general
c. An elderly farmer
d. A young noble, trained for rule from birth

**67. Which of the following was not an effect of the Neolithic agricultural revolution?**

a. The establishment of social classes
b. The building of permanent settlements
c. An overall increase in leisure time
d. All of the above were effects of the Neolithic agricultural revolution

**68. Which of the following US Constitutional Amendments lowered the voting age to eighteen?**

a. The 24th
b. The 25th
c. The 26th
d. The 27th

**69. Which of the following is an effect that mountains can have on a society?**

a. Acting as a source of food
b. Protecting the society from invasion
c. Providing a means of cultural diffusion
d. Providing a source of transportation

**70. Which statement is the best summary of the Monroe Doctrine?**

a. That European powers were not to interfere with the affairs of North America
b. That no European power could forbid the United States from trading with another sovereign state
c. That European powers were to not to interfere with affairs in the Western Hemisphere and that the United States would stay out of affairs in Europe.
d. None of the Above

**71. Who was the first President of South Africa to be elected in a fully representative South African election?**

a. Mahatma Gandhi
b. Thabo Mbeki
c. Kgalema Motlanthe
d. None of the above

**72. Which of the following events was a proximate cause of World War I?**

a. The Japanese bombing of Pearl Harbor
b. The assassination of the Austrian-Hungarian Empire's Archduke Ferdinand
c. The sinking of the RMS Lusitania
d. The British interception of the Zimmerman telegram

**73. Who was Boris Yeltsin?**

a. A Russian politician credited with breaking up the USSR
b. A Russian politician who was instrumental in the Russian Revolution
c. A Ukrainian politician who encouraged his country to break away from the Eastern bloc countries
d. A Scandinavian politician who successfully prevented his country from joining the Warsaw Pact

**74. Which of the following best describes The Truman Doctrine?**

a. The United States has the sole authority to assist other democracies located in North and South America.
b. The United States must not interfere with the internal struggles of countries outside the Western Hemisphere.
c. The United States must support free peoples who are resisting attempted subjugation by armed minorities or by outside pressures.
d. None of the above

**75. In 1955 the Soviet Union formed the Warsaw Treaty Organization to counterbalance which of the following?**

a. NAFTA
b. NATO
c. The U.N. Security Counsel
d. The Four Power Pact

**76. Which of the following was an advantage that the South held over the North at the beginning of the Civil War?**

a. Greater industry and capability to produce war materials
b. Larger population/more available manpower
c. Better railroad system
d. Better military commanders

**77. Which of the following was one of the ways that the Mormon migration was unique among the American pioneers?**

a. They transported an entire culture across the American West.
b. They traveled as highly organized companies.
c. They improved the trail, built ferries and, planted crops as a means of assisting those who would follow them
d. All of the above

**78. Which of the following was a long term effect of the New Deal?**

a. The end of the Great Depression
b. An increase in the role the federal government played in the US economy.
c. Decreased price supports for US farmers
d. All of the above

**79. Who was César Chávez?**

a. The leader of a movement to improve working conditions for migrant laborers.
b. A civil rights leader who worked to improve inner city conditions.
c. A civil rights leader who dedicated his life to immigration reform
d. None of the above

**80. Which of the following is not a result of the Civil Rights Movement's work in the 1950s and 60s?**

a. The government enacted legislation prohibiting racial discrimination in employment.
b. Disenfranchisement of African Americans was declared illegal.
c. Court rulings that segregation in schools violated the Constitution led to a near instantaneous desegregation of public educational facilities.
d. The government enacted legislation prohibiting racial discrimination in the housing market.

**81. Which of the following was an effect of industrialization in the United States?**

a. Large growth in city populations
b. A general shift from self-employment to being employed by others
c. Increased economic/employment opportunities for women
d. All of the above

**82. Which of the following were causes of The Dust Bowl?**

I. Wind erosion
II. Too many cultivated fields being left fallow at once
III. Severe droughts

a. I, II, & III
b. I & II
c. I & III
d. II & III

**83. Enlightenment principles signaled a departure from which of the following types of government rule?**

a. Monarchy
b. Democracy
c. Anarchy
d. Republicanism

**84. What was the first well-known American school of painting?**

a. The Boston Revolutionaries
b. The Savannah Art School
c. The New York Artists' Guild
d. The Hudson River School

**85. What does the Communist Manifesto claim makes up all of history?**

a. Battles between political ideas
b. Class struggles
c. Battles to control the means of production
d. None of the above

**86. In a market economy, what is the theoretical basis for the price of an individual good?**

a. Central Control
b. Supply and Demand
c. Cost Gouging
d. Income and Industry

**87. Which of the following is NOT a way that the Internet has affected worldwide economies?**

a. It made near instantaneous communication possible.
b. It caused an overall increase in the cost of transactions.
c. It increased consumer access to goods.
d. It increased the barriers to entry in retail situations.

**88. Which of the following was a method that the government in Nazi Germany used gain control of German children?**

a. Mandating membership in government sponsored youth organizations
b. Including propaganda in textbooks
c. Mandating activities scheduled to conflict with church services and interfere with family life
d. All of the above

**89. What was the purpose of John Locke's Two Treatises on Government?**

a. To support the results of the Glorious Revolution
b. To provide support for the American Revolution
c. To provide support for the French Revolution
d. To provide support for the Irish Revolution

**90. Which of the following could you NOT infer from the data presented below?**

Median US income by amount of schooling, in dollars
Source: US Census Bureau, Current Population Survey, Annual Social and Economic Supplements.

| Year | 9-12th grade, no diploma | High School graduate | Some College, no degree | Associates Degree | Bachelor's Degree or higher |
|---|---|---|---|---|---|
| 2007 | 24,492 | 40,456 | 50,419 | 60,132 | 84,508 |
| 2002 | 23,267 | 35,646 | 45,333 | 51,058 | 73,600 |
| 1997 | 19,851 | 33,779 | 40,015 | 45,258 | 63,292 |

a. Persons without a high school diploma receive smaller monetary increases in their income than persons with a high school diploma.
b. Increased education increases a person's earning potential.
c. Income generally increases over time.
d. A person with a bachelor's degree will make more money than a person with no diploma.

**91. Which of the following is the most appropriate reason to use audio-visual materials in the classroom?**

a. To fill time when the teacher is not prepared for a class
b. To give students additional insight into the forces that shaped the historical event you are studying.
c. To fill time when a substitute will be teaching your class
d. None of the above

**92. Which of the following was used as a justification for increased US military presence in Vietnam?**

a. France's defeat at the Battle of Điện Biên Phủ
b. The Gulf of Tonkin incident
c. The Fall of Saigon
d. The Geneva Accords of 1954

**93. Researching the history of levee building in the United States is most likely to also touch upon which of the following disciplines?**

I. Economics
II. Geography
III. Sociology

a. I only
b. II only
c. I and II
d. I and III

**94. Which of the following is a purpose of a research question?**

a. To determine if one's topic can be researched
b. To focus a broad research topic
c. To evaluate your research topic
d. None of the above

**95. After reading the journals of several citizens of your home town, you find that several of them share the same opinions on a topic. In your paper, you infer that most of the population shared this opinion. What is this an example of?**

a. Using your sources to create a generalization
b. Using your sources to identify a cause and effect relationship
c. Finding a main idea
d. All of the above

**96. A historian is researching daily life in your home town in the 1840s. What might he do to locate sources?**

a. Contact descendants of people who lived in your town to see if they have any records
b. Go to your home town's court house to see if land or court records are available.
c. Go to your home town's library to see if they have information about the town's history
d. All of the above

**97. In which of the following circumstances would it be appropriate to use a chronological view to understand history?**

a. When discussing the role of religion in ancient civilizations
b. When discussing cultural differences between civilizations in different climates
c. When discussing the US-Soviet race to the moon
d. When looking at the role of families in various civilizations

**98. Which of the following was NOT a cause of the First Crusade?**

a. Constantinople, the center of late-Roman, post-Roman and dark-age culture—and a major trading city—was being pressured militarily by the Muslim Seljuk Turks.
b. Christian feudal Europe was teeming with young men, desperate to prove their honor and valor according to the newly-developing code of honor. A move to war would allay the inter- and intra-national squabbling which was currently taking place throughout Europe amongst Christians.
c. The County of Edessa had been besieged and captured by Imad al-Din Zengi's forces.
d. A new religion had come to control Jerusalem, which the Church and Christian Europe saw as their own right.

**99. Which of the following documents would be most appropriate to determine a historical figure's personal opinion on an event in which he was involved?**

a. A biography written by a close friend of him or her.
b. The historical figure's personal journal
c. A biography written by a noted historian with a related specialty
d. Letters written by the historical figure's aide or assistant.

**100. Which of the following are topics that should be covered in a high school (grades 9-12) US history class?**

I. The Great Depression
II. The Jacksonian Era Indian removal
III. Cold War foreign policy
IV. Progressive era reforms

a. I, II, & III
b. II & IV
c. I, III & IV
d. I & III

# Answer Key and Explanations

**1. C:** The first great human civilization was the Sumerian civilization, which was located in Mesopotamia. Mesopotamia encompasses the area between the Tigris and Euphrates rivers in modern-day Iraq. It is also referred to as "the cradle of civilization" and includes part of the Fertile Crescent.

The Sumerian civilization is credited with being the first to practice serious, year-round agriculture. There is question over whether Sumer or Ancient Egypt was the first to have a written language. Sumerian writing began with hieroglyphics and then developed into a form of writing known as cuneiform.

**2. A:** Anubis was the Egyptian god of the dead, typically depicted as being half human and half jackal. Hatshepsut was an Egyptian queen who declared herself king while acting as regent for her stepson (who was also her son-in-law). She was the fifth pharaoh of Egypt's 18th dynasty. Ramesses (or Ramses) II was the third pharaoh of Egypt's 19th Dynasty, and he was Egypt's greatest, most powerful and most celebrated pharaoh. He is also traditionally considered to be the pharaoh of the Bible's Book of Exodus. His tomb in the Valley of the Kings was discovered in 1881. Tutankhamen was the boy pharaoh whose tomb was found in 1922, intact and untouched by tomb raiders, leading to a surge of popular interest in ancient Egypt.

**3. C:** Pope Urban II's plan for an army made up of previously trained military personnel was thwarted by the popular excitement concerning the First Crusade. This led to the creation of large armies primarily made up of untrained, unskilled, undisciplined, and ill- or unequipped soldiers, most of whom were recruited from the poorest levels of society. These armies were the first to set forth on the Crusade, which became known as the People's Crusade. Even though some of these armies contained knights, they were ultimately ineffective as fighting forces. These armies were prone to rioting and raiding surrounding areas for food and supplies and were viewed as a destabilizing influence by local leaders. They were defeated in battle and many converted to Islam to avoid being killed.

**4. A:** Knights Templar is the name by which the Poor Fellow-Soldiers of Christ and of the Temple of Solomon is more commonly called. The Knights Templar began as a small and impoverished order intended to serve as a fighting force in the Holy Land, but soon grew into a large organization and a favorite charity. As the Templars' resources grew, their operations did and their activities included the management of an early form of banking that permitted travelers to carry less money with them, making the travelers a less tempting target for thieves and increasing their safety.

**5. A:** Mary Wollstonecraft wrote *A Vindication of the Rights of Woman* in the late eighteenth century in response to contemporary events and practices. Wollstonecraft called for equality in education at a time when many people believed that women only required domestic education that would enable them to run households. *The Declaration of Sentiments* was a document addressing the rights of women; it was primarily written by Elizabeth Cady Stanton and then read to and signed by the delegates to the Seneca Falls Convention. *Frankenstein* was written by Mary Wollstonecraft's daughter, Mary Wollstonecraft Shelley. *The Awakening* was written by Kate Chopin and published in 1899.

**6. B:** The Dome of the Rock is the oldest existing Muslim structure and was built on the traditional site of Mohammed's ascent into heaven on Temple Mount. Before this, however, the Temple Mount was the site of the Jewish Second Temple which stood from the 6th Century BC until AD 70 when it was destroyed by Romans in response to a Jewish uprising in Jerusalem. The Temple Mount is also the traditional site of Solomon's Temple (also known as the First Temple) and its one remaining wall, known as the Western Wall or the Wailing Wall is an important Jewish shrine.

**7. D:** The Nile River was the lifeblood of the Ancient Egyptian Empire and is sometimes credited with being the reason this empire was able to become one of history's most stable societies. Its yearly floods replenished the soil by leaving fertile silt that made large scale agriculture possible in the land immediately surrounding the river. The agriculture provided Egypt with goods to trade, further enriching the empire. The Nile was also the center of Egyptian cultural and spiritual life. The ancient Egyptians believed that the pharaoh was responsible for providing the yearly floods as part of his role as the divinely appointed ruler.

**8. B:** The Mongol people have traditionally been nomads living in large white felt tents that are commonly known as "yurts" or "gers" and in Mongolia, many of these people still live in this traditional housing. The term yurt is of Turkish and Russian origins, while ger is the Mongolian term. The Mongol ger is designed, decorated and positioned based on a strict formula determined by religion, tradition, and superstition. Today the Mongol people are spread over the Asian steppe region including Mongolia, and parts of Russia, China Afghanistan and Pakistan.

**9. C:** The Sugar Act of 1764 raised import duties on goods which were not of British origin, including sugar, while reducing the import tax on molasses. The Stamp Act of 1765 was a tax of paper and printed products, intended to help the British government recoup some of the costs of the French and Indian War. It was extremely unpopular with the colonists and was repealed in 1766. Lead was one of the goods taxed under the Townshend Acts, enacted in 1767, but it did not receive its own specific tax act. The Tea Act of 1773 was another unpopular tax and led to tea boycotts and was the catalyst for the Boston Tea Party.

**10. B:** The Founding Fathers decided that because the colonies did not have the right to elect members of Parliament, Parliament should not pass laws for them. The Declaration of Independence recognized the British Empire's government as being headed by the King of England, under whom the various local parliaments and legislative bodies served to enact laws for the peoples whom they represented. By addressing their ills to the King, the Founding Fathers sought to prevent the appearance that they acknowledged the British Parliament in London as having any authority over the American colonies.

**11. B:** *Marbury v. Madison* started with the election of Thomas Jefferson as third President of the United States. The lame-duck Congress responded by issuing a large number of judicial patents, which the incoming president and Secretary of State refused to deliver to their holders. Marbury, who was to receive a patent as Justice of the Peace, sued to demand delivery. What makes this case important is the decision which declared the judiciary's ability to overturn legislation that conflicted with the Constitution. The case states:

"It is emphatically the province and duty of the judicial department to say what the law is. Those who apply the rule to particular cases must, of necessity, expound and interpret that rule. If two laws conflict with each other, the courts must decide on the operation of each.

"So if a law be in opposition to the Constitution; if both the law and the constitution apply to a particular case, so that the court must either decide that case conformably to the law, disregarding the Constitution; or conformably to the Constitution, disregarding the law; the court must determine which of these conflicting rules governs the case. This is of the very essence of judicial duty.

"If, then, the courts are to regard the Constitution, and the Constitution is superior to any ordinary act of the legislature, the Constitution, and not such ordinary act, must govern the case to which they both apply."

Later, the ruling states: "The judicial power of the United States is extended to all cases arising under the Constitution." It was in this way that the Supreme Court achieved its now traditional ability to strike down laws and to act as the final arbitrator of what is and is not allowed under the US Constitution.

**12. D:** Abraham Lincoln issued the Thanksgiving Proclamation on October 3, 1863, in which he specified the last Thursday of November as a day of thanksgiving. The last Thursday in November was the traditional date for the Thanksgiving holiday for the next 76 years.

In 1939, President Roosevelt tried to change the holiday's date from the last Thursday in November to the second to last Thursday in November in order to stimulate the economy by creating a longer Christmas shopping season. This action met with resistance in some parts of the country, and a compromise was reached in 1941, setting the date of Thanksgiving as the fourth Thursday in November.

**13. A:** Historiography can be described as the study of the study of history. It is a term used to describe the entire body of historical literature, the writing of history and the critical examination of past historical writings and historical sources. A typical historiographic essay will be a critical look at the past historical research whether it is a broad look at the study of history as a whole or of a specific subject that is being analyzed.

**14. B:** The philosophy of history is concerned with the ultimate significance of history as a field of study and asks questions concerning how history should be studied, including what social unit is correct to use when studying history—whether it is more important to look at the individual lives of ordinary people or to concentrate on the so-called big picture, looking at the overall trends in a society or culture; only giving personal treatment to people, such as George Washington, who had particular significance to the events surrounding them. The philosophy of history also looks for broad historical trends and progress.

**15. C:** A primary source is a first-hand account that is written by someone directly involved in the event being described. Sources like Wikipedia or a colleague's lecture notes would be considered either secondary or tertiary sources. While a newspaper article by an analyst written weeks following the massacre might cite primary sources (like the interviews from the soldiers who were in the massacre), it is not itself a primary source.

**16. C:** While wounds from war most certainly killed more than a few, European disease laid waste to vast swaths of Native American people who had no immunity to the foreign diseases which the Europeans carried. The forced marches took place in the mid-19th century under Andrew Jackson's presidency and are thus removed from the time frame in question.

**17. C:** The Dome of the Rock is the oldest existing Muslim structure, the shrine having been completed in AD 691. The rock in question is the traditional site for Mohammed's ascent into heaven accompanied by the angel Gabriel and documented in the Koran. The Dome of the Rock is a shrine for Muslim pilgrims and non-Muslims have commonly been barred from visiting the monument. The most recent ban lasted from 2000 to 2006. The religion of Islam was founded in Mecca, which is located in present-day Saudi Arabia.

**18. D:** Gutenberg's press used moveable metal type which he formed casting a metal alloy into molds made for each character. These individual pieces were then organized by letter. The letters were loaded into composing sticks that were then loaded into a metal form to create printing plates. As the printing press spread across Europe, printers began using woodcut prints to include illustrations in their products. While Gutenberg is generally given credit for the invention of moveable type, in the 1040s Pi Sheng, a Chinese inventor and alchemist, created moveable type using clay characters which were then pressed into wax-coated plates for printing.

**19. A:** The US Constitution, Article I, Section 3 states that: "The Senate of the United States shall be composed of two Senators from each state, chosen by the legislature thereof, for six years; and each Senator shall have one vote." This was the practice until the Seventeenth Amendment was ratified on April 8, 1913. The Seventeenth Amendment states that US Senators are to be elected by the people of the states which they serve and that the state executive branches may appoint replacement Senators if a Senate seat becomes vacant mid-term, until the state legislature can arrange for a popular election.

**20. B:** The Erie Canal opened in 1825 and created a water route between the Hudson River and Lake Erie. Water routes have historically been cheaper and easier than overland ones and the Erie Canal was originally proposed in the 1700s as a means of providing a shipping route to assist in settling the areas west of the Appalachian Mountains. The Mississippi River is to the west of the Great Lakes; its source is in Minnesota and it discharges into the Gulf of Mexico approximately 100 miles downstream of New Orleans, Louisiana. The Susquehanna River runs through New York, Pennsylvania, and Maryland and is the home of Three Mile Island, the site of the United States' largest nuclear disaster. The Lehigh River is located in eastern Pennsylvania.

**21. C:** The telegraph was a gigantic leap forward in the realm of communications. Before the telegraph, messages could take days, weeks, or months to reach their intended recipient, based upon the distance that they had to travel. The telegraph allowed people to send messages through use of electric signals transmitted over telegraph wires, allowing for instantaneous communications. The main drawbacks to the telegraph included the need to "translate" the message into and out of the appropriate telegraphic code and that the telegraph could only relay one message at a time. In contrast, the telephone allowed for spoken communication between people at different locations, increasing the efficiency and speed as the people on each end of the conversation could communicate multiple messages quickly and in one telephone conversation.

**22. A:** The Incan civilization was very wealthy and the Incan rulers' individual wealth was used to care for their mummified remains following their deaths in order to emphasize the king's divinity as descendants of the Incan sun god Inti. When an Incan king died not only would his wealth be used to care for his remains, there would also be human sacrifices as the king's servants and favorite wives would be sacrificed so that they could continue serving him in the afterlife.

**23. A:** This picture was taken outside of the White House in 1918 and could be used to show students an example of a woman picketing as part of the fight to win the right to vote. In 1917, Alice Paul had begun organizing her followers into groups in order to picket the White House with signs intended to embarrass President Woodrow Wilson into supporting women's right to vote. These picketers did so at their own peril as many were arrested on charges of obstructing traffic. Those who were convicted served sentences at a local workhouse where they were subject to harsh conditions, including force-feedings.

**24. D:** Besides being Athens' primary marketplace, the Agora also served as a central point where ancient Athenians would go to meet friends, conduct business, discuss ideas and participate in local government. While most ancient Greek cities contained agorés, the Athenian Agora was particularly known for its intellectual opportunities. Socrates, Plato and Aristotle were all known to frequent the Athenian agora. The Athenian Agora is also credited with being the birthplace of democracy. The ancient Athenian democracy allowed all citizens the opportunity to vote on civic matters and serve on juries.

**25. A:** Genghis Khan, also spelled Chinggis Khan, was the son of a minor Mongol chieftain, born circa 1162 AD. His birth name was Temujin and he grew up in poverty, but gradually built his own power base to include a confederacy of Mongol clans. He was named Genghis Khan, or universal ruler, in 1206. Attila the Hun was the 5th Century Hunnic leader who led his people to attack into Western Europe, going as far as Gaul (modern day France). The leader of China's 19th Century Taiping Rebellion was Hong Xiuquan, also known as Hong Houxiu.

**26. A:** Bias is a form of prejudice, and a historical work is considered biased when it is unreasonably shaped by the author's personal or institutional prejudices. It is wise for a teacher to choose material that comes from reputable sources and to verify that all material used in classroom presentations is reliable and appropriate. As long as the teacher is willing to do these things and show a variety of historical opinions, this is not an example of bias.

**27. D:** Chronology can be defined as a list of events organized in order of their occurrence.

An anachronism is a chronological error; something or someone who appears out of order chronologically. Anachronisms are frequently seen in popular entertainment dramatizations of historical events. Anno Domini is a Latin term meaning "in the year of [Our] Lord," more frequently seen as the abbreviation A.D. (e.g., "the Battle of Hastings was fought in A.D. 1066."). Chroma is a word used to describe color.

**28. B:** Sacagawea acted as Lewis and Clark's guide during their exploration of the Louisiana Purchase. She had been separated from her family at a young age and was reunited with her brother on the course of the expedition. Pocahontas was the daughter of Powhatan, the leader of the Algonquian tribes at the beginning of the 17th Century when the colony of Jamestown was founded in modern-day Virginia. Squanto's actual name was Tisquantum. He was the Native American who helped the Pilgrims after their first winter in Massachusetts. Wauwatosa is a suburb of Milwaukee, Wisconsin.

**29. A:** The idea behind *Laissez-faire* was to leave the market alone and let it take care of itself with minimal government intervention. Opponents of this policy often blame it for causing the situation which led to the Great Depression while supporters claim that it was an increase of government interference in the market that led to the Great Depression. Social Darwinism is the idea that the fittest members of society will rise to the top and flourish. Keynesian Economics advocates that the government should use its powers to stabilize the economy through raising and lowering interest rates and creating demand through government spending, frequently leading to deficit spending. Keynesian economic theory is chiefly concerned with macroeconomic trends and short-term solutions. It's founder, John Maynard Keynes, was quoted saying, "[i]n the long run, we are all dead."

Monetarism is an economic school of thought that concentrates on macroeconomic principles and long-term solutions to economic problems. An economist supporting this policy would be in favor of policies that are monetarily neutral in the long term but are not neutral in the short term.

**30. A:** Lyndon Johnson became president following the assassination of John F. Kennedy on November 22, 1963. The Great Society was a series of social programs implemented under the direction of Lyndon Johnson. The Great Society's goal was to eliminate poverty and racial injustice in America. The Great Society began with economic reforms including a tax cut and the creation of the Office of Economic Opportunity. From there, it grew to include the enacting of laws creating the Medicare and Medicaid systems to assist the elderly and poor with their health care costs, respectively. Educational and Housing reforms followed.

**31. C:** Woodrow Wilson's Fourteen Points were set forth in a speech that he gave to a joint session of Congress on January 8, 1918, approximately 10 months before the end of World War I on November 11, 1918. These points set forth his plan for the creation of a lasting peace in Europe. They included open diplomacy; free trade; allowing the peoples of Europe the benefits of self-determination; adjustments of European borders, including the creation of an independent Polish state; and the creation of a coalition that became the League of Nations.

**32. B:** Jamestown, Virginia was originally founded and settled by members of the Virginia Company of London, chartered by King James I of England. The Virginia Company was a profit-making venture and the first settlers of Jamestown were instructed to search for gold and a water route to Asia. Plymouth, Massachusetts was founded by the Pilgrims in 1620. Boston, Massachusetts was founded by the Puritans in 1630. The Pilgrims and Puritans were fleeing religious persecution in England. Providence, Rhode Island was founded in 1638 by followers of Roger Williams, a former Puritan leader, and his followers who had been exiled from Massachusetts due to their break with the Puritans.

**33. C:** Identifying the reasons that the US entered World War I is most appropriate for high school students studying US History. Important events in the European exploration and colonization of North America, evaluating the relationship between past and present conflicts, and creating and interpreting timelines are all lower level skills.

**34. D:** Using maps to show post-World War II migration patterns or using charts and maps to illustrate the growth of US cities would be examples of using appropriate visual aids in teaching history. Discussing the effects of weather on world history would be an example of connecting history with geography. Food shortages and inflation are both connected to economic conditions and discussing their destabilizing influence as a contributing factor to the Russian Revolution in 1917 would be an example of connecting history and economics.

**35. C:** The Great Depression began with the 1929 Stock Market Crash on Thursday, October 24, also known as Black Thursday. This crash was the beginning of a market collapse that continued as investors began panicking and banks began to fail. The crash was due to rampant stock speculation and fraud. Many people had invested in the belief that the Stock Market could only go up, and unscrupulous people had taken advantage of this by creating sham companies or artificially pumping up stock shares. The SEC, or Securities and Exchange Commission, was created in 1934 to regulate stock exchanges.

**36. B:** The Pilgrims' initial intention had been to settle in Northern Virginia where England had already established a presence. As there was no government in place in New England, some Pilgrims believed that they had no legal or moral duty to remain with the Pilgrims' new colony which needed their labor and support. Because of this, the Mayflower Compact created a government in New England and was signed on board the Mayflower on November 11, 1620 by each of the adult men who made the journey. The Compact's life was relatively short, due to its being superseded by the Pierce Patent in 1621 which had been signed by the king of England and had granted the Pilgrims the right of self-government in Plymouth. In spite of its short lifespan, the Mayflower Compact is credited with being North America's first constitution.

**37. A:** Manifest Destiny was the idea that the United States was intended by God to expand to fill North America. There were various ideas on what this meant, yet at minimum it was the belief that the United States should expand to the Pacific Ocean. At maximum, it was the belief that the United States should expand to fill North America and South America. The idea behind why the United States should expand through greater territorial acquisitions was to expand the American ideals of freedom, democracy and self-government.

**38. B:** The Marshall Plan was the popular name for the European Recovery Program, named after Secretary of State George C. Marshall. Marshall had originally proposed the Plan as a solution to the widespread inflation, unemployment, food shortages and general lack of resources following World War II in a commencement speech at Harvard University in 1947. As enacted, it was intended to provide a solution to these problems and to prevent the spread of communism by decreasing Soviet influence.

**39. D:** Early civilizations flourished alongside rivers such as the Nile in Egypt, the Euphrates in Mesopotamia, and the Yellow River in China. Besides providing the ancient settlers with a water source, these rivers also provided the land with the rich and fertile silt that the rivers deposited during their regular flooding cycles, making large scale agriculture possible for the ancient peoples.

**40. C:** The original Magna Carta, signed by King John on June 15, 1215, was meant to protect the rights and property of the few powerful families that topped the feudal system. Its primary purpose was to force King John to recognize the supremacy of ancient liberties, to limit his ability to raise funds and to reassert the principle of due process. The majority of the English population at that time was mentioned only once, in a clause concerning the use of court-set fines to punish minor offences. The last clause, which created an enforcement council of tenants-in-chief and clergymen would have severely limited the king's power and introduced the policy of 'majority rule.' However, the time was not yet right for the introduction of majority rule. In September 1215, three months after the signing of the Magna Carta, Pope Innocent III, at John's urging, annulled the "shameful and demeaning agreement, forced upon the king by violence and fear." A civil war broke out over this, which ended when John died the following year, in October 1216.

**41. C:** Even though the Maya were one of the two cultures to develop an urban civilization in a rain forest, their culture was predominately based upon rural life. Cities were primarily used as religious centers while day-to-day life usually centered around farming in the surrounding rainforest. Due to the rainforest land's relative infertility, Mayans used slash and burn agriculture methods that required them to move to new farming plots every two to seven years. Under these conditions it took a large amount of land to support even one family.

**42. B:** The 95 Theses were part of a letter of protest that Martin Luther wrote to his archbishop in 1517, when Luther was a monk in the Catholic Church. These theses criticized church practices, particularly the practice of selling indulgences. Some sources claim Luther nailed this document to the door of the All Saint's Church in Wittenberg (located in modern-day Germany). Luther's intention was to reform the Catholic Church from within, but his letter soon placed him at the center of a religious and civil revolt. He was excommunicated in 1520.

**43. C:** Alexander Hamilton was the Founding Father who is credited with founding the Federalist Party. Hamilton was a proponent of the idea that the young country required the support of the rich and powerful in order to survive. This party grew out of Hamilton's political connections in Washington and was particularly popular in the northeastern United States. John Adams was a member of this party. George Washington's personal beliefs were most closely aligned with the Federalist Party, but he disliked political parties and refused to become a member of one.

Thomas Jefferson was the founder of the Democratic-Republican Party.

**44. B:** The Shoguns were Japanese military leaders. During the Tokuwaga shogunate, which began in 1603, the shogun held the actual power in the Japanese government even though Japan was technically ruled by an emperor. In actuality, the emperor was primarily a ceremonial leader and access to him was restricted to members of the shogun's family.

**45. D:** The Iroquois Confederacy was a participatory democracy made up of Native American tribes in what is now the Northeastern United States. Each of the member tribes were permitted to send male representatives selected by the tribe's female members to the Confederacy's main counsel where each representative was permitted to vote on matters affecting the tribes. The beginnings of the Iroquois Confederacy are disputed, but it is accepted that the Confederacy was originally made up of the Mohawk, Seneca, Onondaga, Cayuga, and Oneida tribes; the Tuscaroras joined the Confederacy in 1722. The Confederacy was formed with the intention of decreasing intertribal violence and encouraging peaceful resolution of differences between the tribes.

**46. B:** James Oglethorpe was a philanthropist who wanted to give England's "worthy poor" the opportunity to prosper away from the highly stratified class structure in England. The original idea was to include people released from debtors' prison among the colonists, though none of the original 114 colonists were debtors just released. Oglethorpe's intention was to create a classless society so that Georgia would not develop the same problems that had plagued England. Oglethorpe was one of the original colonists, even though the colonial charter prohibited him from profiting from the colony and was frequently referred to as the colony's "resident trustee."

**47. A:** The historical evidence shows that the initial workers on tobacco plantations in Virginia were primarily indentured servants who would eventually receive their freedom. The path to slavery in its later forms was gradual, beginning with slavery as a form of punishment for legal infractions. Massachusetts became the first colony to legalize slavery in 1641, followed by other states, including Virginia. This was followed by laws declaring that any children born to a slave mother would be slaves themselves in 1662 and a later decision that all persons who were not Christians in their "native country" would be slaves in 1705.

**48. C:** The term Five Civilized Tribes came into use during the middle of the 19th Century as a means of referring to the Creek, Cherokee, Choctaw, Chickasaw, and Seminole tribes, each of whom had developed complex social and government systems including written constitutions, judicial, legislative and executive systems, complex agriculture practices and the establishment of public schools.

**49. A:** In 50 BC, Julius Caesar was called back to Rome by the Roman Senate in order to stand trial for treason and corruption. When he reached the Rubicon, he decided to ignore Roman Law and the Mos Maiorum (uncodified tradition with nearly the force of law), and instead took one legion to Rome with him, famously uttering the words "the die is cast." This was the beginning of a chain of events that led to the creation of the first Roman triumvirate and the transition of Rome from a Republic to an Empire, with Julius Caesar as "Perpetual Dictator," until his murder in the Senate. His adopted son Octavius (later taking the regnal name "Augustus") eventually became the first emperor.

**50. B:** Edward Jenner's initial smallpox vaccine was comprised of liquid from a young milkmaid's cowpox sores. Jenner was a country doctor who had noticed that persons who had suffered from the relatively mild disease of cowpox did not later catch the much more serious and deadly smallpox. At this time, the main preventative measure against smallpox was to inoculate healthy people with the liquid from smallpox sores from those who had mild cases of smallpox. Unfortunately, this practice often lead to healthy people having full blown cases of smallpox that resulted in death. Jenner's belief was that if he could inoculate someone with the liquid from cowpox pustules, they would then be immune from smallpox without the risk of contracting a full case of smallpox. In May 1796, Jenner diagnosed a patient, a milkmaid named Sarah Nelmes, with cowpox and received permission from a local farmer to inoculate the farmer's son James with cowpox, and then expose him to smallpox. Jenner made two cuts on James's arms and poured liquid from Sarah Nelmes's sores on them before binding the wound. James came down with a mild case of cowpox six weeks later, after James was well again, Jenner exposed him to smallpox, which the young boy did not contract. Jenner conducted further tests and in 1798 he published his findings in a report which introduced the words vaccination (adapted from the Latin word for cow).

**51. A:** Hiroshima had an atom bomb detonated over it on August 6, 1945, officially beginning the atomic age; Nagasaki was bombed three days later. Both cities were selected for atomic bombing because they had not been previously bombed during the war.

**52. A:** Feudalism was a common practice during the Middle Ages, popular as a means of providing social structure and for maintaining the established government and social order. It was most widespread and systemic in Europe but also practiced in other parts of the world including Persia and the Byzantine Empire. The Norsemen of what is now known as Scandinavia, however, were an exception to European feudalism and lived in a fairly egalitarian society where rank was strongly based on personal merit. This is not to say that the Norsemen were entirely opposed to the class delineations of feudalism; when the French King Charles the Simple ceded to them the land that became the province of Normandy, the Norsemen who settled there settled into a feudalistic structure that their descendants took with them to England during the Norman Conquest, where the feudal system was used to assist with subduing the newly-conquered English people.

**53. C:** The passage describes the reasons why the Constitution has managed to last for over two hundred years and would be an appropriate part of an essay answering question C. It might also be an appropriate part of an essay answering questions A or B, but because this passage directly deals with the Constitution's longevity C is the best answer. The Federalist Party was a distinct group from the Federalists who supported the ratification of the Constitution.

**54. D:** The passage could be best used to describe the attributes of the US Constitution in a government class. The passage does not go in-depth into the formation of the Constitution, the basis of US law or why the US Constitution can be amended.

**55. B:** The passage describes the reasons the US Constitution has survived for so long, including the fact that it provides a set of basic rules but allows amendment so that it can be altered as new situations arise.

**56. C:** The people who were opposed to the idea of having a bill of rights in the Constitution were primarily concerned that by specifically enumerating a set of rights, that there would be an argument that the rights not listed did not exist or were not important. The Bill of Rights did not initially apply to the states even though there was some concern that the states were more likely to infringe upon individual liberties than the federal government.

**57. C:** The Federalist Papers were written and published anonymously by John Jay, Alexander Hamilton, and James Madison as part of their effort to ratify the Constitution. There are 85 letters in total and they were meant to convince normal Americans that they should support the Constitution by explaining what it meant and what it was intended to accomplish.

**58. D:** The New Deal met with conservative opposition, especially in the Supreme Court, whose conservative justices frequently blocked New Deal legislation. The plan that was dubbed the "court packing" plan was to appoint a second justice for every justice over the age of seventy. Because all of the conservative justices on the Supreme Court were over seventy, this would have given Roosevelt the ability to appoint enough justices to swing the Court to his favor. However, this plan was met with extreme popular disapproval which led to its eventual abandonment.

**59. D:** Eli Whitney's cotton engine (or gin) was designed to aid in the cleaning of American cotton. Before this invention, cleaning American short-staple cotton was a long and tedious process as all the cotton seeds had to be removed from the cotton by hand, usually by slaves. Whitney's invention could clean more cotton than an individual person could, thereby increasing cotton's profitability and turning it into a cash crop. As cotton became a viable cash crop, the amount of land dedicated to its cultivation increased, as well as the number of laborers needed to work in the cotton fields, which resulted in an overall increase in the number of slaves held in the southern United States. As cotton production increased, cotton also became a major Southern export as textile mills in both the northern United States and Europe became dependent on Southern cotton.

**60. B:** The Sherman Anti-Trust Act of 1890 was enacted in response to the growth of large monopolies in the period following the end of the Civil War. While its purpose was to prevent restraints on free trade, it was not strictly enforced. Additionally, the wording was vague enough that it was also used to break up labor unions. It was replaced by the Clayton Antitrust Act in 1914.

**61. A:** The Texas Rebellion began in 1835 when a group of Texan leaders declared independence from Mexico. Texas won independence in 1836, but the US initially held back on plans for annexation due to concerns that such an act would lead to war with Mexico. In 1845, however, Congress approved annexation and Texas became the country's 28th state on December 29 of that year. The war with Mexico, which had broken off diplomatic relations with the US in 1844 when the treaty was agreed upon, began in 1846 following news of skirmishes between American and Mexican forces along the Rio Grande.

**62. C:** The US Supreme Court justices had decided that *Brown* would have a unanimous holding (the legal term for a court's rulings or decisions) before they determined what that holding would be, which resulted in a fairly narrow holding that "the plaintiffs and others similarly situated for whom the actions have been brought are, by reason of the segregation complained of, deprived of the equal protection of the laws guaranteed by the Fourteenth Amendment." This decision was used in later Civil Rights cases as a legal precedent for the idea that the doctrine of "separate but equal" was inherently unconstitutional, reversing the precedent set by *Plessy v. Ferguson*.

**63. D:** The French Revolution began in 1789, but its end date has been difficult to define. The Reign of Terror was intended as a means of fighting the revolutionaries' enemies and began with the execution of the Queen Marie Antoinette on October 17, 1793. While there was an economic crisis leading up to the French Revolution, there was also a severe economic crisis during/following the Revolution (depending on one's preferred end date). One of the effects of the Revolution was the ending of feudalism and slavery in France. With regard to the Estates-General, King Louis XVI had called together the Estates-General on August 8, 1788, stated that the Estates General would convene in May 1789.

**64. A:** Under the rule of the shoguns, Japan was primarily a closed country; contact with outsiders was severely limited. As a general rule, outsiders who attempted to go to Japan were killed, as were Japanese people who attempted to leave. The primarily exceptions to this rule were Chinese and Dutch traders who were granted permission to trade with the Japanese people. This situation changed in 1854 when the United States and Japan entered into a treaty of permanent friendship following US Commodore Matthew Perry's entry into what is now Tokyo Bay Harbor in 1853 (albeit with an armed fleet).

**65. B: The** Articles of Confederation granted the federal Congress the power to enter into treaties. It did not grant Congress the abilities to collect taxes, enforce laws or to regulate interstate commerce (it could impose some regulations on commerce with foreign entities), these shortcomings led to the eventual abandonment of the Articles of Confederation in favor of the Constitution, which is still in force today.

**66. A:** In *The Republic*, Plato calls for a philosopher king, selected from the ranks of philosophers who are at least fifty years old and given the power of absolute rule for life. Plato's belief was that in this society there should be no laws as they would interfere with the king's ability to use his judgment.

**67. C:** The Neolithic agricultural revolution resulted in an overall decrease in leisure time, in comparison with people living in hunter-gatherer societies, due to such factors as sustaining an increased standard of living and caring for the increased number of children born to families living in permanent settlements.

**68. C:** The 26th Amendment states: "The right of citizens of the United States, who are 18 years of age or older, to vote, shall not be denied or abridged by the United States or any state on account of age. " The 24th Amendment invalidates poll taxes as a requirement to vote. The 25th Amendment deals with presidential succession. The 27th Amendment deals with Congress members' compensation.

**69. B:** Mountains provide societies with a natural protective barrier, making it difficult for an outside force to invade them. The Swiss Alps are frequently credited with being a reason that Switzerland has managed to maintain its independence and neutrality. The barrier created by the mountains can also discourage trade and prevent cultural diffusion.

**70. C:** The principles held in the Monroe Doctrine were not new when President James Monroe issued it in a speech before Congress on December 2, 1823, however that did not stop them from becoming his namesake and shaping American foreign policy, even through the World Wars to which the US remained aloof until threatened with attack in the Western Hemisphere. Germany's attempt to convince Mexico to attack the United States, promising Mexico that it would receive several US states as a reward, was one of the issues that convinced the US to intervene in what had hitherto been seen as a European war. In World War II, the United States remained officially neutral until attacked at Pearl Harbor. The Monroe Doctrine was largely ignored by European powers, but underscored the American belief that the United States was the appropriate dominant power in the Western Hemisphere.

**71. D:** Nelson Mandela was the first President of South Africa to be elected in a fully representative South African election. He was succeeded by Thabo Mbeki, who was succeeded by Kgalema Motlanthe. Mahatma Gandhi was an Indian who lived in South Africa for a time and greatly influenced Nelson Mandela. He was also the leader of India's independence movement.

**72. B:** On June 28, 1914, Archduke Franz Ferdinand and his wife the Duchess Sophia von Chotkova were assassinated by Gavrilo Princip, a member of The Black Hand, a secret society whose intention was to create an independent Serbian country. This act was the first of a series of events that resulted in the beginning of World War later that summer. The Japanese bombed Pearl Harbor on December 7, 1941, bringing the United States into World War II. The sinking of the RMS *Lusitania* and the British interception of the Zimmerman telegram, in which Germany attempted to encourage Mexico to attack the United States, led to the United States entering World War I in 1917.

**73. A:** Boris Yeltsin was a Russian politician who was instrumental in the breaking up of the USSR and the end of Communism in Russia. In 1991, he was elected President of the Russian Federation in Russia's first democratic election.

**74. C:** This was almost a direct quote from President Truman's 1947 address before Congress which later became known The Truman Doctrine. The address explained his reasoning as to why the United States needed to offer assistance to Greece and Turkey.

**75. B:** The Warsaw Treaty Organization was meant to counterbalance NATO, or the North Atlantic Treaty Organization. Members of NATO included the United States, Great Britain, France and West Germany and pledged to consider an attack on one of them as an attack on all of them. NAFTA (the North American Free Trade Agreement) was signed by President Clinton in 1994 and lifted most trade barriers between the United States, Mexico and, Canada. The Soviet Union was a member of the U.N. Security Counsel which is charged with maintaining international Peace and Security.

The Four Power Pact was a pre-World War II treaty in which the United States, Great Britain, Japan and France agreed to respect each other's Pacific territories.

**76. D:** At the beginning of the Civil War, the Confederacy drew many skilled officers such as Robert E. Lee out of the Union army and used them as the backbone of its military leadership. The Union Army, meanwhile, went through a series of unsatisfactory generals before Lincoln found Ulysses S. Grant. The other options were advantages that the North held over the South.

**77. D:** The Mormon pioneers were members of The Church of Jesus Christ of Latter-day Saints and their trek west was intended to transport their entire culture across the plains to a place where they would be safe from the persecutions they had suffered in their previous settlements, including Missouri's Extermination Order (1838) and the assassination of the church's leader, Joseph Smith, on June 27, 1844 in Carthage, Illinois, while under the protection of Illinois' governor. In moving their culture across the Plains, the Mormons not only moved the people but took care to bring religious and secular books and musical instruments on their thousand mile journey. One of the first buildings in Salt Lake City was a theater. On the trek west, the Mormons divided themselves into highly organized companies and worked to improve the trail and provide resources for those coming after them, including the building of way stations, ferries and the planting of crops. They also kept detailed records of their experiences for the use of future pioneers, and an early Mormon pioneer invented the odometer as a means of calculating how far his company had traveled each day. Their migration is the most highly organized mass migration in US history.

**78. B:** The New Deal did not end the Depression. The Depression only ended after the beginning of World War II when there was a huge increase in demand for goods and manpower. The New Deal increased the agricultural price supports offered to farmers and increased the role that the federal government played in the US economy.

**79. A:** Cesar Chavez was a migrant farm worker who founded the United Farm Workers Organizing Committee. He was instrumental in bringing about several reforms that improved living and working conditions for migrant workers including the banning of certain grape pesticides and of the short handled hoe used in lettuce harvesting.

**80. C:** While Civil Rights Era Supreme Court decisions did declare that segregation in schools violated the equal protection clause of the Constitution, these decisions did not lead to instantaneous desegregation of schools, as people in many locations resisted desegregation even going to the length of closing public schools to prevent it. In other areas the National Guard had to be called in to enforce orders to integrate the schools.

**81. D:** The industrialization of the United States led to an overall decrease in the number of farmers as people moved from the country to the city in search of the new jobs created by industrialization. This move also resulted in fewer Americans being self-employed, as they instead became wage earners working for other people. Industrialization also led to an overall increase in economic and employment opportunities for women. Many of these opportunities took the form of what we now sometimes think of as "pink collar" jobs such as typing and stenography.

**82. A:** The Dust Bowl was a period of time, largely coinciding with the Great Depression, in which severe droughts, poor farming techniques, wind erosion and several other factors led to the collapse of farming in the southern Plains states. High grain prices had encouraged farmers to over-cultivate their fields and to bring previously uncultivated land under cultivation, leading to soil depletion and an overall loss in soil moisture as farmers would frequently burn their wheat stubble. This was a problem because the long grasses in the Plains states had previously been instrumental in keeping the soil in place. This loss meant that windstorms now began picking up soil, eroding fields and destroying crops. The Dust Bowl resulted in thousands of farmers losing their farms. Many of them traveled to California where they worked as migrant farm workers. John Steinbeck's *The Grapes of Wrath* tells the story of one family who lost their farm in Oklahoma due to the Dust Bowl.

**83. A:** The Enlightenment, also known as The Age of Enlightenment and The Age of Reason, occurred in the eighteenth century and centered on a belief in reason. The Enlightenment encouraged the ideals of liberty, self-governance, natural rights and natural law. Both the American Revolution and the French Revolution had their genesis in Enlightenment ideals which encouraged the idea that the common man should have a say in government. This was a departure from the most common types of governance, including monarchy and the belief in the divine right of kings. Enlightenment leaders tended to prefer representative republics as a form of government.

**84. D:** The Hudson River School was the first well-known American school of painting. Its members intended to break away from the European art schools and develop a distinct American art school of thought through their celebration of the American landscape.

**85. B:** The Communist Manifesto claims that history has been a series of class struggles; that the rise of Communism will eliminate class boundaries and end the struggle. Karl Marx, the Manifesto's primary author, ended with a call for the working class of the world to start a revolution against the order of things, forcibly taking over the means of production. The final lines read:

"The Communists disdain to conceal their views and aims. They openly declare that their ends can be attained only by the forcible overthrow of all existing social conditions. Let the ruling classes tremble at a Communist revolution. The proletarians have nothing to lose but their chains. They have a world to win. Workingmen of all countries, unite!"

**86. B:** In a pure market economy, price is typically seen as a reflection of supply and demand. A larger supply will result in a lower price and a greater demand will result in a lower price.

**87. B:** The Internet has increased the number of methods in which near-instantaneous communication is possible, indirectly improving the economy by opening new channels for communication at great distances. The internet has also generally caused a decrease in transaction costs and barriers to entry in retail situations (e.g., it is much less expensive to start a website to sell your goods than it is to open a physical store). The Internet has also increased consumer access to goods by making it easier for consumers to locate what they want.

**88. D:** All of the answers are ways in which the Nazi government attempted to gain control of German children.

**89. A:** John Locke was an English philosopher aligned with the Whig party. He wrote his Two Treatises on Government in support of the Glorious Revolution which occurred when William of Orange took over the throne from James II in 1688-89.

**90. D:** The information in this table shows the median incomes of persons who have achieved various educational levels. Looking at the table, one can see that from 1997 to 2007, persons without a high school degree had their median income increase by less than $5,000 while persons with a high school degree had their median income increase by more than $6,000. One can also see that as a general matter, the more education a person has, the higher their income will be and that income typically increases over time. It cannot be inferred that a person with a bachelor's degree will make more money than a person with no diploma because the number given is the median for each category. There is no indication of the range of income in each category, so no inference about the overlap can be made. Also, it is very possible for someone with a bachelor's to be unemployed, which would mean their income is $0.

**91. B:** The most appropriate reason listed in the question is to give students additional insight into the forces that shaped the historical event they are studying. Audio-visual materials can be used to give students additional perspective; for example, a documentary about the Battle of Gettysburg could be used to provide them with visual representations of historical locations or as a means of illustrating the differences in perspective.

**92. B:** The emergence and increasing acceptance of the Domino Theory became a driving force in how the United States made foreign policy decisions after the Cold War. America's involvement in Vietnam was largely structured around containing the spread of Communism. However, it was not until the Gulf of Tonkin incident in 1964 that provided justification for increased US military presence in Vietnam.

**93. B:** Levees are built to prevent flooding in areas along rivers. They consist of large embankments along the side of a river and typically have a flat top atop which sandbags can be piled to increase the levees' height when necessary. The Mississippi River has one of the world's largest levee systems.

**94. B:** A research question can be used to focus a research topic that is too broad to be appropriately handled in the format for which one is researching.

**95. A:** In this situation, you are using the information you have to create a generalization about the opinions of the population.

**96. D:** All of the listed methods are ways that a historian might locate sources, depending on his actual research question.

**97. C:** The US-Soviet race to the moon is an example of a circumstance where a chronological point of view would be appropriate as each nation's advances fueled the other nation's desire to surpass its Cold War rival.

**98. C:** The County of Edessa fell in December of 1143 after a month-long siege and was the catalyst for the Second Crusade.

**99. B:** The personal journal is the best source in this case because it is the only primary source listed. While a close friend's biography or an aide's letters might include information on the historical figure's personal opinion, the information will be filtered through the other person's memory and personal opinions.

**100. C:** High school US History classes are intended to cover the history of the United States since Reconstruction. The Great Depression, The Cold War, and the Progressive Era all occurred following reconstruction. The Jacksonian era took place during Andrew Jackson's presidency which lasted from 1829 to 1837.

# How to Overcome Test Anxiety

Just the thought of taking a test is enough to make most people a little nervous. A test is an important event that can have a long-term impact on your future, so it's important to take it seriously and it's natural to feel anxious about performing well. But just because anxiety is normal, that doesn't mean that it's helpful in test taking, or that you should simply accept it as part of your life. Anxiety can have a variety of effects. These effects can be mild, like making you feel slightly nervous, or severe, like blocking your ability to focus or remember even a simple detail.

If you experience test anxiety—whether severe or mild—it's important to know how to beat it. To discover this, first you need to understand what causes test anxiety.

## Causes of Test Anxiety

While we often think of anxiety as an uncontrollable emotional state, it can actually be caused by simple, practical things. One of the most common causes of test anxiety is that a person does not feel adequately prepared for their test. This feeling can be the result of many different issues such as poor study habits or lack of organization, but the most common culprit is time management. Starting to study too late, failing to organize your study time to cover all of the material, or being distracted while you study will mean that you're not well prepared for the test. This may lead to cramming the night before, which will cause you to be physically and mentally exhausted for the test. Poor time management also contributes to feelings of stress, fear, and hopelessness as you realize you are not well prepared but don't know what to do about it.

Other times, test anxiety is not related to your preparation for the test but comes from unresolved fear. This may be a past failure on a test, or poor performance on tests in general. It may come from comparing yourself to others who seem to be performing better or from the stress of living up to expectations. Anxiety may be driven by fears of the future—how failure on this test would affect your educational and career goals. These fears are often completely irrational, but they can still negatively impact your test performance.

## Elements of Test Anxiety

As mentioned earlier, test anxiety is considered to be an emotional state, but it has physical and mental components as well. Sometimes you may not even realize that you are suffering from test anxiety until you notice the physical symptoms. These can include trembling hands, rapid heartbeat, sweating, nausea, and tense muscles. Extreme anxiety may lead to fainting or vomiting. Obviously, any of these symptoms can have a negative impact on testing. It is important to recognize them as soon as they begin to occur so that you can address the problem before it damages your performance.

The mental components of test anxiety include trouble focusing and inability to remember learned information. During a test, your mind is on high alert, which can help you recall information and stay focused for an extended period of time. However, anxiety interferes with your mind's natural processes, causing you to blank out, even on the questions you know well. The strain of testing during anxiety makes it difficult to stay focused, especially on a test that may take several hours. Extreme anxiety can take a huge mental toll, making it difficult not only to recall test information but even to understand the test questions or pull your thoughts together.

## Effects of Test Anxiety

Test anxiety is like a disease—if left untreated, it will get progressively worse. Anxiety leads to poor performance, and this reinforces the feelings of fear and failure, which in turn lead to poor performances on subsequent tests. It can grow from a mild nervousness to a crippling condition. If allowed to progress, test anxiety can have a big impact on your schooling, and consequently on your future.

Test anxiety can spread to other parts of your life. Anxiety on tests can become anxiety in any stressful situation, and blanking on a test can turn into panicking in a job situation. But fortunately, you don't have to let anxiety rule your testing and determine your grades. There are a number of relatively simple steps you can take to move past anxiety and function normally on a test and in the rest of life.

## Physical Steps for Beating Test Anxiety

While test anxiety is a serious problem, the good news is that it can be overcome. It doesn't have to control your ability to think and remember information. While it may take time, you can begin taking steps today to beat anxiety.

Just as your first hint that you may be struggling with anxiety comes from the physical symptoms, the first step to treating it is also physical. Rest is crucial for having a clear, strong mind. If you are tired, it is much easier to give in to anxiety. But if you establish good sleep habits, your body and mind will be ready to perform optimally, without the strain of exhaustion. Additionally, sleeping well helps you to retain information better, so you're more likely to recall the answers when you see the test questions.

Getting good sleep means more than going to bed on time. It's important to allow your brain time to relax. Take study breaks from time to time so it doesn't get overworked, and don't study right before bed. Take time to rest your mind before trying to rest your body, or you may find it difficult to fall asleep.

Along with sleep, other aspects of physical health are important in preparing for a test. Good nutrition is vital for good brain function. Sugary foods and drinks may give a burst of energy but this burst is followed by a crash, both physically and emotionally. Instead, fuel your body with protein and vitamin-rich foods.

Also, drink plenty of water. Dehydration can lead to headaches and exhaustion, especially if your brain is already under stress from the rigors of the test. Particularly if your test is a long one, drink water during the breaks. And if possible, take an energy-boosting snack to eat between sections.

Along with sleep and diet, a third important part of physical health is exercise. Maintaining a steady workout schedule is helpful, but even taking 5-minute study breaks to walk can help get your blood pumping faster and clear your head. Exercise also releases endorphins, which contribute to a positive feeling and can help combat test anxiety.

When you nurture your physical health, you are also contributing to your mental health. If your body is healthy, your mind is much more likely to be healthy as well. So take time to rest, nourish your body with healthy food and water, and get moving as much as possible. Taking these physical steps will make you stronger and more able to take the mental steps necessary to overcome test anxiety.

## Mental Steps for Beating Test Anxiety

Working on the mental side of test anxiety can be more challenging, but as with the physical side, there are clear steps you can take to overcome it. As mentioned earlier, test anxiety often stems from lack of preparation, so the obvious solution is to prepare for the test. Effective studying may be the most important weapon you have for beating test anxiety, but you can and should employ several other mental tools to combat fear.

First, boost your confidence by reminding yourself of past success—tests or projects that you aced. If you're putting as much effort into preparing for this test as you did for those, there's no reason you should expect to fail here. Work hard to prepare; then trust your preparation.

Second, surround yourself with encouraging people. It can be helpful to find a study group, but be sure that the people you're around will encourage a positive attitude. If you spend time with others who are anxious or cynical, this will only contribute to your own anxiety. Look for others who are motivated to study hard from a desire to succeed, not from a fear of failure.

Third, reward yourself. A test is physically and mentally tiring, even without anxiety, and it can be helpful to have something to look forward to. Plan an activity following the test, regardless of the outcome, such as going to a movie or getting ice cream.

When you are taking the test, if you find yourself beginning to feel anxious, remind yourself that you know the material. Visualize successfully completing the test. Then take a few deep, relaxing breaths and return to it. Work through the questions carefully but with confidence, knowing that you are capable of succeeding.

Developing a healthy mental approach to test taking will also aid in other areas of life. Test anxiety affects more than just the actual test—it can be damaging to your mental health and even contribute to depression. It's important to beat test anxiety before it becomes a problem for more than testing.

## Study Strategy

Being prepared for the test is necessary to combat anxiety, but what does being prepared look like? You may study for hours on end and still not feel prepared. What you need is a strategy for test prep. The next few pages outline our recommended steps to help you plan out and conquer the challenge of preparation.

### Step 1: Scope Out the Test

Learn everything you can about the format (multiple choice, essay, etc.) and what will be on the test. Gather any study materials, course outlines, or sample exams that may be available. Not only will this help you to prepare, but knowing what to expect can help to alleviate test anxiety.

### Step 2: Map Out the Material

Look through the textbook or study guide and make note of how many chapters or sections it has. Then divide these over the time you have. For example, if a book has 15 chapters and you have five days to study, you need to cover three chapters each day. Even better, if you have the time, leave an extra day at the end for overall review after you have gone through the material in depth.

If time is limited, you may need to prioritize the material. Look through it and make note of which sections you think you already have a good grasp on, and which need review. While you are studying, skim quickly through the familiar sections and take more time on the challenging parts.

Write out your plan so you don't get lost as you go. Having a written plan also helps you feel more in control of the study, so anxiety is less likely to arise from feeling overwhelmed at the amount to cover.

### Step 3: Gather Your Tools

Decide what study method works best for you. Do you prefer to highlight in the book as you study and then go back over the highlighted portions? Or do you type out notes of the important information? Or is it helpful to make flashcards that you can carry with you? Assemble the pens, index cards, highlighters, post-it notes, and any other materials you may need so you won't be distracted by getting up to find things while you study.

If you're having a hard time retaining the information or organizing your notes, experiment with different methods. For example, try color-coding by subject with colored pens, highlighters, or post-it notes. If you learn better by hearing, try recording yourself reading your notes so you can listen while in the car, working out, or simply sitting at your desk. Ask a friend to quiz you from your flashcards, or try teaching someone the material to solidify it in your mind.

### Step 4: Create Your Environment

It's important to avoid distractions while you study. This includes both the obvious distractions like visitors and the subtle distractions like an uncomfortable chair (or a too-comfortable couch that makes you want to fall asleep). Set up the best study environment possible: good lighting and a comfortable work area. If background music helps you focus, you may want to turn it on, but otherwise keep the room quiet. If you are using a computer to take notes, be sure you don't have any other windows open, especially applications like social media, games, or anything else that could distract you. Silence your phone and turn off notifications. Be sure to keep water close by so you stay hydrated while you study (but avoid unhealthy drinks and snacks).

Also, take into account the best time of day to study. Are you freshest first thing in the morning? Try to set aside some time then to work through the material. Is your mind clearer in the afternoon or evening? Schedule your study session then. Another method is to study at the same time of day that you will take the test, so that your brain gets used to working on the material at that time and will be ready to focus at test time.

### Step 5: Study!

Once you have done all the study preparation, it's time to settle into the actual studying. Sit down, take a few moments to settle your mind so you can focus, and begin to follow your study plan. Don't give in to distractions or let yourself procrastinate. This is your time to prepare so you'll be ready to fearlessly approach the test. Make the most of the time and stay focused.

Of course, you don't want to burn out. If you study too long you may find that you're not retaining the information very well. Take regular study breaks. For example, taking five minutes out of every hour to walk briskly, breathing deeply and swinging your arms, can help your mind stay fresh.

As you get to the end of each chapter or section, it's a good idea to do a quick review. Remind yourself of what you learned and work on any difficult parts. When you feel that you've mastered the material, move on to the next part. At the end of your study session, briefly skim through your notes again.

But while review is helpful, cramming last minute is NOT. If at all possible, work ahead so that you won't need to fit all your study into the last day. Cramming overloads your brain with more information than it can process and retain, and your tired mind may struggle to recall even previously learned information when it is overwhelmed with last-minute study. Also, the urgent nature of cramming and the stress placed on your brain contribute to anxiety. You'll be more likely to go to the test feeling unprepared and having trouble thinking clearly.

So don't cram, and don't stay up late before the test, even just to review your notes at a leisurely pace. Your brain needs rest more than it needs to go over the information again. In fact, plan to finish your studies by noon or early afternoon the day before the test. Give your brain the rest of the day to relax or focus on other things, and get a good night's sleep. Then you will be fresh for the test and better able to recall what you've studied.

### Step 6: Take a Practice Test

Many courses offer sample tests, either online or in the study materials. This is an excellent resource to check whether you have mastered the material, as well as to prepare for the test format and environment.

Check the test format ahead of time: the number of questions, the type (multiple choice, free response, etc.), and the time limit. Then create a plan for working through them. For example, if you have 30 minutes to take a 60-question test, your limit is 30 seconds per question. Spend less time on the questions you know well so that you can take more time on the difficult ones.

If you have time to take several practice tests, take the first one open book, with no time limit. Work through the questions at your own pace and make sure you fully understand them. Gradually work up to taking a test under test conditions: sit at a desk with all study materials put away and set a timer. Pace yourself to make sure you finish the test with time to spare and go back to check your answers if you have time.

After each test, check your answers. On the questions you missed, be sure you understand why you missed them. Did you misread the question (tests can use tricky wording)? Did you forget the information? Or was it something you hadn't learned? Go back and study any shaky areas that the practice tests reveal.

Taking these tests not only helps with your grade, but also aids in combating test anxiety. If you're already used to the test conditions, you're less likely to worry about it, and working through tests until you're scoring well gives you a confidence boost. Go through the practice tests until you feel comfortable, and then you can go into the test knowing that you're ready for it.

## Test Tips

On test day, you should be confident, knowing that you've prepared well and are ready to answer the questions. But aside from preparation, there are several test day strategies you can employ to maximize your performance.

First, as stated before, get a good night's sleep the night before the test (and for several nights before that, if possible). Go into the test with a fresh, alert mind rather than staying up late to study.

Try not to change too much about your normal routine on the day of the test. It's important to eat a nutritious breakfast, but if you normally don't eat breakfast at all, consider eating just a protein bar. If you're a coffee drinker, go ahead and have your normal coffee. Just make sure you time it so that the caffeine doesn't wear off right in the middle of your test. Avoid sugary beverages, and drink enough water to stay hydrated but not so much that you need a restroom break 10 minutes into the test. If your test isn't first thing in the morning, consider going for a walk or doing a light workout before the test to get your blood flowing.

Allow yourself enough time to get ready, and leave for the test with plenty of time to spare so you won't have the anxiety of scrambling to arrive in time. Another reason to be early is to select a good seat. It's helpful to sit away from doors and windows, which can be distracting. Find a good seat, get out your supplies, and settle your mind before the test begins.

When the test begins, start by going over the instructions carefully, even if you already know what to expect. Make sure you avoid any careless mistakes by following the directions.

Then begin working through the questions, pacing yourself as you've practiced. If you're not sure on an answer, don't spend too much time on it, and don't let it shake your confidence. Either skip it and come back later, or eliminate as many wrong answers as possible and guess among the remaining ones. Don't dwell on these questions as you continue—put them out of your mind and focus on what lies ahead.

Be sure to read all of the answer choices, even if you're sure the first one is the right answer. Sometimes you'll find a better one if you keep reading. But don't second-guess yourself if you do immediately know the answer. Your gut instinct is usually right. Don't let test anxiety rob you of the information you know.

If you have time at the end of the test (and if the test format allows), go back and review your answers. Be cautious about changing any, since your first instinct tends to be correct, but make sure you didn't misread any of the questions or accidentally mark the wrong answer choice. Look over any you skipped and make an educated guess.

At the end, leave the test feeling confident. You've done your best, so don't waste time worrying about your performance or wishing you could change anything. Instead, celebrate the successful completion of this test. And finally, use this test to learn how to deal with anxiety even better next time.

**Review Video: Test Anxiety**
Visit mometrix.com/academy and enter code: 100340

## Important Qualification

Not all anxiety is created equal. If your test anxiety is causing major issues in your life beyond the classroom or testing center, or if you are experiencing troubling physical symptoms related to your anxiety, it may be a sign of a serious physiological or psychological condition. If this sounds like your situation, we strongly encourage you to seek professional help.

# Online Resources

Due to our efforts to try to keep this book to a manageable length, we've created a link that will give you access to all of your online resources:

mometrix.com/resources719/texeshist7-12

# It's Your Moment, Let's Celebrate It!

Share your story @mometrixtestpreparation